The Heave
of Boston

The Heavenly Twins of Boston Baseball

A Dual Biography of Hugh Duffy and Tommy McCarthy

Donald Hubbard

Foreword by Richard A. Johnson

McFarland & Company, Inc., Publishers
Jefferson, North Carolina, and London

LIBRARY OF CONGRESS CATALOGUING-IN-PUBLICATION DATA

Hubbard, Donald, 1959–
    The heavenly twins of Boston baseball : a dual biography of
Hugh Duffy and Tommy McCarthy / Donald Hubbard ; foreword
by Richard A. Johnson.
      p.   cm.
    Includes bibliographical references and index.

    ISBN 978-0-7864-3455-8
    softcover : 50# alkaline paper

    1. Duffy, Hugh, 1866–1954.   2. McCarthy, Tommy, 1863–1922.
3. Baseball players— Massachusetts— Boston — Biography.
I. Title.
GV865.A1H83   2008
796.3570922 — dc22 [B]   2008028900

British Library cataloguing data are available

On the cover: (top) Hugh Duffy; (bottom) Tommy McCarthy
(both photographs from the Library of Congress)

Manufactured in the United States of America

McFarland & Company, Inc., Publishers
  Box 611, Jefferson, North Carolina 28640
  www.mcfarlandpub.com

To Tony C.,
who hit a home run
on my first visit to Fenway Park

Acknowledgments

I would like to extend special thanks to the staffs of the National Baseball Hall of Fame, Harvard University, Boston College, Holy Cross, Dartmouth and the Boston Public Library. Peter Nash was very gracious in answering my questions about the Royal Rooters and in tracking down art work for me. Richard A. Johnson was a constant source of assistance and inspiration.

The *ESPN Baseball Encyclopedia, 4th Edition*, served as my statistical resource throughout, even if the editors concluded that Hugh Duffy actually did not win a triple crown in 1894.

There is nothing cooler than talking to people you knew only from their baseball cards, and special thanks go out to Teddy Lepcio, San Mele and Johnny Pesky, the Hugh Duffy of our time.

This project would never have been conceived without the terrific detective work of Suffolk County (MA) Probate and Family Court Register Rich Iannella, who took prompt and effective action after he discovered that someone had stolen wills of dead baseball players and helped restore many of them to their rightful archives. Rich, Assistant Register Dan Gibson and the late Bob Kavin were always helpful in answering my questions.

Final and most heartfelt thanks and love go out to my Heavenly Triplets, Lori, Billy and Caroline.

Table of Contents

Foreword

by Richard A. Johnson

For most of the nineteenth century, a portion of the twentieth, and what we have seen of the twenty-first, Boston has reigned as baseball's royal city. During this time not only has Boston been home to clubs known as the Red Stockings, Beaneaters, Unions, Braves and Red Sox, but it is also home to the nation's oldest amateur baseball league. Boston can boast of champions in five of the six major leagues in which it has been a member, including the single season of the Players' League in 1890 and the first-ever World Series champions (Boston Americans) in 1903. Boston teams have also played in a variety of epic settings, including the victorian manse that was the first South End Grounds, the quirky, compact Congress Street Grounds, the ramshackle Huntington Avenue Grounds, the wide expanse of Braves Field, and the baseball Shangri-La that is Fenway Park.

One might imagine that with all this baseball heritage Boston would claim at least a dozen native Hall of Fame ballplayers. After all, our rivals in New York can point to numerous hometown heroes, such as Lou Gehrig, Rod Carew, Whitey Ford, Hank Greenberg, and Sandy Koufax, to name but a few who made the trip from the five boroughs to Cooperstown. However, one could win many a bar bet by asking the name of the one and only native of Boston enshrined alongside his New York brethren.

By way of a hint I will inform you that he started his career as a pitcher, became an infielder (who earned the lasting respect of the legendary John McGraw, who called him the master of the hidden-ball trick), and achieved glory as the right fielder on two of the greatest teams of the nineteenth century. This native of South Boston batted .294 in 1,258 games and is often described as the least accomplished member of the Hall of Fame. Many writers and historians have even called for his plaque to be removed from the shrine.

Back in the day Thomas Francis Michael McCarthy was nothing less than a prince in his hometown of Boston, Massachusetts. During the 1890s McCarthy was a star outfielder for the Boston Beaneaters, known to one and all as half of the "Heavenly Twin" duo along with fellow outfielder Hugh Duffy. During this era the club became one of baseball's greatest dynasties along with their bitter rivals, the Baltimore Orioles of John McGraw, Hughie Jennings and Ned Hanlon. In five seasons with Boston, McCarthy was a beloved member of two championship teams.

McCarthy's best friend, Hugh Duffy, played much longer for the old Boston Beaneaters and worked well into his late eighties in the front office of the Boston Red Sox. To this day he commands the highest single-season batting average of .440, set in 1894. While Duffy and McCarthy hailed from similar backgrounds and shared many of the same close friends, Duffy always knew how to bat better, make money more effectively, and live much longer and healthier than his friend.

In the pages that follow, historian Don Hubbard introduces us to McCarthy, this most misunderstood of Hall of Fame members, and skillfully weaves a compelling story of a ballplayer who rose from the humble ranks of the factory team at the Chickering Piano Company to the plateau of baseball hero in the city where it mattered most in America. Hubbard recounts the life of a ballplayer whose sad journey seemingly created the template by which all too many future players lived their lives following retirement.

Hubbard also relates that while Hugh Duffy was infinitely more successful at baseball and living a happy life than McCarthy, he was anything but a retiring soul. Duffy liked to argue and fight and was always good for a joke or to light up a smoke; he was an eminently fun-loving person. Later in life he reinvented himself and became the modern-day equivalent of Boston Red Sox legend Johnny Pesky. But before then there were battles to win as a ballplayer during a rough era and as an Irish-Catholic in a prejudiced age.

F. Scott Fitzgerald said it best when he once remarked, "Show me a hero and I'll write you a tragedy." In contrast Hubbard has written a tale that captures both the heroism and melancholy of Boston's only native Hall of Famer, a player worthy of such a fine biography, while also demonstrating that with Hugh Duffy, one can be heroic and never boring.

Braintree, Massachusetts

Preface

In the 1990s, an enterprising baseball fan drove all over the country, merrily stealing the wills of long-dead baseball players so that he could sell their authenticated autographs. Certainly the signatures of Hall of Famers netted the highest financial yield, but the thief did not discriminate based upon talent as he eventually stole wills of very obscure baseballists as well.

Eventually the will thief was caught and punished, and many but not all the wills were returned to their rightful public archives. I personally took great pride in locating the will of Ned Hanlon, and with an assist from more powerful folks than myself, saw that the will was returned as well. In the midst of this unusual caper, the thief had filched the wills of Tommy McCarthy and Hugh Duffy.

I had heard enough of each to know that I knew very little about either. So I started to research their lives and discovered two very colorful and often controversial players. They became famous as "the Heavenly Twins" in the old Boston championship teams of the 1890s, ancestors of the Atlanta Braves.

Trouble is, McCarthy played only four full years on those terrific teams (he had a brief unsuccessful stint with them in 1885), and during that time he only had two good seasons, while Hugh Duffy starred for years in the major leagues. But that did not deter the voters from honoring McCarthy with a posthumous induction into the Baseball Hall of Fame in 1946, one year ahead of a then very alive Duffy.

That tells the reader a bit about them, but why a dual biography? To paraphrase the immortal Ernie Banks, "It's a great day, let's write two." On a more scholarly note, much of their historical records was destroyed years ago, and McCarthy's will, which would have provided some key insight into the final years of his life, has never been returned to its rightful place in the Suffolk (MA) County Probate Court Archives. Fortunately, Duffy's will was located and is now under lock and key, but as you will see, Duffy always was luckier than his Heavenly Twin.

In the Baseball Hall of Fame Library in Cooperstown, New York, I saw an entry in one of the files that had a comment to the effect that many of the ballplayers of the nineteenth century remain shadowy and obscure figures. Hughie Duffy and Tommy McCarthy were too vibrant to remain considered that way forever. Hopefully, by using the resources that still remain, I have been successful in bringing them figuratively back to life. To the extent that I have not, I beg the reader's forgiveness, pointing out by way of defense that the great Hugh Duffy, who still holds the record for the highest single-season batting average, only hit .440.

Prologue

Thomas Francis Michael McCarthy had a momentous decision to make. Should he remain at his job at the piano factory at $18 a week and help support his Irish immigrant parents and six younger siblings, or should he take an offer from a fly-by-night professional baseball league named the Union Association in its first (and final) year of existence?

Born an Irish-American on July 24, 1863, in Boston, Massachusetts, shortly after the Union and Confederate armies bitterly fought the decisive battles of Gettysburg and Vicksburg in the Civil War, McCarthy's life to date had met its limits early.

While Boston in that era had become, along with New York, one of the havens for Irish emigrants from the Great Famine, their numbers had not yet translated into power, influence or anything resembling respect from most of their Yankee neighbors. Upon escaping the prospects of almost certain starvation, the Irish emigrants to America experienced nearly identical forms of oppression they had suffered at the hands of the British Empire.

For instance, in 1839 a mob had attacked the Ursuline Nun's Academy in nearby Charlestown and had burned it to the ground. In 1854, the Know-Nothings, a supremacist movement hostile to Irish-Americans, had taken over the governor's office and the legislature of Massachusetts. For even menial jobs, advertisements often stipulated, "Positively No Irish Need Apply!"

Noted religious leader, transcendentalist and abolitionist Theodore Parker advocated in this era quarantining the Irish for 31 years because "[c]ertainly it would take all this time to clean a paddy on the outside.... To clean him inwardly would be like picking all the sands of the Sahara." Apparently, the benign impulses which supposedly guided Parker's advocacy against slavery did not extend to the Irish-Americans in his midst.

Baptized a Roman Catholic, McCarthy was raised as the oldest child of seven in South Boston, which then and now serves as an enclave of Irish-American pride and defiance. The neighborhood has at times lived uncomfortably

with the conflicting sentiments of religious devotion versus a tolerance of hooli-
ganism. Universally beloved Cardinal Cushing, archbishop of Boston from 1944
to 1970, hailed from Southie as did serial murderer Whitey Bulger. It serves as
the background of the uplifting hit movie *Good Will Hunting* as well as the
equally popular gangster flick *The Departed*.

While Southie buffered McCarthy against some of the most overt hatred
of the day against Irish-Americans, it did not provide for him a foundation for
success in the fields of law, medicine or banking. Indeed, after he completed
his studies at the John A. Andrews Grammar School, he began working as a
clerk in a clothing store in nearby Summer Street, as noted in the United States
Census of 1880.

Intervening years did not measurably improve his job prospects, as at age
20 he subsequently labored at a piano factory. Fortuitously for McCarthy, at
this time he also began to play baseball at nights on Boston's historic Common,
and in the midst of one of his pitching performances, he received an offer to
play a home game for the Boston Unions against the Chicago club. Although
he roamed the outfield and did not pitch in the game, as has often been mistakenly reported, McCarthy started another home game against St. Louis, and
at that point received a firm offer from his hometown team to join it on the
road.

To modern readers the choice might seem embarrassingly simple — get on
the first train out of Boston!

Not so for McCarthy. While George Wright, the legendary Cincinnati Red
Stockings shortstop and founder of the Wright and Ditson sporting goods company, backed the Boston Union Club financially, the new league operated on
shaky foundations. As a new baseball league in competition with the established National League and American Association, many of these issues came
with the territory.

Comically, these problems plagued the fledgling Union Association from
its inception through its demise. Established stars did not flock to the new
league and many of the ballplayers who did barely could put a bat to the ball
or field their positions. The owners' enthusiasm did not always translate to sufficient financial backing for clubs and attendance often did not materialize in
numbers conducive to future franchise operations. Some teams, like the Washington club at 12 wins and 51 losses, were dreadful beyond comment, and in
the midst of utter chaos, it is not even clear if that was indeed their record. Other
clubs folded in midseason and morphed into new entities while at least one
team had trouble raising its train fares home. Apparently no central organization guided the league.

At this career threshold, young Tommy McCarthy weighed his decision.
Did reason mitigate against forsaking a safe position at a factory that helped
support six younger siblings at home and with no guarantee that his boss would
hold his job after the baseball season ended? What were the prospects that he

might find work anywhere else? Or should he cast his lot with a team which promised little in the way of instruction or competent coaching in a hopelessly mismanaged and unprofessional league?

Tommy McCarthy got on the first train out of Boston.

Chapter 1

The Silver King

Years after the hunt, most of his friends regarded Tim Murnane's stalking and the running down of his prey as the defining moment in his early life. Murnane carried neither rifle nor bow as he stealthily drew a bead on his victim and pounced. Caught between first and second base, the swiftest baserunner in baseball, Ross Barnes, belatedly scurried away from the outstretched arm of Murnane, clutching the deadest of dead ball baseballs in his hands.

Timothy Hayes Murnane never starred during his four years of professional baseball and in his many years of semi-pro ball. In the infant National League of 1876, he possessed little prestige or star power to help cultivate the new organization for its potential fans, or cranks as they were known then. In the 100th year anniversary of the signing of the United States' Declaration of Independence, he was a centennial ham-and-egger.

Not so for speedy luminary Ross Barnes, one of the biggest stars in the firmament that passed for the highest level of professional baseball. Barnes hit for the highest season average in the 1870s and had a national reputation for having the fastest set of wheels on the diamond. He out-ran everyone and out-hit everyone, and almost every Caucasian boy in America idolized him and wished to emulate him.

When Barnes ran from first base to second base on behalf of his Chicago club, he feared little in the path of his rather modest goal. Certainly a plodding fellow like first baseman Tim Murnane had no chance to run him down and tag him out. Why didn't anyone tell Murnane what Barnes and everyone at the park already knew, that he had no chance of tagging out the greatest baseball player in America? He should have saved himself the effort and returned the ball to the pitcher or thrown to the third baseman to deter Barnes from contemplating the double steal.

Of course, no one told Murnane anything he did not wish to hear because he loved baseball, and in honor of the institution alone, he had to make the effort. He was the little train that couldn't, but with his arm outstretched and clutching the baseball, he persisted in racing after his prey. In folklore the tortoise defeated the hare in a race, but that was storytelling and Barnes had no intention of lazing about like the hare as he motored toward the safety of second base.

And then a funny thing happened. The much faster Barnes heard the footsteps of the handsome Murnane beating down upon him. Maybe his adrenalin coursed through him with more immediacy or maybe he simply wanted it more, but Tim Murnane relentlessly pursued until he lunged at Barnes and tagged him just short of second base for the out. Barnes did not want to get tagged out but Murnane had to tag him and that made the difference.

This one run-down constituted the pinnacle of Tim Murnane's playing days. Born in Naugatuck, Connecticut, in 1852, the son of an Irish immigrant father, Murnane carried his father's brogue as his own throughout life. Although his boyhood home increasingly became the center of the state's industrial revolution, he received his education in the traditional New England "little red schoolhouse." Later in life, his hair whitened, and that fact together with the respect that he eventually garnered in the sporting world earned him the universal sobriquet "the Silver King."

By 1869 he had begun playing ball for nearby Stratford, Connecticut, and the next year forayed to Savannah, Georgia, in pursuit of his career. The dream quickly segued into a nightmare when during one of his first games with the club he caught a foul tip in the eye that quickly swelled shut. Since the team carried no spare parts, his manager shifted him to the outfield where he promptly split his finger trying to catch a foul ball, opening up a naughty two-inch gash.

During one of his team's tours of the eastern seaboard, he played in Middletown, Connecticut, and the local baseball club duly procured his services and brought him closer to his home, which allowed him the perspective to assess his fortunes. More than a century before the Houston Astros' Jeff Bagwell curried the scouts' attention playing varsity baseball for Xavier High School in that Connecticut River Valley city, Murnane worked in the Douglas Pump Works while moonlighting as a member of the Mansfields nine in the early 1870s.

From Middletown, he shifted to Philadelphia as a member of one of the early incarnations of the Athletics and played a couple of years. Perhaps the most important step he took in advancing his prospects came when he joined the Boston team for a two-year stint, from 1876 to 1877, and met famed shortstop and future entrepreneur George Wright. A merry soul, Wright seems to

Opposite: Tim Murnane (spelled "Murnan" here) is pictured in the second row at the right in this team photograph of the 1877 Boston Professional Team. Team captain George Wright is pictured in the center of this row. Collection of Richard A. Johnson.

JAS. WHITE 1ST B.

BROWN. C.

LEONARD. L.F.

THE

MORRELL 2D B.

GEO WRIGHT. S.S.

BOSTONS

MURNAN. C.F.

SUTTON 3D B.

BOND. P.

1877.

O'ROURKE R.F.

W.H. WHITE.

SHAFFER.

MANING.

have remained on cordial terms with Tim Murnane from that point forward, an important contact to make as Wright became an influential and wealthy sports figure after his ball-playing days ended. Rounding out his own career, Murnane played a final year in Providence in 1878, and seemingly retired from baseball altogether by 1880.

Not content to visit New England mill towns and cities or take a single junket beneath the Mason-Dixon Line, Murnane conjured distant horizons. Indeed, he even traveled to England on a tour of American baseball but the tour did little to excite interest in the sport the British felt they had discovered (called rounders) and then ignored. Not everyone fared so well in these foreign goodwill junkets. Pitcher Cannonball Crane accompanied Al Spalding once on a trip across the world, and according to legend, went from teetotaler to habitual drunkard by the time he returned. But Murnane did make an impression because he went native, playing a game of cricket and making a catch so outstanding in the field that his hosts talked about little else until the next tea break came around. Murnane got along with everyone.

An intelligent man, he must have surmised that he had little future as a professional ball player, particularly as the game caught hold and more folks gave it a try. After 1878, he began to look for work elsewhere, running a saloon at one point, a natural for his garrulous demeanor, but not gratifying enough to sate his considerable intellectual and organizational strengths.

Because Murnane wove words together so well in his later incarnation as a sportswriter, folks not of his acquaintance often perceived him to be a rebel, but his love for institutions belied such romantic notions. Although he had at least one priest in his family, he did not become a prince of the church but rather, when the occasion arose, became one of the dynamic forces in the founding of St. Aidan's Parish in Brookline, Massachusetts.

While he certainly observed the demands and expectations of the Catholic Church of nineteenth- and early twentieth-century Boston, the institution he cherished most was organized baseball. From 1886 until the end of his life, Murnane served as the *Globe*'s sports editor, devoting his efforts primarily to explaining the game of baseball to his readers.

Eschewing the brief but boring simple game by game encapsulation of his day, he expanded coverage of each game and then followed up with a larger picture analysis of the developments in local and national ball. He virtually invented a more in-depth exploration of baseball, its players, its owners and its business side. For many of these years he simultaneously served as the president of the New England Minor League Association and perceived no conflict of interest in assuming both the role of league official and independent correspondent. After all, Murnane was the conscience of his sport and never knowingly undertook any action to damage his great love.

No romantic, Murnane despised the outlaw image that baseball projected too often. He found the intimidation and occasional physical assaults on umpires by players and fans moronic, and did not cater to umpire baiting, particularly when it threatened the individual safety of an ump or sullied the reputation of organized baseball in general. If he saw an umpire call a particularly atrocious or one-sided game, he pounced him in the next day's edition of the *Globe.*

He did not in maudlin terms portray baseball as a sacred vessel, but rather sought to alleviate its unbecoming and objectionable features and inject respect for authority and lawfulness into a sport whose participants too often resembled British soccer hooligans of the future. Murnane wrote hundreds of thousands and perhaps millions of words about baseball (well worth the read), but his most eloquent line was one of his shortest: "Base ball has a history, and in many respects it is one to be proud of." Murnane helped develop the sport's glorious tradition and sailed into anything or anyone who sullied his cherished sport.

Tim got along with folks who did not like each other very much. In the early twentieth century, two opposing Boston politicians—James Michael Curley and John "Honey Fitz" Fitzgerald—dominated the city's political system. Curley almost always prevailed in this competition because although he was a corrupt figure who managed to go to prison on two separate occasions, he observed a Spartan moral life which his opponent did not.

Honey Fitz had an eye for the ladies. Although married and the father of a lovely and extraordinarily devoted daughter named Rose, he managed to stage a very public affair with a much younger bimbo named Elizabeth Ryan, nicknamed Toodles. A popular jingle of the day went like this: "A whisky glass and Toodles' ass made a horse's ass of Honey Fitz." In one aborted contest against Curley, Honey Fitz withdrew from the race because Curley threatened to deliver a series of public lectures centered on Fitz' infidelity.

Honey Fitz laughed loudest and last, however, as Curley's heirs proved to be mediocrities, while Fitz' daughter Rose married Joseph Kennedy from East Boston and spawned a political dynasty which produced the country's first Catholic president. Although these two clans battled bitterly with each other and caused most politicians ("pols" in Boston lingo) to take sides, only Tim Murnane successfully maintained strong friendships with both politicians and their camps.

No back-slapping bullshitter, Murnane intuitively understood what each person needed in terms of companionship and provided it. In a city not known for embracing non-natives, Murnane inherited his father's Irish lilt and never lost it, winning over the flintiest of Hibernian hearts. He had a sunny disposition and loved to have fun, taking particular pleasure in delivering after-dinner speeches to baseball magnates as well as common men lining the Knights of Columbus halls throughout New England.

Although now widely regarded as the premier sportswriter of the nineteenth century and a groundbreaking investigative talent, Murnane did little to suggest in the first thirty-three years of his life that he might someday wield influence and befriend sports stars, politicians and princes of the church alike. However, in 1884 an opportunity arose for him to exploit his talents when a group of renegade capitalists attempted to form a new baseball league, the Union Association, to challenge the more-established National League and American Association. While Hall of Fame legend and entrepreneur George Wright provided much of the capital for the establishment of a Boston team, Murnane acted as the team manager and sole talent scout, and it was in that capacity that he came into contact with a promising young ballplayer from South Boston named Tommy McCarthy.

Tommy McCarthy, as a first-generation Irish-Catholic American, loved growing up with his fellow Irishers in the enclave of South Boston, Massachusetts, affectionately known as "Southie." While the Lowells of nineteenth-century Boston talked only to the Cabots and the Cabots talked only to God, young McCarthy did not lack for wonderful boyhood friends culled largely from his fellow Irish-Catholic neighbors.

It did not take very long for the parents of Tommy McCarthy or Hugh Duffy to whisk their newborn sons to the local church to have them baptized into the Catholic faith. Immigrant families both, they kept as their rock the same faith that Jesus asked Peter to build upon as tenaciously in the face of their Yankee employers as they had with their British Empire overlords. Since McCarthy (known throughout life as "Mac") had been born in late July, the priest did not have to break the ice in the baptismal font for the baptismal ceremony as the priest in Rhode Island most likely had to do for Duffy, a late November baby. Mac got the break on that one, an exception in his later relationship with Duffy.

Both babies missed out on Vatican II, the event that somewhat liberalized church practice, so their first memories of Mass centered on inscrutable Latin phrases. Their priests said Mass with their backs turned to the congregation, with wreaths of incense filling the pews. Women wore hats and even the poorest of laborers dressed their families up for weekly services and special Holy Days of Obligations.

A medieval church in many ways, it still possessed tender merits for the congregants. All were equal in the eyes of the Lord, a Lord who listened to and answered prayers. Each person was unique and possessed his or her own soul. Angels hovered liberally about, and not only did everyone have his own soul, but possessed his own guardian angel who watched over him day and night and was known to steal a kiss on the cheek while his charges slept.

The church united the Irish and the Italians in Rome and the poor folk in the missions in Africa and China in the face of the enemies, real or not. Eire's own Saint Patrick had preached the concept of the Holy Trinity, a central tenet for Catholics worldwide by plucking a three-leaf clover and explaining that the shamrock, like God, had three constituent parts to a whole mystical unity.

Throughout their lives, Duffy and Mac kept their religion close to them as one prong to the trinity that guided their existences.

In chronicling the lives of people who became famous but who sprung long ago from obscure circumstances, the recitation of their early years is incomplete and maddening. Our heroes did not receive trophies for every athletic accomplishment or write-ups in the local community newspapers, but they did not live obscure lives as much as undocumented ones. They generally show up only in birth records or census records, and the numbers often failed to jibe with each other, so the ages of children could sometimes be estimated within a year or two of accuracy.

It would be rewarding to unearth reams of information about our heroes' childhoods, but unfortunately such records simply are scant. Frankly, with children born in the nineteenth century, unless they came from wealthy families like Teddy Roosevelt or future kings and queens, where every fall from a pony was duly noted when it occurred, most children did not have extensive permanent records or vast correspondence from which we can fathom how they lived. Even George Washington has only the chopping down the cherry tree story for his entire childhood, and that story is hogwash.

From what little historical records exist, Tommy McCarthy's parents, Daniel and Rose, decided to make their home in South Boston and raised all of their children there. Irish emigrants both, Daniel found work as a laborer and Rose kept house, a job that became more challenging after she gave birth to their first child, Thomas Francis Michael McCarthy on July 24, 1864, on the Vigil of St. James the Greater.

Or 1863. The older baseball encyclopedias invariably list McCarthy's birth date in 1864, but the City of Boston certified records have him coming into the world a year earlier, which might suggest he shaved a year off his life throughout his career in order to appear younger and more of a phenom for prospective employers.

Controversial dates of birth aside, the McCarthys subsequently augmented their family through the additions of siblings John, Mary, Daniel, Sarah, Hannah and Julia. There may have been more children, particularly if one or more died in infancy, but the children listed formed the family in 1880 at least, when the U.S. census was taken.

Then as now, South Boston is perhaps Boston's most insular neighborhood. The homes, tenements really, in its Gates Street neighborhood fairly leaned into each other like the medieval Shambles of York, England. After a short walk to Telegraph Street and down the road, the McCarthys mustered every Sunday at St. Augustine's Church, a brick structure that stands to this day with its three doors, one for God the Father, one for God the Son and one for the Holy Ghost.

It does not appear that Tommy advanced past grammar school, as he began to work in a clothing store by at least his 17th birthday, and probably much sooner. It seems that he dedicated his free time to playing baseball, primarily on the old Constitution Grounds in South Boston, where he was later recalled to have been a prodigy who played with boys twice his age. Among his boyhood friends who later continued to play baseball professionally were Arthur and John Irwin, Frank Butler, Miah Murray, "Big Mike" Sullivan, Tommy Smith, Jim McKeever and minor leaguers "Dinzi" Sullivan and John McDonough. Although it never appears in the obituaries for these players, local ball-tossing-maven Cannonball Crane also hailed from Southie. Commendably, Mac kept many of his friends throughout his life.

In modern-day South Boston, very few baseball players ascend to the National or American leagues, although the area continues to produce excellent hockey players. Indeed, across town the Red Sox drafted Manny Delcarmen, who made news as the first Boston high school player in decades to become a major leaguer.

Nevertheless, the plethora of South Boston baseball stars born in the middle of the nineteenth century suggests at a minimum the hold that baseball had over the era's youths in that area. The Irish-Americans in Boston became part of a nationwide movement of first-generation Irish in the country to seize the opportunity that a potential professional career in baseball promised while removing them from the factories and mills that beckoned.

It also suggests something more. In isolation, the sheer numbers of ballplayers who came from "Southie" demonstrate the bonds they formed both on the sandlots and in their neighborhoods and churches to watch out for each other. The networks increased with time as the individual athlete made his way to other parts of Massachusetts, or if lucky and good enough, to cities throughout the country. The Irish in that period of American history often adopted an "us against them" mentality and followed the leads of their increasingly big-city politicians by doing favors for their own kind. McCarthy's life is replete with instances where he was assisted by his co-religionists. He threw punches at a lot of people, but he rarely or never reached that point of rage with another Irishman, even as pugnacious a soul as John McGraw. The Irish understood each other back then.

Nonetheless, McCarthy's first advancement came while playing for the Chickering Piano factory team. At that time, Chickering had the world's largest factory and had already produced approximately 50,000 pianos by the time he began working there. The main plant bordered South Boston, while the showroom overlooked the Boston Common. While employed there, he served as a clerk, and although many of his company games may have occurred on the Common, it seems that his employer stationed him back at the factory, even if that left him less than fresh for the important games at night. Otherwise, Chickering approached its baseball almost as actively as it did its pianoforte manufacturing, and as late as the 1920s still fielded a squad in the local commercial league.

Developing somewhat of an expertise in piano manufacturing and as a ringer on the company nine, Mac later shifted his allegiance to the nearby Emerson Piano Company. Thus Tommy McCarthy had a day job and an opportunity to elevate his level of play beyond the level of the Southie sandlots. While Tommy McCarthy was not making beautiful music, he was helping manufacture the instrument to aid others to do so while he tentatively plotted his unlikely destiny beyond the borders of his neighborhood.

Whereas Tommy McCarthy came from a large Boston family, Hugh Duffy hailed from a very small one. In the 1870 and 1880 censuses, Duffy is listed as living with his Irish immigrant parents Michael and Margaret in West Warwick, Rhode Island. There is some suggestion in public documents that Duffy had a sibling, and certainly he surrounded himself with dear cousins, but primarily he received the almost undivided attention and affection from his parents. In his will, Duffy makes direct references to his wife's nieces and nephews but also specifically speaks of two nieces of his own, which may suggest that he had a brother or a sister who had children.

Born in 1866 or 1867, Hugh Duffy did not share in the rich sandlot tradition of South Boston or the high caliber of fellow players. His birth date is even harder to ascertain than McCarthy's, because in the 1950s when Duffy was pushing 90, he told people that if his employers, the Boston Red Sox, knew his true age, he would be out of a job. That is ridiculous, of course, because his employer at that time was Tom Yawkey, who did not disqualify people from working for him due to their ages.

Despite the dubious birth date, Duffy developed an early interest in baseball, having witnessed many of the old Providence Gray games as a boy. Quite likely, he witnessed Hoss Radbourn win some of his record-setting 60 games in 1884, a feat necessitated when the team's other star pitcher, Charlie Sweeney, went on a bender and either jumped or was pushed into the upstart Union Association.

Hugh Duffy did not need St. Patrick or his three-leaf clover to teach him about the Holy Trinity, which in his experience as a boy consisted of his Catholic faith, baseball and some undefined "something else" as elusive as the Holy Ghost. His trinity never demonstrated any signs of rending or having one devotion supplant another, and as a boy quite often he attended church with his mother and father while donning a baseball uniform underneath his suit for a quick change at the sandlots or the ball fields. Like McCarthy, baseball formed quite early the second constituent element in his personal trinity.

Although Cranston, Rhode Island, is universally listed as his birthplace, Duffy resided in a village called River Point from at least his adolescence until nearly his thirtieth birthday. Now part of West Warwick, mill towns such as River Point, Phenix and Arctic formed a constellation of small communities catering at that time mostly to cheap Irish immigrants and first-generation labor, most of whom lived and worked there.

By age 13, he had already begun to work full time in a print shop, most likely the Clyde Print Shop in River Point. His baseball skills spared him a life in the mills, though according to lore, he gained his strength by working 60 hours a week in the print works and may have also hauled large bundles of blue-dyed fabric in a clothing dye factory. In 1884, during his latter teen years, he is rumored to have played in the Rhode Island State Association for $5 a week. This league housed clubs in East Providence, Lonsdale, Pawtucket, Woonsocket, Winship, Bristol and Perry College.

Curiously, while Duffy's participation in this association is dubious, apparently the inclusion of Morgan Murphy (a minor figure in baseball before the turn of the century who intersected Duffy's path early on) with East Providence is established. Duffy claimed that "[i]n 1885 and 1886 I was in short pants playing semi-pro ball," but made no mention of joining the Rhode Island State Association.

Of course, had he worn short pants in 1885, he probably would have been killed by fellow factory workers or rough ballplayers since it appears that he traveled across the border to Eastern Connecticut that year to work and to play ball in Jewett City. Along with his daytime chores of lifting heavy fabric in a linen dye factory, he reportedly received $30 a month as a baseballist.

The next year Duffy most likely relocated from Eastern Connecticut to that state's far northwestern corner to play in the Winsteds' club for $50 a month plus room and board. If true, this constitutes a remarkable relocation for this still very young man, far from any support system that his family or friends once provided him. Many young men his age drifted off to the monastery, and although Duffy was more religious than most of them, his path led to a small but burgeoning Connecticut Yankee mill town. He had his baseball and his deep life-long Catholic faith, but most abidingly in this stage of his life he had his loneliness.

It is unclear if he also had to labor during the day for a factory or a mill. But an exciting development occurred nearby in the much more prestigious minor league team in Hartford when the team owner sold five of his best players (including a catcher named Connie Mack) to the Washington major league team in September 1886 for $3,500. Running a baseball franchise was not for the faint of heart, and the sale of these players not only brought capital into the Hartford team coffers, it also represented a salary dump of their best players.

And what better way to obtain new talent than recruit a ballplayer who had gladly served his team for a $50 a month fee? Although the accepted version is that Hugh Duffy played just one game for Hartford that year, in an October 1 game in Newark, New Jersey, this is erroneous. The contemporaneous box scores of the *Sporting Life* do not support this misconception, because as early as September 20, Duffy was batting ninth in the order and catching for his new team. He played at least another three games before his historically attributed debut in the minor leagues. He even hit a double in one of these contests.

With the move from a small town to the Nutmeg State's capital, he significantly increased his odds of being evaluated by someone from a larger and more prestigious professional association. While he most likely secured another job after the conclusion of the 1886 baseball season, Duffy by this time had established sports as his principal career pursuit.

Although Duffy later gained fame as a swift base runner and rangy outfielder, he volunteered for the dangerous job of catcher as a means to advance his career. Once he demonstrated his hitting ability and his indispensable contributions to later teams, he rarely donned the rudimentary and totally insufficient tools of ignorance of late nineteenth-century baseball.

While Duffy and McCarthy later became fast and enduring friends, there is no evidence to suggest that Duffy and McCarthy met or even saw each other until Mac recruited him to play for St. Louis in the off-season of 1890. They did not grow up together and their paths to the major leagues took different turns. Still, similarities abound. They both rose above their anointed lot in life as children of Irish immigrant laborers to assume positions in companies that fielded competitive baseball teams, offering scant pay and no promise of a significantly better outlook.

Religious faith was one of the cornerstones in the lives of Hugh Duffy and Tommy McCarthy. This stained glass window was donated to Sts. Peter and Paul Parish in Phenix (West Warwick), Rhode Island, in honor of Duffy's parents. Pawtuxet Valley Preservation and Historical Society.

While Duffy and Mac relied on their church and baseball, they still lacked the third side of the triangle, the missing element to their trinities. Without it, a life of toil and poverty centered on their narrow neighborhoods beckoned them, an embrace fraught all too often with Rome, sottishness and the lash. Life only made sense after they found the third part of the clover, not an institution like their church or their favorite sport, but in a man named Tim Murnane.

Chapter 2

The Union Association

If you ever have the opportunity to travel to Cooperstown, New York, and visit the Baseball Hall of Fame, appreciate beforehand that Tim Murnane invented the Tommy McCarthy who is immortalized there. Without the Silver King, you would never see McCarthy's plaque and read about his exploits on the diamond. Read the plaque knowing that Tim Murnane forged it.

Tommy McCarthy's first memory of him took place in 1876 when Murnane, playing the infield, ran down and tagged out the much swifter Ross Barnes. The Silver King even had a poem written about him, albeit posthumously, which concluded, "[w]hen we turn to the Final Scorer to be judged each at his worth, God grant that Tim will greet us — a Prince — The Salt of the Earth."

But during the Union Association season of 1884, club manager Murnane cared little about creating more than a competitive ball club. As the player/manager and minority investor of the upstart Boston team, Murnane had a unique opportunity to revive his professional baseball career while simultaneously burnishing his resume as a field general and a factor in the ground floor of a third major league.

More then one hundred years later, we can laugh at the ill-fated Union Association, set up to challenge the established National League of Cap Anson and Spalding and the American Association. Commencing in late 1883, serious investors, managers and players endeavored to establish something lasting and profitable in a third league.

In Boston, for instance, majority investor George Wright, the star of the legendary 1869 Cincinnati Redlegs, strove to cultivate his franchise, with the help of local impresario, Frank Winslow. After he completed his distinguished baseball career, Wright founded the lucrative Wright and Ditson Sporting Goods Company, and in his spare time became the acknowledged father of American golf. On a less altruistic note, the Union Association not coincidentally agreed to use the Wright and Ditson brand baseball for all its games.

Contractors were hired to build the Boston Union grounds, and although they were not ready for the start of the 1884 season, moneys were expended in a sincere effort to provide the team with a professional foundation, albeit on a sunken lot.

The Union Association attracted recruits by advocating the termination of the reserve clause, a legal concept that theoretically bound a player to his team through eternity, or at least until the team decided to trade or release the individual. Had the promoters adhered to this noble goal and taken a long-term view of the challenges ahead, they may have not only solidified their league, but also eliminated an odious and unfair labor practice long before Curt Flood was born. In addition, properly paid athletes may have had less incentive to throw baseball games, an all-too-common occurrence until the 1919 Chicago Black Sox famously fell down due to the conspiracy of eight players and the organized crime elements of the gambling world.

From the league's inception, problems in the Union Association arose. The moving force behind the creation of the league, Henry Lucas from St. Louis, always seemed more interested in advancing his own franchise at the expense of the greater good of the other teams in the league. While the Union Association never stockpiled great players, Lucas signed up the best available talents for his St. Louis Unions. He also ensured that the bulk of his team's games in the early season occurred at home.

No one equated the Union Association with the other established leagues, but organizers still held out hopes for their new organization. The established league leaders countered this by threatening to blacklist Union Association players who wanted to return to the fold. Conservative newspapermen also accused the new congregation of "such crimes as prostituting the game by using lively balls, inflating batting averages and tolerating drunkards among its players." Claiming that

George Wright was the star shortstop on the 1869 Cincinnati Red Stockings team and then moved to Boston where he continued to star. He later founded Wright and Ditson Sporting Goods Company and has been dubbed the Father of American Golf. Collection of Richard A. Johnson.

the Union Association leaders conducted many of their tryouts in gin joints is not a total embellishment.

Comically, franchises came and went. For instance, the Altoona club stopped doing business and morphed midseason into the Kansas City club. A team in St. Paul supposedly played a few games and then vanished. By contrast, Milwaukee made a late entry to the league and actually did quite well in the time allotted to it. In a different vein, the Wilmington team missed the starting time of one of its games in Boston but played a game anyway, and it is not clear whether or not they forfeited. The league did not keep good books.

But in the 1884 season, Murnane had scant time to ponder the greater forces at work in the fortunes of the Union. He also had a responsibility to play his best on the field as well as recruit and manage his club to its optimal level.

Accounts of the time emphasize that Murnane worked out scads of athletes in a worldwide talent search to create the finest team in the league, but the truth belies the efforts made. Closer to home and reality, the Silver King whittled the wannabes down to 10 men, nine of whom were from Boston and one of whom hailed from nearby Worcester. The starting ten of the Boston Unions were:

Tim Murnane, first baseman/outfielder. Tim had not participated in professional ball since 1878, and even at that juncture he had not dazzled anyone. A former saloon keeper, one suspects that he rounded up most of his recruits from his bar.

Tommy Bond, pitcher/right fielder. A native of Ireland, the staff ace had won 40 games or more on three previous occasions, but in 1880 he lost 29 games; he did not pitch much and did not win at all in 1881 or 1882. He misinterpreted his modest success with the Boston Unions by staging a comeback with Indianapolis in the American Association, where he got shelled and disappeared to live a very long life in Boston.

Charles Daniels, pitcher. The devil went down to Georgia but this Roxbury native never went anywhere, apparently losing both games he pitched for the Unions. He never played anything even pretending to be major league baseball before or after his stint with Boston.

Thomas O'Brien, second baseman. He played six seasons in the National League, Union Association and American Association but never hit well wherever he went. He was among the original weak-hitting utility infielders.

John Irwin, third baseman. Arthur Irwin's little brother and probably the best player on the original Boston Unions, he managed to play seven more seasons in professional ball after the Unions' 1884 season, yet never as a starter. Like his older brother, Arthur, he was always considered a good baseball man.

Walter Hackett, short stop. Other than his experience with the Unions, he played only a bit for the Boston National League team in 1885, and then faded away. He ran a baseball squad at the *Boston Globe* where he worked for many years, and may have bumped into Murnane (in his later incarnation as a writer) occasionally. His cousin was mentally unstable Hall of Famer John Clarkson.

M.J. Slattery, center fielder. An enigma because he stunk while playing for the Union but actually batted fairly well in stints with the New York clubs in 1889 and 1890, but he never played well thereafter. He died before his 39th birthday of stomach trouble after spending his post-career as a salesman in a clothing store.

Cannonball Crane, left fielder. One would expect a superstar with a name like Cannonball Crane, but the Unions got a toy cannon, although he almost always won long ball tossing contests. Still, Crane caught on as a pitcher with a number of professional teams for almost a decade after his stay with the Unions losing far more than he won and walking more than he whiffed. An habitual drunkard, Crane went on a six-week bender a few years after he stopped pitching and died due to what was ruled an accidental ingestion of chloral. Few people attended his funeral and probably fewer believed his passing to have been accidental.

Lew Brown, catcher. Speaking of cannonballs, Brown once offered to catch one shot at any chosen speed for $2,500. He had played a number of years in Boston, Providence, Detroit, Baltimore and Louisville before he ended his career with the Unions. Before the year was out he would be accused and tried for stealing a janitor's gold watch and chain, and ultimately was acquitted. At the age of thirty he injured his knee while playfully wrestling at work and died from pneumonia while ensconced in the hospital.

James McKeever, catcher/right fielder. This Southie sandlot legend stunk in his short time with the Unions and never played major league ball again. Like Slattery, he died a young man.

The original Boston Unions posed no threat to be remembered with the 1927 Yankees. Nonetheless, once the season began, they did not compete particularly well with the other Union Association teams.

Parenthetically, a review of the original Boston Unions' roster reveals in some cases a marked abuse of alcohol by some of its membership. Supposedly Cannonball Crane lived a sober life until he accompanied Albert Spalding's world tour of baseball, at which time he fell in love with the spirits that would ruin his life. In reading about ballplayers of this era in general, one can not avoid appreciating the extent to which chronic alcoholism permeated the ranks of these ballplayers. Nevertheless, many of the ballplayers on the team were at least enabled in their alcoholism by management, which often looked the other way at transgressions in an effort to field the strongest team possible.

Certainly by this time, temperance societies had begun to unite and agitate against this societal ill, and yet too much of their efforts centered on the supply aspect to the issue. Carrie Nation and others later resorted to vigilantism, literally busting bottles of alcohol. In other words, cut off the flow of alcohol and the scourge would evaporate. Ultimately these efforts culminated a generation later in the passage of the Eighteenth Amendment to the Constitution; of course, Prohibition failed miserably.

Unfortunately, little access to support systems and counseling existed in the late nineteenth century, and the disease of alcoholism largely went untreated unless a particularly strong individual could quit using alcohol of his or her own volition. Alcoholism was a moral failing in the eyes of many Victorians.

The Providence team of the National League in 1884 serves as an example after its star pitcher Charlie Sweeney meandered through too many lost weekends during the season and left the team. Slightly more abstemious pitcher Hoss Radbourn stepped to the breach, formed a one-man staff the remainder of the season, and proceeded to earn an all-time major league record of 60 wins. Overlooking Sweeney's rampant disease, the St. Louis Unions snapped up the pitcher and he dominated the circuit. Baseball used him sparingly over the next three years and he died a young man, but not before he allegedly murdered another young man.

As an astute student of the game, Tim Murnane knew his team had numerous flaws, drunkards aside, as he tried to cope with the mediocre fare of his league. Uncharitably, the press corps critiqued the quality of his team in late June, with one article proclaiming, "It seemed as if the members of the Boston Unions were indulging in a trial on the Union grounds yesterday afternoon to see which could do the worst throwing. Over half of the nine took part in this kind of a contest, and succeeded in pretty well disgusting the 700 people present." To stem criticism heaped upon his charges, Murnane began to tinker in earnest with his creation in mid–July.

At this point in the saga, pitcher and Boston native Fred "DuPee" Shaw alienated the management of his Detroit club. Back in that era, no players had agents nor did they particularly feel the need for them, as quite often they heeded the advice of their liquor bottle and drinking cronies in forming their professional decisions.

It is not known whether DuPee Shaw followed the advice of Old Grandad but he did shoot off his mouth by leaving his team and returning home after he had been fined $30 for making an errant throw during a game, which his team refused to rescind. As a poor pitcher with the worst team in the National League, the ax fell on him soundly. Since no one in the National League nor the American Association came searching for him, he "listened" to his friends in Boston who persuaded him to join the Union team. After ascertaining that Detroit had irrevocably released Shaw, Murnane signed him and made him a starter.

Murnane appreciated that a poor pitcher in one of the other leagues might prove to be a superstar in the Union League. Upon signing Shaw, he also reinstated catcher Lew Brown, who had been dismissed from the team for unspecified reasons, although with the irresponsible Brown, alcohol abuse likely provoked the crisis.

Of more significance, the Silver King also attempted to improve the team in the field. Many of the local baseballists had disappointed him, and like other Union managers, he began to scout around for more qualified recruits. While the Union team enjoyed a level of immunity from criticism as they toiled during an almost unimaginable five-week road-trip, when they returned home, they met their fans, read their reviews from their home newspapers, and had to face facts.

Either Arthur or John Irwin referred young Tommy McCarthy to Murnane for a tryout. In July of 1884, needing an outfielder badly, the Silver King arranged to view the new prospect. McCarthy impressed him enough to earn the opportunity to play in the Unions' game against Chicago on July 10. Reportedly, a gaggle of onlookers stood in awe and asked where he came from, whereupon McCarthy proudly proclaimed, "From the sandlots!"

By this point in time, McCarthy had begun to demonstrate his highly ambitious nature, a trait that accompanied him for the remainder of his lifetime. Unfortunately for him, his driving nature too often interfered with sound judgment concerning how to navigate his life at a particular time. Having come from a commercial league with the Chickerings, McCarthy should have considered playing with one of the many fine teams from the industrialized towns

Baseball on the Boston Common in the shadow of the State House, most likely depicting a scene a few decades before Tommy McCarthy was born. Sports Museum of New England.

ringing Boston rather than jump to the Unions, which at least had pretensions of being a major league.

While Bill James has convincingly argued that in modern-day terms the Union Association was not a major league, McCarthy basically jumped from a very competitive high school team or the American Legion to Double- or Triple-A ball. And the demands of his new team outstripped the development of his talent to that date.

Later lore held that McCarthy had first thrilled the Unions fans with a shut-down performance as a pitcher against the Chicago team, but no evidence exists to suggest this event ever happened. He did, however, play right field and received some press when one of the dailies discovered that "[t]he home team put in a new man, McCarthy, who made two good [throws] in right field, and nearly tied the game in the ninth by daring base running but was left on third." In fact, the opposing pitcher, Hugh Ignatius Daily, also know as One-Armed Daily, hurled a one-hitter against the Boston Unions, and Mac came up hitless.

That is where matters stood until July 14, 1884, when McCarthy excelled in his next chance for the Boston Unions against the "gilt-edged" St. Louis team, titans of the new league. Murnane placed McCarthy in right field again and he made three putouts and "did good work for the Union team." Although the two teams combined for an embarrassing 29 errors, he played flawlessly in the field. More auspiciously, Tommy in his five trips to the plate rapped out two hits and led his team to a 12-10 slugfest victory over the cream of the league.

In a loss to St. Louis on July 17, Murnane made an unlikely appearance in right field and booted two balls. Clearly, this situation had to change and change it did two days later when the Silver King wisely returned to first base, and McCarthy started in outfield, socking two hits in three at-bats. Although St. Louis shut out his team, the papers noted that "McCarty [sic] did the best hitting of the game."

Having passed his audition, Murnane handed McCarthy a ticket to accompany the Boston Unions on a road trip to Washington, D.C., to play the Nationals. The train ride proved exciting, but once there, he met the hottest and muggiest weather he had ever encountered. In late July the humidity in Washington reaches its height and no air-conditioned hotel rooms or visiting clubhouses existed to provide respite for the young ballplayer and his teammates.

Once there, the desultory dew points did not deter McCarthy, who during an exciting ten-inning game hit cleanly to left-center field and then scored the winning run when his old South Boston sandlot friend Frank Butler drove him home decisively with a triple. Life was proceeding very rapidly for the young man.

That scenario continued until July 21, when McCarthy went 0-for-4 against the Nationals and began to discover how cold D.C. can be in the middle of summer. He also exhibited signs that became more apparent as the season continued, namely that while the Union Association had several shortcomings, McCarthy had not played any competitive level between the Boston Commercial League with the Chickering Piano Company and Emerson Piano squads and the Unions. While no formal minor league system existed at that time, several teams competed in eastern Massachusetts mill towns that bridged this competitive gulf. McCarthy's wonderful start against St. Louis showed promise, but masked his lack of seasoning and inhibited his growth, particularly at the plate.

In the Boston Commercial League, McCarthy worked all day and played at nights primarily against other folks who earned their main money as laborers. Even compensating for the inconsistent level of play in the Union Association, most of these players threw the ball harder and ran faster than the competition McCarthy had seen. At the least, they had dedicated their lives to baseball and did not treat it as an avocation or a part-time job.

He also had to adapt to traveling away from home as a young man — the youngest player on the team — and dedicating himself to his chosen profession, all the while playing in front of much larger crowds. Bringing up a player to a higher echelon can often bruise one's confidence and, in some cases, destroy careers. And the former scenario played out in McCarthy's case as he struggled with his limitations.

Taking heed of this situation, Murnane took two seemingly divergent paths in dealing with his young right fielder. First, he kept McCarthy out of games, and then tried to restore his confidence by inserting him to a higher place in the batting order. Most importantly, the Silver King reacted to McCarthy's shortcomings and slumps with patience. McCarthy, even early in his vocation, exhibited a quick wit which his manager, a very articulate man himself, could not fail to appreciate. On a team of drunks and misfits, Murnane had not only found himself a swift outfielder; he had begun to develop a life-long friendship.

Murnane gifted another treat to McCarthy on August 23 by permitting him to start as a pitcher in Hudson, Massachusetts, against the town team. He pitched well, earning a 4–1 victory. He not only mesmerized the opposing batters, but also stabbed a shot that appeared to the appreciative crowd to be a certain hit. Although no one knew it that day, one of the batters he consistently retired was Wilber Robinson, a future teammate of McCarthy's and member of the Baseball Hall of Fame. At the time, Robinson worked in a slaughterhouse.

Buoyed by his strong performance against the Hudsons, McCarthy starred again at the Union Grounds against the Wilmington club. Consistent with the operations of the typical Union franchise, Wilmington forfeited the first game because its players arrived too late at the park. In the second game, Dupee Shaw shut out Wilmington, with McCarthy earning kudos for his baserunning, throwing and his prowess at the plate.

Rewarding his protégé's success, Murnane moved McCarthy up to the second spot in the order in the game against the Pittsburgh Unions (formerly the Chicago team) and their pitcher, One-Armed Daily. That day, McCarthy generally acting as the catalyst for the winning rally, scored two runs and hit a crucial single to seal a 4–1 victory for Boston. Indicative of the lack of quality equipment, several lazy fly balls that afternoon fell for base hits because the sun distracted the outfielders, who were only a few generations removed from fielding competency by the popularization of sunglasses, or smoked glasses as they were known then. Tellingly, the journalist excused poor performances in the field the next day due to the sun "getting in the eyes" of the fielders, including our hero, who threw a ball from the outfield to second baseman O'Brien, who had his back turned to him at the time.

One can go fairly paralytic in trying to squarely analyze fielding statistics, one of the most difficult aspects of late nineteenth-century baseball playing to gauge accurately. By way of example, McCarthy earned another starting nod in an exhibition against a local team, the Roxburys, and did remarkably well, notching a complete game three-hitter and striking out 17 in the course of a blow out. The Roxburys did not help their cause by committing 19 errors in one inning and 34 muffs throughout, but the professional Unions committed 11 errors during the game.

Much of the scorn for late nineteenth century baseball springs from this seemingly inscrutable inability to stop the ball and throw to a base correctly. Certainly, in this exhibition, the crowd witnessed remarkably sloppy play even allowing for their standards, but it does confound the modern reader to understand why so much sloppiness occurred. In what will be a recurring theme, there were factors that explain in part these lapses. The sun did cause errors and the fielders did not always use "smoked glasses," so some curving of the grades must occur to appreciate the skills that these players possessed in the absence of safe and effective equipment. McCarthy, for one, supposedly never used a glove during his entire baseball career. That does not in any way, however, excuse 19 errors in one inning.

Thereafter, the *Boston Globe* teed off on local Boston sandlotter Jeremiah Sweeney, who came to town as the first baseman of the Kansas City team. Sweeney, the original legend in his own mind, received before the first inning "an elegant design of flowers" made to depict a diamond and a baseball bat. Although he played only 31 games in the Union Association and never served in a colorable major league before or after, he was the captain of the team, and proudly drove a ball past Tommy McCarthy in an apparent inside-the-park home run, if not for two stubborn facts: he missed touching second and third base. The *Globe* dubbed his act "making himself as sublimely ridiculous as ever did a player in this city." When called out, Sweeney "began a disgraceful amount of kicking," parlance of the day for arguing vociferously with the umpire. They liked McCarthy, though, celebrating his "long backward running catch in the fifth inning." The eventful day ended with the game called in the sixth inning due to darkness.

Toward the end of the season, McCarthy received more opportunities to pitch against actual league rivals instead of local squads. Against Cincinnati, he pitched wildly, and sometimes pitcher and current catcher Cannonball Crane also threw the ball all over the place. Eventually losing, 13–7, McCarthy pitched the entire day, undoubtedly because the team's other two pitchers had to play in the field. While young Tommy twisted slowly in the wind, DuPee Shaw committed two errors in right field and Crane accounted for six more against a team with at least one quality player — second baseman Jack Glasscock.

Interestingly enough, in the midst of playing in frustrating conditions in an unprofessional league, the Boston Unions instituted a lasting innovation to the national pastime as "[t]hey use[d] two balls and when one is knocked over the fence, the second ball is brought into use until the first one is returned."

Although late in the season, no true pennant race existed, as St. Louis still led the league in wins with Boston fourth in a seven-team league. By then, Wilmington had folded and the Milwaukee was about to be born. Sadly, the *Globe* noted the fact "[t]hat St. Louis should have taken such a long lead at the start is unfortunate, as the other clubs are now in a condition to make the fight a pretty one."

Emphasizing the lack of intensity in Union Association games, in Kansas City DuPee Shaw and Lew Brown "failed to materialize" for the afternoon ballgame at Athletic Field. Pressed into service, McCarthy suffered from "an inability to pitch a good game," which is a charitable way of describing a performance in which he made seven of his team's errors that day. Apparently a local umpire also was recruited for duty that day and performed with similar inconsistency. Still, McCarthy only lost by a score of 5–2, and while batting second he hit well and scored his team's only runs. It is not known where the two Boston Union players disappeared to that day.

Murnane apparently shared the press' evaluation of the game as he started his protégé again in Kansas City, and this time the Unions lost by only 2–1, with McCarthy adding seven assists in his defense. Perhaps as punishment, Murnane rested his own misshapen hands and started Lew Brown at first base in his stead. McCarthy again pitched well in Milwaukee a week later, initiating a double play with a stab of a hardliner while losing only 2–0 against "the best pitchers [the Unions] ever faced."

By late October 1884, the wheels were falling off the trolley in the Union Association. Prior to the final game of the year before 7,000 fans in St. Louis, Cannonball Crane engaged in a long ball throwing contest against a stiff cold breeze, narrowly losing after making several throws. To add to the carnival atmosphere, local sprinters staged foot races. After getting down to business, Crane incredibly pitched a shutout, and more amazingly, it was the first shutout sustained by the St. Louis Unions.

Altogether it was not a bad year for young Tommy McCarthy, who started the spring as a pitcher for the Chickering Piano Company in the Boston Commercial League and ended up pitching and playing the outfield on diamonds throughout the country. He ingratiated himself with Tim Murnane, a relationship that only grew in importance after his manager cultivated his talent with words into a long-term and very successful tenure as sportswriter at the *Boston Globe.*

It is perhaps his friendship and association with Murnane that ensured McCarthy's ultimate election into the Baseball Hall of Fame. Paradoxically, their friendship and common bond also may have contributed to the phenomenon that exists to this day, which is that while Tommy McCarthy made the Hall of Fame, he did not deserve to gain induction there. He received the equivalent of a kid making a team not based on ability, but because the coach was friends with his old man. In other words, he got what he wanted, or what his old man wanted, but people would never stop grumbling that he did not deserve the recognition.

As events transpired, most of McCarthy's enduring fame revolved around his additional association with Hugh Duffy as Boston's "Heavenly Twins," but as we shall see, with Tommy McCarthy, heaven can wait. Had he followed more of a deliberate path to the major leagues, as Duffy later did, McCarthy may have developed into a more mature and better-conditioned player. He may have even legitimately earned his entry into the still-uncreated Baseball Hall of Fame.

Still, Boston was and is a sweet place to be for a successful sports star. With no major league football, basketball or hockey teams in the town at that time, baseball ruled supreme. And by all appearances, Tommy McCarthy was a star despite the fact that he barely batted .200 and lost all seven of his pitching decisions in a notoriously weak league.

Compared to his neighbors in South Boston or his co-workers at Chickering Piano, he had obtained startling success. He had traveled the country as a major leaguer, and he expected to never see another sandlot or minor league facility except if, by chance, he drove past one. He would proudly list his occupation as a baseballist in the *City of Boston Street Guide.* As he returned to his family's modest home on Gates Street in South Boston, he could only envision the future becoming ever brighter once spring rolled around again. Tommy McCarthy had arrived.

Chapter 3

Oshkosh by Gosh

St. Louis Unions owner Henry Lucas brokered a deal whereby he sold out on all of his alleged beliefs concerning the reserve clause in exchange for his being allowed to sever his team from the Union Association and graft it onto the National League as a new franchise. Like many pacts with Satan, it provided only temporary joy, as his superstars proved largely unable to play in their new league, and their gaudy statistics plunged precipitously. Most knowledgeable baseball fans patronized the crosstown Browns, featuring such genuine stars as Charlie Comiskey, Tip O'Neill and Parisian Bob Caruthers. In two years, Lucas' team was consigned to the dustbin of history.

By his typically selfish actions, Lucas did not only doom any long-term chance of success for his own team, he also effectively killed the Union Association. Dreams died, and suddenly players like McCarthy had to determine if they had any right to believe they were baseball players any longer.

Strangely enough, in Boston, for instance, no one seemed to tell them the news, and in the spring of 1885, an incarnation of the old Union team survived and started searching for games. On April 7, 1885, for instance, Mac played for a Unions squad (composed almost entirely out of his former sandlot chums) against the Boston National League team, and he won kudos for "the splendid catching of McCarthy in left field." The two teams played again shortly thereafter, but instead of playing for the Unions, "[t]he Bostons presented McCarthy, their latest acquisition, in the field." He had just taken a jump from a dying pretender major league to the real thing literally overnight. Call it the luck of the Irish.

Or was it? Having barely survived against weak Union Association pitching, he now had to struggle against the best arms in the land. For instance, Chicago had John Clarkson, who would win 53 games that year, while New York answered with two future Hall of Famers, Mickey Welch and Tim Keefe.

Additionally, for large parts of May and June, he disappeared from the daily lineup, this despite a promising start that had the *Sporting Life* proclaiming at the end of April that he "has done very good work for the Boston thus far and doubtless answer all that can be expected of him." Matters had become so dire that on July 8, 1885, the same publication commented that "McCarthy is still under agreement to the Boston club. He is not with the club on their Western trip, but draws his money with the utmost regularity and waits for the chance which never comes."

A break came his way with the chronic injuries befalling his team. On July 12, 1885, Mac returned to the lineup but went hitless in three at-bats against future Hall of Famer Pud Galvin, whose curveball perplexed most of the other batters as well, ironic since Galvin was experiencing perhaps his worst year as a hurler.

McCarthy's lack of success proved relentless, and in late July, the directors of the Boston club scheduled a meeting with him, chastising him for "not playing better ball." He responded positively at first, hitting a timely double to win the game against Detroit on July 30, an effort that led the *Globe* to gush, "But to McCarthy, the popular little left fielder of the Bostons, is due the credit of finally winning the game."

He continued to receive encouraging notices in print in early and mid–August for his good hitting. In actuality, that month proved unforgiving as McCarthy watched his average dip below what today we refer to as the Mendoza line, sinking to .182. Facing the inevitable, Manager Morrill released Tommy McCarthy and teammates Manning, Hackett and Davis due to their collective and individual lack of a "sufficient amount of strength in a very essential point, namely batting."

Strangely enough, the press at that time did not focus on the loss of the skillful McCarthy, but instead fixated on the popular but woefully inept Jimmy Manning. The hype of the moment propelled Manning into a contract almost immediately with the Detroit National League entry, where he soon perpetuated his incompetence until his downside eclipsed his upside.

One of the new players brought in proved to be the foundation for the championship Boston Beaneater teams of the 1890s, one Billy Nash, infielder extraordinaire from Virginia. Tommy McCarthy too would play a critical role on those squads in the future. At the moment, he had to start looking for new work in the minor leagues. It is not known if Mac and Nash met at that time, with one on his way out the door and the other headed to a major league team.

Although it was late in the baseball season, McCarthy hooked up with the local minor league Haverhills. At least one account placed him that year playing for a Maine minor league team, the Biddefords, but this appears to be an error, perhaps caused by the fact that about the time the Boston Nationals signed Mac, the Biddefords successfully recruited eight of his old Union teammates. The Biddefords gained their lasting notoriety that year by appointing as their mascot an African-American steward, who received $2 a day for his efforts, with a $50 deduction from his pay if someone caught him swearing.

Although it was late September, Mac played out the string that year for the Haverhills. The club instantly became one of the strongest in the Eastern New England League thanks to his inclusion on their roster.

In retrospect, Mac had been rushed to the major leagues and had to find a suitable level commensurate with his talents. Perhaps he had not wasted the past two years, but he had not spent them wisely, either. Thus, in 1886, he began the baseball season with the Haverhill entry in the New England League, managed by a novice named Frank Selee. In addition to regular pay, one fan gave each player a box of cigars for every stolen base, an exciting prospect for the fleet afoot on the team.

He did not stay for long, however. On April 25, McCarthy received a nice press notice for his work at second base with his new team in its victory over the Dartmouth College club. A couple of days later, he batted second and played left field for the Providence team in the National League.

Baseball in Providence had taken a precipitous drop in fortunes since Hoss Radbourn's magnificent performance in 1884 when he won 60 games and carried the team to the league pennant. Providence stayed in the National League in 1885, but could not approximate their success, and by 1886, they were a minor league town. This did not deter the ambitious Mac, who calculated that while this was no longer a major league club, it was definitely a step above the Haverhills and not that far from his ultimate dream.

Unfortunately for McCarthy, Providence not only failed to regain its glory, it could no longer sustain a baseball franchise, and in the first week of June, it disbanded. The directors of the club unanimously decided they could not make payroll. Despite paying only a quarter for admission, few people bothered to stop by and watch a game. They magnanimously permitted the ballplayers to sign with whatever team they wished and agreed to pay their fare out of the city.

Poor McCarthy had to humbly return to the New England League, where he had been employed recently by the Haverhills. They either did not want him back or he did not crave free cigars, and after a two-week hiatus, he joined a competitor in the New England League, the Brocktons.

Unlike Providence, Brockton never developed much of a reputation as a baseball town, particularly since its most famous citizens — boxers Rocky Marciano and Marvin Hagler — were yet to be born. Still, playing ball beat working, and unlike his last club, the Brocktons were able to pay their players. In mid–June of 1886, he began to work for his third team that year.

This is where the legend of Tommy McCarthy really begins. Before long, he started to light up the daily box scores with multiple-hit games, and even on a bad day, he usually posted at least one hit. On July 13 he hit for the cycle, and the *Boston Globe* began paying attention to him again, noting that his hitting "is simply phenomenal." By the end of the month, he led the Brocktons at the bat with an average of .329.

Other people noticed, too. The manager of the Haverhill club, a novice named Frank Selee, was building his own Hall of Fame career step by step, and along the way he had to figure out a way to defeat a Brockton team featuring a speedy and rejuvenated McCarthy. Unfortunately, Selee did not finish the year with Haverhill, and with John Irwin installed as new manager, his own career appeared to stall. Supposedly he and Irwin operated a "chop and oyster" joint in the off-season, but at this time, Selee's future appeared quite murky.

In contrast, the only bump in Tommy McCarthy's path was a fear in early August that the Brocktons were on the verge of disbanding, but the rumors of their demise are slightly exaggerated and the team continues to exist with their star thriving. On September 21, his 4-for-4 batting is a special feature in an otherwise meaningless game before 200 people. But the day was noteworthy because the major league Phillies manager, Harry Wright, was seeking a new player. He purportedly wanted a player named Esterbrook (probably Dude Esterbrook of the New York National League team), but is firm that he will not pay much for his services, a rather backhanded compliment to make public.

At this point a terrible thing happened to Tommy McCarthy — he was picked up by a major league club, namely Wright's Phillies, who apparently never acquired Esterbrook. Mac had experienced a terrific year for Brockton and needed a bit more seasoning and confidence to fully establish himself as a major leaguer, but he instead joined a club with a manager that did not elicit the best from him. Playing for the legendary Wright must have seemed exciting, but Harry Wright no longer had his health, and he did little for McCarthy. One good note is that his old South Boston sandlot friend, Arthur Irwin, was a starting infielder for the Phils.

In eight games in his cup-of-coffee tryout with the Phillies, McCarthy batted only .185 and strangely enough, earned a chance to pitch, at which time he got shelled. Somewhat encouragingly, even though he had not played enough to demonstrate his progress, at the beginning of the next season McCarthy donned a Phillies jersey once more.

The situation in Philadelphia should have been ideal for McCarthy. Old Southie friend and team captain Arthur Irwin stood firmly in his corner and the team manager, Harry Wright, had a knack for collecting premier talent. Along with his brother, George, Harry Wright starred in the legendary undefeated Cincinnati Red Stockings of 1869 and later led teams in Boston to preeminence throughout the 1870s.

Wright relocated to Philadelphia in 1884 and managed there for the next ten seasons, but did not approach his previous levels of success. Meanwhile, his brother George wisely founded his lucrative sporting goods company. Part of the futility that Harry Wright encountered resulted from other teams and team owners recognizing the potential for financial windfalls in becoming baseball magnates and luring star players to adorn their rosters in order to attract throngs of paying customers. In Chicago, for instance, Wright's old protégé and

Tommy McCarthy as a "second baseman" for the Philadelphia Phillies. His versatility in many ways hampered his development under manager Harry Wright, who shifted McCarthy all over the field, not allowing him to concentrate on hitting and fielding one set position.

ace pitcher Al Spalding had become a mogul and assembled a formidable squad built around Cap Anson.

In a different vein, some of Harry Wright's wounds were self-inflicted. He did not build stellar squads in Philadelphia, and his handling of Tommy McCarthy stands as a microcosm of this development. In late March, after the Phillies had played in Savannah in preparation for the 1887 campaign, the *Sporting Life* commented, "Mr. Wright pays little McCarthy a glowing tribute by saying his playing at second base could not be excelled. He is as agile as a cat, takes big chances, is correct in fielding and throws accurately. He is likewise doing wonderful work with the stick."

As soon as the teams headed back home to play an extended series of exhibition against the Philadelphia Athletics, Wright proceeded to conduct a frontal campaign on Mac's confidence by not playing him in several of the 12 games, shifting him all over the field (when he did play, he fielded at second base, shortstop and all outfield positions), and having him bat all over the order. At the end of the twelfth game, of the 26 players that batted in the series, McCarthy stood at .276 and a respectable 13th position, but the die is cast. In the twelfth and final game, it is reported that the Phillies tried to put their strongest team together, and in doing so, they omitted McCarthy in that important game.

Astoundingly, even though most teams of that era carried little more than a dozen players, at that juncture the Phillies had twenty men under contract. Immediately, Wright tried to parcel a player to a Lynn, Massachusetts, team and attempted to sell another man to a Toronto club. He had shown little confidence or patience in little McCarthy, his most naturally talented player, and had no surfeit of superstars in the wings to guide his team to a title.

By the time the regular season began, McCarthy stood on the cusp of being cut at any moment and had been publicly embarrassed by his manager by not having the foresight and confidence in starting him in the ultimately worthless exhibition series against the Athletics. It was not that Wright had somehow lost the ability to evaluate talent. He correctly praised McCarthy in late March, and was only a couple of years away from building an outfield with three future Hall of Famers in its ranks, namely Ed Delahanty, Big Sam Thompson and Sliding Billy Hamilton.

Yet in his ten years with the Phillies, Wright never won the National League pennant. The closest he came was in 1887, when his team fell four games short of the title-winning Detroit juggernaut. Arguably Delahanty, Thompson and Hamilton were all better players than McCarthy, but the Phils did not have those players on their roster yet and they did have a very good player in Mac. In 1887, Harry Wright plugged holes with mediocrities like Charley Bastian and screwed a young and promising player, marring his entire team in the process.

Under Harry Wright's lack of tutelage, McCarthy did not get off to an auspicious start in the 1887 season. Essentially used as a utility fielder (playing outfield, second base, shortstop and third base), his struggles with his hitting caused him to virtually match his average with the Phillies at the end of the previous season. In the third week of June, an opportunity to play more developed as the Oshkosh minor league team, managed by his old Haverhill manager, Frank Selee, offered $800 to Philadelphia for McCarthy's services.

At first he refused to report to his new club, creating a bit of a controversy in the process. He decided to straddle the fence and negotiated his salary with his new suitors. He eventually headed up to Wisconsin once he was apprised of his options, or lack thereof, where he was greeted by team manager Frank Selee.

Born in 1859 in Amherst, New Hampshire, Selee was only four years older than McCarthy. At the time he caught up to him in Oshkosh, and indeed throughout their relationship, Selee always seemed much older than his protégé. Although early in Selee's life his family moved to Melrose, Massachusetts, not all that far away from South Boston, Mac seemingly had little in common with the manager.

A Protestant minister's son, Selee played baseball briefly and unsuccessfully, and somewhat surprisingly found himself in his mid–20s managing minor league baseball teams in New England. Unlike the majority of the players and managers in what passed for organized baseball, he was not uncouth nor overbearing, possessing instead almost a boundless calm and serenity about him. He always guided his actions by his simple philosophy that "[i]f I make things pleasant for the players, they reciprocate."

Plainly, this man appeared cut out to attend divinity school and succeed his father as pastor of some quaint old parish. Instead, he not only loved baseball, he had the talent to change it, improve it, and excel in dispatching the responsibilities assigned to him as a baseball manager. Because he maintained such a placid exterior, he had to wait nearly a century after his death to quietly gain induction into the Baseball Hall of Fame. Beneath the calm, however, lay an absolute devotion to winning and an innate skill for evaluating baseball players for their ability and hunger to share in his need to win.

Something Selee saw in McCarthy in 1886 convinced him that this seemingly lost soul on the diamond might serve as a valuable component in a winning franchise. Even before Philadelphia released Mac, Frank Selee had brought his Oshkosh team from the doldrums in the Northwestern League, and team ownership had committed itself to spending reams of money to obtain the finest minor league talent in America. Selee, therefore, brought McCarthy on board.

The Northwestern League not only housed Oshkosh, but also included teams from Des Moines, Duluth, Eau Claire, LaCrosse, Milwaukee, Minneapolis and St. Paul. The later incarnation of the Northwestern League in the early twentieth century contained squads from the Great Northwest coast and Canada, but in 1887, Iowa, Minnesota and Wisconsin formed the northwestern border of the known professional baseball world.

Selee started McCarthy in right field, next to a deaf mute teammate who later enjoyed a long and successful major league career (and lived to be almost 100 years old), Dummy Hoy. Due to his deafness, Hoy worked out a system for avoiding crashes in the outfield involving him, infielders and fellow outfielders, and it worked quite well throughout his career. Hoy also had an intense fear of dying in a fire, so his teammates always let him have the lower bunk on the Pullman train car and one player was always designated as the contact person to run after Hoy in the event of a fire. The system evidently worked as Hoy lived to the age of 99 years.

In an article published toward the end of his life, Selee admitted that despite his calm exterior, "I always entered every game with an intense desire to win, and I think it had its influence upon the players, keeping them keyed up with the determination to win at all odds." In this pursuit of excellence, McCarthy proved a welcome addition and a willing ally, and he made his imprint on the club in his first game with the team. Selee recalled that

"McCarthy was in his prime at that time. I think he opened in Oshkosh with two triples, a double and a single, which was going some even in those days."

Any disorientation or loneliness for Mac was quickly alleviated by the arrival of his wife Margaret, "a handsome lady, about twenty-five years of age," although truthfully she was closer to being between seventeen and nineteen years old. Still, if she was handsome so was Mac, who during his early career was as good looking as a star of the stage, described by the local paper the *Daily Northwestern* as "a fine formed a man as there is in the team." While they obviously made a striking couple, more importantly, she provided him a home life far away from his home and ambition to play major league ball.

Little is known about Tommy McCarthy's wife, and her first appearance in this story apparently was as abrupt as it occurred in real life. It appears that she was the daughter of John McCluskey and Hannah McCluskey and was probably born sometime between 1868 and 1870, as the records which document her conflict with each other. She grew up in South Boston, Irish-Catholic just like Mac, but unlike the case of Hugh Duffy, where his marriages are trumpeted in the newspapers, it is not clear when the McCarthys wed. What we do know is that when she joined McCarthy in Oshkosh, she was about two months pregnant with the couple's first child.

Although the presence of his wife comforted McCarthy, he had new friends to meet. Fans like C.P. Salisbury, who traveled with his favorite team on road trips. Teammates like Dillworth, who was committed to St. Barnabas Hospital after "crashing everyone in the hotel" during a road trip upon suffering from an apparent attack of delirium tremens. And a brief mention must be made of Bill Loveland.

Bill Loveland was an Oshkosh superfan who had an incredibly long beard that he liked to play with. When Oshkosh fell behind in games, he tied knots in his beard and on occasion started chewing on it. In one particularly tense match, Loveland tied 107 separate knots in his beard, to no avail, however, as Minneapolis defeated his team.

Meanwhile, finding the team way behind league-leader Milwaukee, Selee and one of the team owners, a chap named Sawyer, went on a talent run and not only bought out Mac's contract, but also obtained a few players from the Bridgeport, Connecticut, club. Encouragingly, the team gelled into an instant winner. The *Sporting Life* quipped that the Oshkosh owners were spending as much money assembling their team as a National League or American Association team.

The unlikely pairing of Selee and McCarthy flourished. Selee saw that his younger Bay Stater possessed one of the game's keenest strategic baseball minds. As their relationship developed over the years, McCarthy became the preeminent sign stealer on the Boston championship teams, and also developed the hit-and-run play. They shared first-class baseball minds and worked quite harmoniously together. Most importantly, unlike John Morrill and Harry Wright,

Selee channeled McCarthy's cockiness into true confidence and turned his upside into fully realized potential.

The match proved a perfect fit for McCarthy, who had made poor career choices to date and needed a mentor, who unlike Tim Murnane, was not a personal friend. In Oshkosh, Selee and McCarthy matured in their profession together. Selee channeled McCarthy's ambition into enhancing his personal and team-oriented goals, and as Oshkosh won, Selee's reputation soared. Selee was a winner, and he bestowed his magic touch upon Tommy McCarthy, who under his tutelage crushed the ball.

With McCarthy aboard, the Oshkosh team began to challenge for the Northwestern League pennant. McCarthy hit everything, almost never going without a hit in a game and generally making multiple hits in each contest. Batting third ahead of Dummy Hoy, his confidence grew as he blossomed into an offensive playmaker.

On July 19, he used his bat and his considerable speed to leg out a triple, as his team nipped St. Paul, 6–5. Four days later he went 5-for-7 at the plate, including a home run, as he and his mates outslugged Eau Claire, a proud minor league town that one day would welcome Hank Aaron as one of its players.

The management of the Oshkosh entry in the Northwestern League funded a virtual minor league all-star team under manager Frank Selee, who is sitting in the middle row of the photograph, third from the left, with Tommy McCarthy fourth from the left in the same row. Dummy Hoy is seated on the ground in the far left of the first row. Almost all of these players at some point played in the major leagues. Wisconsin Historical Society.

By August 10, the *Sporting Life* reported that Oshkosh was pushing the St. Paul squad hard for third place in the Northwestern League standings. This constituted progress, but the quiet, mild-mannered manager Frank Selee only wanted titles for his teams, so he pressed his team further to battle for the top.

Baseball became fun again for Mac. At about the same time that Hugh Duffy hit a 450-foot home run for the Lowell team halfway across the country, Mac went 3-for-4, including a double, as his team edged out Duluth, 4–2. Duluth had recently been outed as having on its roster a number of players "who nightly visit houses of ill repute and who are great 'lushers.'"

Fortunately for the Oshkosh team, all of the claps its players received emanated from cheering fans. But as August wound down, Oshkosh lost badly to Des Moines, 14–1, seemingly stalling the Wisconsin's team's momentum for the flag.

And then Oshkosh did what every great club must do to secure a pennant by going on a seven-game winning streak in early September. In a doubleheader against Eau Claire, McCarthy went 2-for-5 in one game and 3-for-6 in the second to lead his team to a sweep. By early October, Oshkosh had vaulted to second place in the standings, a bare point behind league-leading Milwaukee.

Finally, on the final day of the season, Oshkosh edged Milwaukee out for the lead, securing the pennant in the Northwestern League. The purchase of McCarthy by the team for only $800 proved a steal, as he provided the impetus for his club's unlikely sprint to the finish. Meanwhile, in Philadelphia, Harry Wright's team lost out on another championship, deprived of the spark that Mac could have provided at the plate and on the base paths.

As a reward for winning the championship, the Oshkosh franchise was faced with the threat of being voted out of the Northwestern League, primarily at the insistence of the Milwaukee club ownership. This unpleasantness did not prevent Oshkosh from staging a huge party for the team and its fans with plenty of speeches and cheers for the boys as the whole town came out to applaud them.

Tommy McCarthy loved being around fans and teammates, and perhaps for the first time in his professional career, baseball began to make sense. He finally had the confidence needed to succeed at the next level, as he had received excellent coaching from Frank Selee and had been given a chance to thrive. Tommy McCarthy was a baseballist.

Chapter 4

A Star Is Born

A most woeful sight presented itself to the greatest hitter in baseball history as he peered for the first time at the playing field at Hampden Park in Springfield, Massachusetts. A proper Englishman would never have considered taking Queen Victoria to a pigpen, but no such propriety accompanied the invitation to the greatest hitter in baseball history to see these dismal grounds, quite literally a baseball diamond in the rough.

No field of dreams, Hampden Park contained more craters than could be found in Blackburn, Lancashire. When it rained, puddles formed all over the place, and when it showered heavily, one part of the field disappeared under up to three feet of water. Balls were lost, uniforms became muddy, and players felt embarrassment.

But while Queen Victoria had known from an early age that she was special, Hugh Duffy did not yet appreciate the dimensions of his talent. Instead of expressing umbrage, he gamely navigated the ruts as he ran to the outfield, to shortstop or behind home plate to catch, wherever his manager deemed he must play on that day.

While Duffy played all over and frequently batted as low as seventh in the batting order, he did as his team's bidding. Before the 1887 season ended, major league franchises throughout the country scouted Duffy, making him the subject of a bidding war between at least two clubs. In the spring of 1887, though, when his Springfield baseball team lost to most everybody, including the varsity of nearby Williams College, few people perceived his gifts. As the year progressed, at least one sportswriter mused that Duffy's play was not exceeded by anyone in the United States, and by year's end, many folks agreed with that scribe. Until then, Duffy avoided the potholes.

The Eastern League of which Springfield was a part constituted a strange organization, and the facilities at Springfield's Hampden Park proved hilarious. The Springfields were particularly inept in the field as they sank quickly to last place in the six-team league, formed entirely from clubs in the Connecticut River Valley or west of the river.

Still, even as soon as one week into the regular season, Hugh Duffy exhibited his natural leadership skills. After saving his team with fine defensive play behind the plate in the tenth inning, his team went on a rare scoring surge in the twelfth to lead by several runs over rival Waterbury, 17–10. But Waterbury had a gambit — if they could extend the game to a point where the umpire had to call it because of darkness, they might at worst salvage a draw.

At one juncture the Waterburys gave up entirely and did not even try to put the Springfield hitters out in an attempt to keep the game going forever, or at least until the umpire had had enough. First they used up fifteen minutes trying to kick reporters, official scorers and even fans out of the park, and then smiling broadly, their fielders began to toss the ball back and forth to each other. Even when play resumed, the circus atmosphere prevailed as they deliberately let balls fall and failed to field grounders around them. The Springfield players even began to walk around the bases in an attempt to get tagged out, but even this did not work when a Waterbury fielder held the ball and did not tag the Springfield runner who walked right past him on the base line.

The remaining fans began to hiss loudly, and the Springfields could only stop the nonsense by having their hitters deliberately strike out. By the time Waterbury came back on the field it was "then so dark that Duffy couldn't see the ball and after putting one man out he threw aside his mask and declared that he couldn't play any longer." Only then did the umpire call the game a draw. More importantly, two things became very clear about the young Duffy, soon dubbed "Sir Hugh." He was smart about his safety as he wore a mask and did not want to sacrifice his health in this ridiculous contest. He also had the good sense and courage to call the farce to an end before someone got hurt. In so many ways, Sir Hugh was a natural.

A few days later "Little Duffy, who is by all odds the safest hitter on the nine," displayed leadership by example by hitting his team's first home run of the season to lead it to a rare victory past his old team, the Hartfords. The press, however, constantly carped on him about his fielding at shortstop, claiming he was better suited at catcher, ignoring totally the fact that with his speed he belonged in the outfield.

Nevertheless, he played his heart out on a ridiculous team in a disorganized league. For instance, in one game against Danbury, the league umpire never appeared at the game, so the Danbury team doctor served quite partially to his own team in the arbiter role. The joke reached such a point that many of the 1,200 home fans were permitted to stand behind the plate from first to third, and when a ball got past their catcher, they kicked it back to him. When the ball got past Duffy, who caught that day, the fans would kick it away from him. The Springfields left the game early to catch a train back home, thereby putting the worthless exercise behind them.

On May 25, 1887, Springfield hosted the Danbury team at Hampden Park before a pathetic crowd of 100 people. After the game, the team abruptly ceased to exist. Duffy and his teammates were free agents. With the hapless Springfields Duffy demonstrated his mastery at the plate, batting .350 in 17 games. Balancing power and speed, he hit four doubles, two triples and a home run in addition to stealing 17 bases. It came to naught, however, because ball clubs before the turn of the century often existed in a terminal state for months or even years before they padlocked their gates and shut down forever, often in the course of an ongoing season.

And so it was with the Springfields, who ceased operations before the end of May, leaving their players to look for new teams to join or new careers outside of baseball to pursue. Fortunately, Duffy had made a good account of himself. When he searched for new opportunities, he did not have to wait long before one of the Salem team operators gave him a rehearsal.

In 1692, the Massachusetts Court of Oyer and Terminer sitting in Salem put to death twenty people upon suspicions that were witches or warlocks. In 1887, much of the angst and guilt from the community had been purged, or at the least had helped create great literature by one of the judge's heirs, Nathaniel Hawthorne. By 1887, most people prepared not for mea culpas, but for great baseball, a wish fulfilled when a diminutive Hugh Duffy came to their home ball field as their newest ballplayer, late of the disbanded Springfield club.

Had the witch trials still been in operation and force, judges may have had much difficulty believing that such speed on the base paths and power from the plate emanated from such a small player, but Duffy never saw much in his talent that confounded him. His approach was very simple: swing the bat and try to make contact. Still, since the Salem team was nicknamed the Witches, Duffy became a witch.

While Salem is on the eastern shore of Massachusetts, clear across the state from Springfield, its minor league team closely resembled Duffy's defunct club. Poorly financed, run by people with little knowledge of sports business and entertainment, and lacking adequate facilities, the Salems did not have even a shoe string on which to budget themselves. In retrospect, it was a wonderful place for a young athlete to cast his fate because the franchise was so disorganized, the players had a chance to show themselves off to other more stable clubs.

According to folklore, Hugh Duffy almost returned to the mills before his career in baseball really began. A most merry soul, Hugh Duffy became a very good story-teller with age, and when he recalled his first game with the Salems, his tales became broader and more improbable as time progressed. Apparently one of the team leaders, "Wally" Fessenden, wanted to give Duffy a tryout, but a major team backer, a cheapskate named George Vickery, wanted no part of this tiny little guy on his team (almost every early Duffy story is embroidered in David-versus-Goliath terms, with the short ballplayer overcoming great odds to achieve stardom).

Historically, in his first game for the Salems, Duffy bombed out, making several errors and failing to hit at all. The folklore has falsely established this as his first game in organized ball, overlooking his experiences in Hartford and Springfield, and that it was almost his last. In these accounts a superstar of the day, speedy infielder Arlie Latham, is on the opposing team and gleefully watches the young upstart struggle. Supposedly, too, Vickery and the fans loathed Duffy and wished to send him to the gallows, but Fessenden adamantly refused to ditch Duffy without giving him a second chance to prove his mettle. In his second game, of course, Duffy starred, the fans fell in love with him, and he belongs to the ages.

The little tale is true in its broad strokes, as Duffy did have a bad first day and redeemed himself thereafter. Other parts of the story do not stand up to scrutiny, however. George Vickery apparently had little influence over the team and either had nothing to do with it after Duffy's first game or had a cameo role to play at best in club operations. Duffy did not embarrass himself before one of the game's greats, Arlie Latham, for on that day Latham played on the roster of the major league St. Louis Browns, nowhere near the site of the epic tale. Most importantly, Duffy was on the verge of becoming one of the greatest hitters in baseball, and his raw talent and ambition generated his career ascent, not the luck of the draw.

Still, the Salems were just glad to have him on their team, because they needed stars due to the club's financial condition, which hovered very close to subsistence levels. At that time, the Salems played in the fluid New England League, which at one or another time consisted of the Lowells, Portlands (ME), Manchesters, the Haverhills, the Haverhill Blues, the Lynns, the Boston Blues, the Salems and the Old Salems. While the New England League rated as a minor league, it probably differed little in talent level from the late Union Association, and in fact some of Tommy McCarthy's old teammates and opponents from the Unions filled out the rosters of the New England Leagues.

Unlike the major leagues of the late nineteenth century, which at times could attract as many as 30,000 fans and gate-crashers (although generally the games did not have anywhere near that many cranks), the New England League rarely ran more than 4,000 people through its turnstiles, even to critical games.

On July 5, for instance, only 500 people attended the Salems game against the Lowells, but of much more import, on that day Hugh Duffy served as a labor agitator. He and his teammates went on strike and refused to play since they had not received pay for quite some time. Some creative collective bargaining ensued and it was agreed that the players would split the game proceeds after Lowell had received its share of the gate. As events transpired, the game went on and Salem won the contest, 16–9, behind the fielding of Duffy and the inspired hitting of his rejuvenated teammates.

Flush with success, on the next day the Salems played the Boston Blues, a team created by the old Boston Unions manager, Tim Murnane, and got

Was King Kelly America's first rock star? From this nineteenth century baseball card, it appears that he was. Here he belts out a solo on air guitar while his manager decides whether to play him at first base or catcher. Like Carlton Fisk, King Kelly arguably played his best years in Chicago, but he will be forever remembered as a Boston ball player, and in fact is buried in the city of Boston.

hammered, 15–9. The game might not otherwise deserve even a footnote, but at this game as a spectator was larger-than-life Boston Nationals superstar Mike "King" Kelly, later a teammate of Duffy and ultimately a Hall of Famer. Duffy concealed any awe he might have felt around this great player by winning kudos the next day in the press both for his slugging and his remarkable play at shortstop. Duffy must have been thrilled at playing so well before the legendary Kelly, and Kelly probably left the game almost as impressed with Duffy as he was with himself.

Frustratingly, on the evening of that historic game, the Salems directors met to ponder the future of the club. Apparently, the team owners had earned the contempt of their players for not paying them in a timely manner, a development that squeezed Duffy more than many because he did not have a permanent home near Salem and had less financial leeway to exhibit patience. The directors recommended either selling to interested parties in Salem, or barring that, to parties in Concord, New Hampshire, or Brockton, Massachusetts. Within a week both the Salems and the Boston Blues had disbanded, the latter team becoming the Haverhills.

Fortuitously for Duffy, within a week's time of the directors' meeting, he donned the uniform of another New England League club, the Lowells. Playing right field in his debut, he hit well and watched his team's pitcher get sick in the fifth inning and have to leave in the eighth due to having fairly swooned due to the heat. Sir Hugh must have smirked a bit because he never begged out of a game.

Then as now, Lowell is an uncommonly special place to watch a baseball game. Today it houses the Spinners, a minor league affiliate of the Boston Red Sox, which once famously issued Jack Kerouac bobblehead dolls to honor its acclaimed native, author of *On the Road*. The city loves its teams, as exhibited in 1887, when, although the Lowells were stuck in fourth place, one of the local papers proudly predicted that its team would rise to first place by August 1.

That did not occur, and yet in a magical game in late July, for instance, Duffy's team defeated the Haverhills, 5–4, in a tough game in which he hit a long fly ball to center field that struck the top of the fence, shot up high in the air, and then settled outside of the fence for a home run. He did not need luck but he received it in abundance after making the simple move from Salem.

While the Lowells began to win regularly and threaten the league-leading Portland team, the conditions under which the team played bordered on the bizarre. In a game at Manchester, the Lowells contended with about 1,000 New Hampshire cranks, many of whom "rushed onto the field to bother [the Lowell fielders] while catching flies swore at our men as they came to bat and talked fight from the beginning to end."

This moronic rowdyism is not a singular occurrence. In another game that Lowell played in New Hampshire that year, the Manchesters' Johnny Troy shouted at the umpire, a chap named Lynch, for calling him out at second base. Troy's comments became heated and the umpire fined him $10, at which time Troy stormed off second base, clenched his fist, and punched Lynch in the face. Lynch fined Troy another $25 and resigned from the game, while the local fans shouted out three cheers for Troy, stormed the field to shake hands with him, and took up a collection to pay his fines. If this were not surreal enough, to replace Lynch as umpire, Morgan Murphy, who either had just signed or was about to sign as a player with Lowell, stepped in and umpired the remainder of the game, which Lowell won of course.

In another unrelated disturbing development at this time, one of the Lowell club's directors allegedly began to overtly bet against his own team winning. If true, he lost his shirt because his team had pulled close to the leading Portland team. Even if this story were apocryphal, it indicates that long before the 1919 Black Sox scandal, gambling had infected baseball beyond cranks laying down money at the ballpark or at a pool. By the time these allegations became public, Duffy had carried his team from a fourth-place outfit to a challenger with his league-leading .431 batting average and his stellar play at third base.

Relentlessly, Duffy led his team to triumph. In a 14–2 victory against the Lynns at River Park, Duffy hit two home runs, one of which constituted the longest hit in the ballpark that year. For this titanic effort, Duffy won a new hat. However, in a game against Manchester, the umpire proved to be his kryptonite as he called Sir Hugh out when he supposedly was struck by a batted ball while running from second to third. Duffy yelled to his manager that he had out-jumped the ball, and received a $10 fine for his impudence, after which he became rattled and committed several errors. Amazingly, he could submit to almost inhumane abuse from opposing fans and baiting from the other team, but at the least provocation from an umpire, he quite often went ballistic. Hugh Duffy hated umpires.

Nevertheless, by late August 1887, Tim Murnane took notice of the caliber of play in the mill towns of Maine, New Hampshire and northeast Massachusetts by dubbing Hugh Duffy, Hatfield and Davin the "kingpins of the New England League." While Duffy generally batted sixth with Salem and had not set any fires at the plate, with the Lowells he quite suddenly became the superstar of the New England League, and Murnane (who probably was already in bed with the major league Chicago team) began to scout the New England League assiduously. Not coincidentally, the rumors shortly thereafter floated around that Anson and the Chicago Colts might make an offer to the Pride of Lowell.

At the same time that Murnane endorsed the Lowells' new star, Duffy led his team to a 7–7 tie in Portland, again with a multiple-hit game. His teammate, center fielder Cudworth, led the kicking (arguing against the umpire's decision-making) and perhaps helped inculcate this tendency in Duffy, later to become one of the most notorious umpire baiters of his generation. Portland tied the game in the ninth, which ignited the hometown fans to cheer themselves hoarse while throwing cushions and hats in the air in jubilation. Neither team won as the game was called due to darkness in the 10th inning, but Duffy kept pounding the opposition with his drill-press hitting.

In a game against Lynn, for instance, Duffy swatted two hits, stole four bases and impressed one of the scribes so much that he was moved to write the performance "couldn't have been exceeded by any player in the country." To top matters off, a screaming line drive came his way and Duffy tried to catch it, but it came out of his hand, at which point he acrobatically caught it for an out before the ball hit the ground.

Back to the pennant race. On August 31, the Lowells narrowly lost to the Manchesters, which coupled with a Portland victory provided some respite for the Portlands. Most significantly, for the first time ever, a player hit a home run over the center-field fence in that New Hampshire ball field and, of course,

Duffy hit it. The ball traveled at least 450 feet, an impressive distance in that era, and was an early indication that although small in stature, Duffy was a powerful young man with a quick bat. As an incentive to its hitters, the Manchester management promptly promised a new gold watch to any of its players who hit a round-tripper in that same area.

Similarly in a 21–5 mauling of Manchester, Duffy hit three home runs, two of which were inside-the-park shots, not surprising due to his great speed on the bases. He probably would have hit his fourth home run but the opposing outfielder played "100 feet" out of position and grabbed the hit after it hit a carriage parked nearby and caromed over to the fielder, stopping Duffy at third base. This account is how the newspaper called it at the time.

As part of Duffy's storytelling, he later told his listeners that he actually had hit four home runs that day, but that after the third homer, the opposing outfielder hid a ball in the field. In the later inning when Duffy hit what was apparently his fourth home run, the outfielder picked up the hidden ball and threw that ball into the infield to hold an incredulous Duffy to a triple. In another story regarding the same incident, Duffy had the opposing outfielder either standing or sitting in the carriage lucking out when Duffy hit it almost right to him.

On September 2, the Lowells defeated league-leading Portland and Duffy again lit up the scorecards with his multiple hits and his catch of a screaming line drive. His ego may have suffered a bit when he read the *Boston Globe* the next day and saw that the newspaper referred to him as "Henry Duffy," but on a team level, the victory brought the Lowells to within one-half game of the leading Portlands. Association President Howe was so tickled pink over the victory that he took Duffy and his teammates out to the theatre that evening as a reward. Portland stood at 57-30, with Lowell threatening at 56-30.

As a welcome respite to the pennant race, Lowell hosted the National League major league club with its stars Monte Ward, Orator Jim O'Rourke, Roger Connor and Silent Mike Tiernan and beat them, 6–3, undoubtedly because New York did not start one of its legendary pitchers. Still, Duffy banged out three hits and shined in his effort to impress the big leaguers with his ability to play in their ranks.

In a different vein, in mid–September the major league St. Louis Browns banded together and refused to play "the negro club the Cuban Giants," simply another example of the hardening Jim Crow attitude descending upon American baseball. Encouragingly, the Giants split two exhibitions against Lowell a week later, although a local rag noted, "The coaching of the Giants was the funniest exhibition we have ever seen outside of the minstrel stage."

On the final game of the season Portland defeated Lowell and the pennant race ended in a dead tie. In a league meeting in Boston, the Lowell ownership argued that it had already won a contention hotly disputed by Portland ownership and upon a league vote the six remaining teams deadlocked. As a compromise, Lowell and Portland agreed to play a five-game playoff to decide the league championship, a deal which profited the owners since teams loved scheduling exhibitions to earn more money.

On September 29, Lowell defeated Portland in the first game of their championship series before an uninspiring crowd of 1,003 cranks. Duffy fielded well but provided little help with the bat and was thrown out trying to steal. Tensions ran particularly high, and around this time a Portland team official had to deny rumors that his fans had chased an umpire around the field with "anger, canes and carriage cushions." The Lowells squeezed out a run in the tenth inning to defeat Portland in the second championship game, 5–4, and although Sir Hugh did not push the winning run across the plate, he did receive a commendation for his "good work."

The Lowells finally won their championship after two partially played rain-outs by defeating the Portlands, 7–0, in Boston. The game was a blow out from the beginning, and Duffy swatted three hits and scored two runs to lead his team to the coveted award of the *Boston Globe's* gold medals, symbolic of supremacy in the New England League. The most remarkable play occurred before the game when one of the players was hitting fungos to his Portland teammates and managed to get knocked unconscious by chasing one of his own pop-ups and running into the Portlands' star player, Hatfield. The Lowells formally received their gold medals at a ceremonial banquet in their honor at the American House in Lowell, as their management went off scrambling for post-season exhibition games.

At this event, Duffy apparently exhibited his more cantankerous side, and what a wonderfully colorful nature it was. On the evening of the party at the American House, the *Lowell Weekly Sun* reported that "Duffy was slouching around with a dirty flannel shirt on." At this point, "A gentleman advised him to put on a linen shirt as it was hardly the proper thing for him to appear in the one he was wearing. 'What the h— do you take me for?' said the champion batter in the New England League. 'Ain't I as good as any of them d— blokes?' And he didn't change his shirt, but sat through the whole evening when he wasn't shoveling food into his mouth with a look of bored indifference on his face." Hugh Duffy was a delightful guy, but particularly at this stage of his life he did not take well to people giving him orders.

Plus, by this time, Duffy probably knew he would not be playing ball next year in Lowell, as Tim Murnane had been working surreptitiously to land the young player (and Charley Farrell, of one of the Salem incarnations) with Cap Anson's Chicago team. Supposedly, Duffy had promised Arthur Soden and the other two Boston major league owners (called the Triumvirs) that before taking any offer from any other major league team, he would speak with them. Apparently their telegrams and other communications to him went unanswered.

Duffy harbored reservations concerning the sincerity of Boston's willingness to let him play regularly in 1888. Murnane may have placed some of those doubts in his mind, perhaps in part from watching his friend Tommy McCarthy languish with the Bostons in 1885 and sitting out while mediocrities populated the outfield. On a more remote level, perhaps Duffy had by this time met McCarthy and received word of this himself, although the possibility that Murnane sabotaged Boston seems more plausible. After all, Murnane had definitely seen Duffy play and harbored no love-loss for the Bostons, with whom he competed for the entertainment dollar in the 1884 Union Association year. Plus, Murnane worked for Cap Anson.

In the end, Duffy made the decision. He may have relished the opportunity to play for Chicago team owner Al Spalding and legendary captain Cap Anson, in addition to believing he had more of an opportunity to play there. Certainly, Duffy specifically said he did not believe Boston meant to give him much time in the field in at least one interview he gave, and signed with Chicago for a $500 advance and a further promise of a relatively lucrative salary.

In late October, Lowell played the National League Boston club for the mythical championship, and the Bostons had little trouble handling their minor league neighbors, beating them in each exhibition game. Few fans took the exhibition seriously and even fewer, a scant 400 at one game, braved the advancing cold weather for the second game. In the first game, played in Lowell, many disgusted fans marched off the field before the game ended. Those that did watch invariably fixated their attention on resident superstar King Kelly, but hopefully a few of them averted their gaze to the finest player on the field by that time, Hugh Duffy.

Duffy's ascent did not resemble McCarthy's rise for a number of reasons. While the two young men each possessed ambitious natures, Duffy took a much more calculating and cerebral approach to personal advancement, while Mac permitted his appetites to exceed his grasp. If one placed their early baseball careers on a bar graph, Duffy's rise could be charted by a line that gradually but without break shot upward, while McCarthy's would bounce up and down like a lie detector test sheet.

Mac needed mentors, whether it be Tim Murnane or Frank Selee, and even there he did not always follow their advice or take their orders with equanimity. Duffy did what he was told, whether it involved playing second base or shortstop or the outfield, never deviating from his principal goal. Most importantly, Duffy possessed better natural talent and almost always out-trained his heavenly twin.

Instead, Duffy made the most of the opportunities that presented themselves to him. In the early part of the season he joined up with a Springfield team so weak financially that it barely survived past the opening game before disintegrating. He latched onto a Salem team firmly entrenched in last place in the New England League with financial issues so severe that the players had to strike to get paid. The Salems also planted their best player in the sixth

DUFFY, S. S., Chicago's

OLD JUDGE

CIGARETTE FACTORY

COODWIN & CO., New York

Hugh Duffy had high expectations for his career after leaving Lowell for Cap Anson's Chicago major league club. The look on Duffy's face helps inform us whether his expectations were met.

position in the batting order until that team too went bust.

In this momentous year, Duffy joined a mediocre Lowell club, seemingly entrenched in fourth place, and by sheer force of his skills and leadership, led the club to the pennant. In the course of his experience with Lowell, he transformed himself from a footnote on an obscure Springfield club to arguably the finest baseball player in the world. That is exhilarating stuff, but the gentleman who told Duffy to put on a linen shirt during the pennant-winning celebration at the American Hotel in Lowell got it all wrong. Duffy did not have to change a thing, not even his ratty shirt. With an ornery streak married to remarkable talent and an ambitious will to figure out what it took to succeed, Duffy was the perfect ballplayer for his age. He carried the Lowell team to the pennant as he later carried his Boston Beaneaters to glory in the next decade.

Chapter 5

Mac and the St. Louis Browns

The superstar of the defending American Association champion St. Louis Browns in the spring of 1888 was not team manager Charles Comiskey, 32-game winning pitcher Silver King, ace hitter Tip O'Neill, speedster third baseman Arlie Latham or colorful second baseman Yank Robinson. The straw that stirred the drink did not even play the field but rather owned the team — Chris Von der Ahe.

Born in Germany, Chris Von der Ahe became wealthy by buying up businesses in St. Louis until ultimately he bought the Browns, the local professional baseball team. Like old man Noah, Von der Ahe knew a thing or two, but thought he knew it all. He did not know it all.

The danger in approaching Von der Ahe as a person is that there is a tendency to pigeonhole him based on one of his central characteristics, an approach which prevailed in the mid-twentieth century and remains a threat today. It is easy to write off Von der Ahe as a clown, but by doing so, this obscures his considerable devious side. If he is portrayed solely as a schemer, then the aspect of him that helped keep the American Association alive (in contrast to another St. Louis magnate, Henry Lucas, whose duplicity and ambition ensured that the Union Association lasted only one year) does not receive its proper due.

Similarly, viewing him as a complex character also fails because he was a very simple person underneath. He personified impulse, and whatever his impulse encouraged him to do, he did it. Like many people who want to be nice but do not possess a charitable soul by nature, Von der Ahe sometimes did accomplish good things. At his essence, he was a very egotistical man whose considerable strengths clashed constantly with the tragic flaws in his constitution. He screwed other people and in the end screwed himself, a modern-day Charles O. Finley.

On occasions, Von der Ahe fell into luck, none more prominently than when he partially dismantled his 1887 champions and somehow came up with a strong substitute version. Acting upon a tip from Yank Robinson (who knew

McCarthy, having played against him in the old Union Association), Manager Comiskey sought out the services of Mac to replace star outfielder Curt Welch. Among his issues with the Browns, Welch liked to drink alcohol to an unhealthy degree, an occupational hazard for too many baseballists of the era. Considering some of the drinkers on the Browns, not to mention their owner, Welch must have truly stood out.

Thus, McCarthy's entrance had been orchestrated beforehand as the Browns, after winning their third straight pennant in 1887, traded Welch and another player for three Philadelphia Athletics and cash. The Browns needed an outfielder, and Von der Ahe found a capable replacement for Welch. In the spring of 1888, the defending American Association champion St. Louis Browns welcomed Tommy McCarthy as the savior of the franchise. All this occurred after four brief and generally unsuc-cessful partial seasons of major league play by their new player; the spirit of St. Louis spawned the leg-end of Tommy McCarthy.

McCarthy had come into camp well conditioned, having worked out all winter with his South Boston friends at Boston College, sparing a week from conditioning in January only to celebrate the birth of his daughter Sadie. In later years, he did not always come to the ball field in excellent shape, but at this stage of his development, he generally worked hard during the off-season and liked training among his old Southie friends.

Without McCarthy even having appeared in St. Louis, the *Post Dispatch* had this to say about their much-hyped new addition: "Thos. McCarthy, the Browns' new right fielder, who is regarded by ball players as a faster base-runner than Latham, is expected here tomorrow. He is said to be a peer of Nicol in the field, and if he turns out as well as his friends here think, he will be the best right-fielder the Browns have ever had."

The matinee idol as a young St. Louis Brown. The year before a newspaper in Oshkosh, Wisconsin, had fairly gushed about Tommy McCarthy as "a fine formed a man as there is in the team." National Baseball Hall of Fame Library, Cooperstown, N.Y.

The honeymoon continued in his first appearance for the Browns, in an exhibition days later, as "the little outfielder is a marvel of physical strength ... can cover an immense amount of field. Capt. Comiskey has a veritable jewel in him." His popularity soon extended to the fans as he became a local favorite.

Early press clippings emphasize his speed and say little about his batting, and McCarthy certainly read his sports articles because soon he made base-stealing his forte, culminating in a fourth-place finish in the association leaders in stolen bases. His slowness to develop hitting prowess was excused in large part, as old manager Frank Selee weighed in an interview in late May, explaining "he played as fine a game as was ever played in the outfield.... Wait til he gets his eye in, then your people will have an opportunity to see him at his best.... He is a terrific hitter."

Still, by June 2, 1888, McCarthy had only raised his average to a very pedestrian .270, and by early July, cynics compared him unfavorably to the departed Curt Welch. The criticism most famously emanated from another former Browns star from 1887, Bob Caruthers. Parisian Bob (so named because he once supposedly had visited Paris, France) had won 29 games the year before and also hit over .300 playing in the outfield, but in 1888, had accounted for himself very well with the Brooklyn club, the Browns' main rival in the association. While conceding McCarthy's greater speed, Caruthers preferred Welch, supposedly for his better "judgment." As events transpired, McCarthy's and Welch's statistics at the end of the season differed slightly, which worked well for Von der Ahe, as all he needed to do was to replace Welch.

Although Brooklyn led the association in early July, the judgment of the team's management came under scrutiny as it brought onto its roster second baseman Black Jack Burdock, one of the most out-of-control drunkards in baseball history. Burdock returned the Brooklyn team's confidence in him by batting .122 for the rest of the pennant race. This was a truly horrible acquisition, particularly when viewed with the presence of at least one other problem drinker on the roster, namely Curt Welch. While that acquisition proved disastrous in the long term, it did not immediately affect the Brooklyn team, which proceeded to sweep the Browns in a four-game series ending on July 10.

Not happy with Brooklyn's lead in the association and the sweep of his team, Von der Ahe injected himself into the race by staging a diversion and accusing his rival's owner, Charles Byrne, of tampering. More important for the Browns' fortunes than their owner's jackass behavior was the return to their lineup of Tommy McCarthy from an unspecified illness. The tampering charges went nowhere, but McCarthy went right from being sick to getting filleted after Kansas City's Sam Barkley badly spiked his hand in a game on July 17, 1888. Stoically, McCarthy stayed in the lineup, bad hand and all.

While Mac went down, the entire Brooklyn team went into a profound downspin after sweeping St. Louis, playing .400 ball for the rest of July and well under .400 ball throughout August. Late in the year, McCarthy acted in a most ferocious manner in Philadelphia after finding fault with a call by Umpire Ferguson. He began furiously arguing his point, charitably interspersing his comments with profanities, for which he received a fine of $25 per expletive until he rang up a $75 bill, a relatively stiff fine. At one point he told Ferguson to go to hell, pretty much par for the course in terms of the abuse umpires of that era endured.

After going back to his bench to grouse, Mac grabbed a baseball and reportedly threw it full force at Ferguson's head, missing by a foot. Since the umpire's back was turned, he did not see the missile and levied no further fine, but the fans gave McCarthy a hard time, and the *Philadelphia News* laid it on pretty thick. The *Philadelphia Inquirer*, reporting the same incident, makes no mention of the attempted fragging, and it may have never occurred. The *St. Louis Post Dispatch* defended Mac, adding that "a more quiet, gentlemanly and diffident player than McCarthy never walked on a ball field."

Polite yes, but Mac never walked away from an interview, and when the *Sporting News* came to call, he had this to say: "Yes, I am the freshest man in the business, that is if [umpire] Ferguson is banned. There's a man I have no use for. Yes, I had a short interview with Ferguson in Philadelphia and it cost me seventy-five. The fine ought not to go. I could not even speak in the coaching base. He made me keep still all through the game. I have got about as much use for him as I have for a chump. The umpires ought to get fined once in a while for their rotten work. It would keep them down a bit."

Around this time the national sports press analyzed the incongruity in Mac's actions as he "is getting the name of being a 'tough' in the East. Mac is one of the most gentlemanly ball players on the diamond today — at least he has always behaved himself like a gentleman while in St. Louis — both off and on the field, and why he should be called a tough and a thug by the Eastern press is something that I cannot understand."

What seems to run through all of these accounts is that he lost his temper, and the more people came to know him, it did not constitute an isolated incident for him to do so while he roamed the ball field. Throwing the ball at the umpire's head almost certainly never occurred because at that stage, McCarthy's throw would not have missed. St. Louis fans in time came to appreciate the ambitious and sometimes hot-headed competitiveness that the generally mild-mannered star brought to his game. Had he been taller and been born a bit later, Mac would have made one hell of a hockey player.

In a down year for batting in the association, Tommy McCarthy batted .274, second on his team behind the stellar batting of Tip O'Neill, who excelled at an association-leading pace of .335. McCarthy also stole 93 bases, good for fourth overall in the league.

There was one tiny bit of business left for the Browns to conduct and that was to engage in a championship series with the New York club, pennant winners of the rival National League. St. Louis had played and lost a series at the end of 1887 against the then-champion Detroit squad, and these events never went well for Browns players.

Other than the championship series, Von der Ahe found every way to degrade his players and not pay them. St. Louis did not play well against the New York team, although McCarthy acquitted himself rather well. At the end, the Browns lost, and the players hated Von der Ahe even more than before. For Mac's part he returned home as soon as possible to wife Margaret and daughter Sadie in South Boston.

Having won four straight American Association championships and not lost any key personnel in the off-season, most baseball fans and scribes felt confidence in the Browns five-peating in 1889. The previous year's version had lost a number of stars but seamlessly added new players like McCarthy into a dynamic winner. And with this team gelling under capable manager Charlie Comiskey, virtually nothing stood in its way of waltzing over the opposition.

The only obstacle in their path was their mercurial team owner, Chris Von der Ahe, whose hubris had assumed mythological proportions. The Browns had met their enemy and increasingly it was "der Poss." Still, on opening day in St. Louis, he made his appearance reportedly as happy as a clam, having decorated the park with bunting and lacing his owner's box with American flags. The band regaled the crowd with renditions of "The Conquering Heroes Come."

With those bold notes still in their ears, the players started off their new campaign in an extraordinarily encouraging way as the club sailed to 13 victories in its first 15 contests, and had apparently sewn up another title in the first week of May. Instead, at this point they lost it, and it all started with an elderly ticket-taker.

In a home game against Louisville, Browns second baseman Yank Robinson noticed before the game that his pants did not fit. He sent a boy to the hotel to pick up a pair of padded trousers for him, which the boy duly did, but when he returned to the park, the gate-keeper refused to let the boy back in. Hearing about this, Robinson left the dressing room in his uniform and started screaming obscenities at the gate-keeper, reportedly within the earshot of several ladies.

And in microcosm, we have the classic Von der Ahe stalemate, where the owner quickly draws a line in the sand, and subsequently can only with difficulty dig himself out of the mess that he impulsively created. Robinson should not have browbeaten the man, particularly in the presence of ladies. But rather than let the matter fade away, Von der Ahe accelerated the unpleasantness. Hearing this he publicly upbraided Robinson near the grandstand and fined him $25. It was a classic shoot from the hip Von der Ahe move — embarrass the player publicly (ostensibly the same sin that Robinson had recently committed with the gate-keeper) and then hit him in the pocket book. Had Von der Ahe possessed any tact and a minimum of common sense, he would have contacted Comiskey, who most likely would have asked Yank to apologize to the old gent and watch his temper.

Instead, Robinson dug in his heels and refused to play again until Von der Ahe reversed the fine. The matter took on a life of its own at this stage because in that era, the fans generally ponied up the money for a player's penalty. But rather than find a way to permit Robinson to not lose face, the owner publicly demanded that the fine come out of his pay. With the team standing on the train tracks, prepared to embark on a series in Kansas City, the players held a meeting and virtually to a man refused to embark on the trip. The sole exceptions were Manager Comiskey and center fielder Charlie Duffee, a certifiable "cigarette fiend" who accompanied a steaming Von der Ahe on the excursion across state.

Back at the station, more responsible front office officials prevailed, and the remaining teammates changed their stance and decided to jump on a later train, but the incident had metastasized. Von der Ahe looked very bad in the public's opinion, and the Browns' players had conspired at some point to play in Kansas City, but not necessarily exert themselves with an excess of skill or élan.

In fact, they made a mockery of the ongoing fiasco by tanking three games to an opponent they towered over. In the first game the Browns sloppily lost, 16–3, and McCarthy had to play second base to replace the departed Robinson, and then moved back to right field when Nat Hudson was called in to relieve as the runs began to curiously pile up. Tip O'Neill in particular did all the speaking necessary in the house by booting ball after easy ball hit to him; the papers deduced the situation immediately by stating the obvious: "The Strike Caused It."

Believing it far better to win a battle than win a war, Von der Ahe accelerated the decline by threatening to penalize the players, fine Robinson $25 each day he refused to play (with expulsion from the team promised on the fifth day of his intransigence), blacklist some players, and trade away a number of other players.

In this whirl, Tommy McCarthy undoubtedly sided with his teammates but played rather well in spurts. In one of the other odd games, he played second base, center field and right field, and went two-for-five at the plate. Still, at least three games carried a distinct odor, and probably the fourth game in Kansas City was tainted, but the opposition played so poorly that the Browns could not give the game away.

No one even tried to claim the Browns were playing on the up and up. On May 6, 1889, the *St. Louis Post Dispatch* ran a headline that read "Playing Ball to Lose — The Browns Continue Their 'Queer' Work At Kansas City," and editorialized that "[t]he team is, as team, playing to lose, playing to get even with President Von der Ahe, in the Robinson matter."

The next day the *St. Louis Post Dispatch* ran another yellow headline, proclaiming that "The Quitters Return." However, by this point, someone finally began to persuade Von der Ahe that he had lost his team and that perhaps a plethora of other clubs might pay (at a discount, of course) for the Browns' disgruntled players. Von der Ahe went on an untruth offensive, claiming that his team had merely played in bad luck, that the Kansas City park was in horrible shape because it doubled as a gun-shooting ground and that the sun was so bad that Tommy McCarthy had to wear smoked glasses to deflect its harmful effects.

No one bought this prattle, of course, but it did finally calm tensions a bit, as Robinson and his padded trousers slinked back to the team, and presumably the gatekeeper was able to continue to abuse young boys and assorted whippersnappers, blatherskites and poltroons who annoyed him. The problem that remained was the players genuinely hated Von der Ahe and he knew it, and the club had lost three games that might come in handy in a tight pennant race in October.

There were other problems, with star third baseman Arlie Latham providing headaches to players and management alike. A good-hit, no-field third baseman, Latham juggled his life as a clown, a drunk and an expert base-stealer, and the fans loved him. During the 1889 season, though, Latham's behavior became increasingly erratic and objectionable, as Mac witnessed on May 27, in a game against Kansas City. With Comiskey and McCarthy on base, Mac called out to Latham to coach behind third base, but Latham outright refused to do so.

This incident would have meant little in isolation, particularly in that rowdy era of baseball, but like most of Latham's hijinks, it did not stand alone. For more important reasons, Von der Ahe suspended Latham, and while it is difficult to side with der Poss in any labor matter, his wayward player had probably deserved it with his unreliability and drunkenness. Ultimately, it served to make the struggle to win a pennant even more difficult for the Browns, with the rival Brooklyn team tough to put away.

The previous year, the Brooklyn team with its many Browns castoffs had choked in the clutch, but in 1889, they let their stars play with a minimum of distractions and ultimately edged out St. Louis in the American Association race by two games, or one fewer than the team had thrown in their early-season games in Kansas City. All this because a ticket-taker did not let a young boy back into the park with Yank Robinson's pants. While Von der Ahe had worn down his players, he still had an ally in the *Sporting News*, which referred late in the campaign to der Poss' "true and manly characteristics."

Labor unrest quickly overtook the public's attention to the American Association or National League races. Led by John Montgomery Ward, the Players' Brotherhood decided to form a league of its own, establishing eight teams and stockpiling them by luring stars from every established leagues' rosters, with few exceptions. Shortly after the 1889 imbroglio ended, Tommy McCarthy and teammate shortstop Shorty Fuller signed new contracts with the Browns. As a result, when the Players' League formed, they had already bound themselves to their old team.

Having let the championship slip away by clearly throwing three games in Kansas City and their team owner fining everyone in sight, the 1890 edition of the St. Louis Browns found themselves severely weakened by the scourge threatened the previous season by the Players' Brotherhood and brought to fruition in the off-season, which was the creation of a separate Players' League to compete against the established American Association and National League.

St. Louis did not stand alone in losing most of its best players, as every other team saw the majority of stars defect to the Players' League. In Chicago, for instance, Hugh Duffy and all of the other key fielders, save Anson, defected to the new league.

With Fuller and pitcher Happy Jack Stivetts, Mac endured a forced loyalty to the St. Louis Browns, although he "could have been with the [Players' League] this year, but foolishly tied himself up early last fall." Needing a captain/manager after Charlie Comiskey jumped to the Chicago Players' League team with Tip O'Neill, Silver King and Arlie Latham, Von der Ahe appointed Mac the new manager of the St. Louis Browns. After four years of futility in the major leagues and only two fairly successful years there, Mac had his own team, at least for fifteen minutes or so.

Von der Ahe made no secret in the pre-season as to whom manipulated the levers for the Browns as he stormed into the team clubhouse after they lost an exhibition to the Omaha minor league contingent. Fuming every which way as he bolted into the dressing room, he encountered McCarthy who "pulled him aside and talked earnestly to him for a few minutes, after which the President walked away." McCarthy probably saved his men from a severe "roasting." Der Poss held his peace. For now.

McCarthy soon appreciated the type of work that Comiskey had to perform to keep the team owner at bay, and it did get to Mac. During one exhibition, J. Thomas Hetrick related that "[d]uring a particularly argumentative series with Columbus, Tommy McCarthy wiped out opposition pitcher Jack Easton, who was backing up third base. With clenched fist, McCarthy barreled into the diminutive Easton, who got up and charged McCarthy. With St. Louis fans howling, Easton's teammates corralled their enraged pitcher and prevented further fisticuffs."

Once the season commenced, the Browns shot out of the gate, triumphing in nine of their first 13 games. Unfortunately, the reconstituted Browns quickly developed a reputation as an undisciplined lot prone to keeping late hours in bars after the game. Or in other words, they reflected the excesses of their owner, an unwarranted charge given the number of serious drinkers who populated the Browns' roster, both before and after Mac joined up with them.

Since Von der Ahe could not fire himself (although this would have been his wisest move), he decided that Mac was too much of a player's manager. After the team meandered to a .500 record, he fired McCarthy, appointing Chief Roseman as his replacement. Like many of his moves, this one by Von der Ahe was stupid, impulsive and spiteful, and had the opposite effect of what he wished.

Von der Ahe messed up his own team in other ways too. Without Comiskey as a buffer, he dumped on all of his players. In 1890, the *Sporting News* dropped its deference to der Poss and started to refer to him as "Von der haha." On May 31, the magazine ran the headline "Demoralization in the Camp of the Home Club [Browns]." McCarthy and some teammates had attended a ball in Syracuse, which Mac claimed the owner endorsed. When they returned from the fete, the owner fined the players as was increasingly his custom to do. An anonymous player rhetorically asked how any of the Browns could be expected to play ball for Von der Ahe.

In addition to the meddling of the owner, the team did not win because it was largely a collection of replacement players; the real stars had essentially gone on strike and ran their own league. Given the way this owner treated his players, one can understand why so many bolted from his team. Rather than face reality and reward Mac, one of the few old Browns who stuck with him, Von der Ahe chose to humiliate him and bruise his ego, all the while continuing to own a team with inferior players. Before the season had ended, he had also disposed of Roseman, thus saddling his club with three managers during the course of the campaign.

The firing needlessly humiliated Mac, but in addition to bruised feelings, the *Sporting Life* also pointed out that the termination of McCarthy as manager meant "a loss to the little right fielder of several hundred dollars for the season's work as he was to receive extra compensation for looking after the boys when they were at play." Von der Ahe had largely received positive press as he rose to prominence and his clubs repeatedly won championships, but without Comiskey to lead, the shortcomings of the owner became more apparent, an observation made this season by the estimable baseball writer Henry Chadwick. As the seasons passed, the criticisms of Von der Ahe continued to increase, although the plight of his players continued to deteriorate.

On a positive note, the *Sporting Life* commended the Browns for the completion of their "grand stand, with all the spirit and beauty of St. Louis ... complete with the many-colored handsome toilets, [which] presented a striking appearance." Say what you wish about Von der Ahe, but at least he got the bathrooms right.

Although Mac had to remain as a player for the Browns after losing his position and presumably much of his salary, to his credit, he did not roll over. Instead, he played at a high level, generally positioning himself in second place for the league batting title for most of the season before falling to third at the very end. He finished in the top five in most offensive categories and led the American Association in stolen bases with 83.

Copyright 1887.
Goodwin & Co.

McCarthy. C.F. St. Louis Brown's.

OLD JUDGE CIGARETTES Goodwin & Co.,
New York.

Tommy McCarthy exhibits an unorthodox batting stance for this early photograph.
He probably never used this stance in a ball game unless he wanted to irritate Chris
Von der Ahe.

Nevertheless, playing for an increasingly irrational Von der Ahe continued to wear on McCarthy, a sentiment that his old manager tried to exploit when St. Louis opened up a series in Rochester, New York. Supposedly, Mac had sent Comiskey a letter expressing disdain for Von der Ahe and evidencing a desire to leave the Browns. In response Comiskey and Silver King (both of whom had jumped to the Chicago Players' League club) checked into Rochester's Hotel Bartholomew under assumed names and met privately with Mac and another Brown player, Fuller, in an attempt to get them to jump to their Chicago team, or at the least, sign up with them for the 1891 season.

Mac zestily played the situation, staying out with Comiskey all night and not returning to the Browns' team hotel at all that evening. Von der Ahe, of course, found out about the meeting and scurried all over Rochester to return Mac to the fold, to no avail. Neither Mac nor Fuller jumped to the Players' League team, but they did serve notice to Von der Ahe that in the next year, they might consider doing so. No one denied that McCarthy and Fuller had signed up as players for the Chicago Players' League club for the next season, either. Comiskey let it drop that Mac and Fuller "have been sick of Von der Ahe for some time and anxious to get away from him."

In St. Louis, everyone naturally assumed that a strong union man like Tommy McCarthy would cast his lot with the new league and terminate his affiliation with the hated Von der Ahe, but he did not do so in 1890 and he denied rumors that he was prepared to join the Players' League in 1891. In that they greatly underestimated the independence and more likely the burning ambition of Mac, who complained that such rumors were lies "of the whole cloth so far as I am concerned.... There is plenty of time between the ending of this season and the opener of the next, and I would be foolish to sign this early. I will go where it pays best to go next season. It may be in St. Louis or it may be somewhere else." Rather than contend for the association pennant, St. Louis limped to a third-place showing.

Mac never had a chance to test the market because the Players' League soon folded and most of its members returned to their former teams. Hugh Duffy proved a stubborn exception to this rule as he in no way wanted to return to the Chicago Colts and the hated Anson and Spalding. Sir Hugh went his own way, and it ended with him clashing for the first time in competition against Tommy McCarthy.

Chapter 6

See You in Chicago

A twice-told tale concerning Hugh Duffy's introduction to Chicago Colts manager Cap Anson has happily come down to us, and here is the version that Duffy himself related:

> I was a tiny mite when Anson greeted me. He said to me, "We've got a bat boy, what are you doing here?" When I told him I was the Eastern League outfielder Tim Murnane had recommended and that I was on his salary list for thousand a season he didn't say anything at all but let me sit on the bench for two months before I worked myself into a game.

We know now that Duffy, correctly or not, has received credit as the first Triple Crown winner, but his introduction to his new boss differs little from the experience of the last Triple Crown winner when Carl Yastrzemski met then–Red Sox general manager Joe Cronin:

> Cronin couldn't believe my size—five-eleven, 160 pounds—and the amount of money I was getting. The first thing he said—and I could never forget it—was "We're paying this kind of money for *this guy*?" I guess he expected somebody six-two and 210 pounds to walk in.

There is a wonderful symmetry to the stories, of course. Both Anson and Cronin were Hall of Famers in the making, and they expressed incredulity that their clubs had committed themselves to these seemingly undersized specimens. Unlike Duffy, Yaz did not sit on the bench but had time to mature in a minor league system, as he contemplated the formidable task of replacing Ted Williams.

Initially, Duffy welcomed the opportunity of playing under such a luminary as Anson, but quickly chafed under his tutelage. Not only did he sit on the bench, he began to see Anson not purely as a tremendous ballplayer but also as a very flawed and prejudiced character. Most baseball fans know that Anson worked feverishly to bar African-Americans from playing in the major leagues without appreciating the full import of his biases.

Unless one was a white Anglo-Saxon Protestant, Anson had little use for the individual ballplayer as a human being. Although Anson had matriculated at the University of Notre Dame and presumably had met his share of fighting Irish students, he never cottoned to them. Indeed, Duffy always believed that Cap detested Irish-Catholics, and in addition to the height issue, he and his manager never saw eye to eye.

As bigoted a soul as Anson was, Duffy was only partially correct. Anson exhibited ugly biases, true, but he also appreciated baseball talent, and ultimately his love of the game trumped his biases, at least if the ballplayer was Caucasian.

Until Anson measured Duffy correctly, superstition superseded sound judgment as the Chicago team calculated that it lost all but one game by mid–June after it had worn its dress jackets, upon which the players consulted their haberdashers and made the proper adjustments. Anson for his part went off potatoes for good. At the end of June, the Colts actively shopped Duffy, as "Anson is willing to sell young Duffy to the Bostons, whose infield the old man believes needs strengthening. New Orleans had her eye on the youngster, but Spalding wanted too much for his release, and the brilliant young player's ideas of salary were too far advanced." Since the Colts and Duffy were stuck with each other, Anson decided to get some use out of his rookie.

Plus, talent won out over voodoo eventually as the *Sporting Life* noted in July 1888, "Anson has played Duffy at right

ADRIAN C. ANSON.
ALLEN & GINTER'S
RICHMOND. Cigarettes. VIRGINIA

Say what you want about Cap Anson, he could have been a superstar in whatever era of baseball he played. While he and Duffy often clashed, toward the end of his life Anson dined with Sir Hugh at a small gathering sponsored by Boston's legendary Mayor Curley. David Fleitz collection.

field during the past few games, and the promising young outfielder has shown himself capable of playing the position as well as any man who has yet filled it for Chicago. He is also a reasonably reliable batsman and an excellent baserunner." And then a large segment of hell broke loose.

Literally, fireworks went off during the second game of a doubleheader Chicago played against Philadelphia on the Fourth of July. More than 21,000 fans went to the two games, a massive crowd at that time, with the majority attending the second game. So many fans arrived for the second game that they overflowed onto the playing field, necessitating the implementation of special ground rules to account for their presence in the outfield and along the base lines.

Many of the cranks were drunk by game time and the imbibing did not cease with the first pitch. Flasks were opened and drained, and upon the commencement of the game, the patrons set off thousands of firecrackers and continued to do so for the duration of the contest. One Philly fan tossed a rather large and powerful "cannon" firecracker at Anson that exploded at the foot of Anse, fortunately not causing him any injury other than ticking him off. Of course, the Chicago fans retaliated by making the Philadelphia players targets of their own explosives, and so the holiday was observed. For his part, Duffy singled but got caught stealing second base, as his team lost, 6–5.

Making most of his opportunities, on the next day, Duffy went 2-for-5 and stole a base, demonstrating his potential as an offensive playmaker. Although this game constituted one of Duffy's earliest starts in the major leagues, his manager instilled confidence in the young player by batting him second. Anson said and did many stupid things in life, but he knew how to maximize the abilities of each player and motivate them to excellence.

Contrast this with Harry Wright batting McCarthy sporadically and playing him at every position. Duffy did not take to riding the bench, but Anson's coaching prevented him from experiencing the many false starts that marked Tommy McCarthy's early career. Anson did not jack Duffy around with infrequent playing time at numerous different positions in the field, but rather waited until he had reached a level of comfort with Duffy's play before inserting him into the lineup. Harry Wright was a much better man that Cap Anson — most people were — but he nurtured Duffy effectively while Wright botched McCarthy's development.

Although legend has it that Duffy became a regular for life once Anse gave him a chance, it did not happen quite like that. After this promising start, Anson benched Duffy for about two weeks, as he reverted to his favorite veterans. During Duff's limbo, he busied himself with fellow benchwarmers Petit, Borchers and Darling in "chasing grounders and catching flies." Unfortunately for Anson, the 1888 edition of his club did not resemble his earlier powerhouses, and had to resort to his star rookie as a starter due to the sheer force of the team's shortcomings. Having just endured a six-game losing streak,

Anson, as was his custom, dramatically announced to the press on July 27 that from thenceforward, Duffy would start in the outfield. The next day, Chicago won.

While the Chicago team had dominated in the early 1880s, the lure of money had caused team owner Al Spalding to unload star catcher and outfielder King Kelly to the Boston team for $10,000, and in early 1888, he sold excellent pitcher John Clarkson to the same team for the same amount. At the time Spalding boasted that the team had won before Clarkson and would win without him, a prophesy that proved utterly wrong.

In essence, Chicago had begun to adopt a nineteenth-century policy of "Moneyball." The Colts sold Kelly and Clarkson, believing that the players had passed their primes, with a view to securing youngsters like Duffy for a pittance. Unfortunately, it did not take long for Duffy to gauge his value in the marketplace, and Spalding's stinginess proved his franchise's undoing.

In addition, second baseman Fred Pfeffer openly rebelled against Anson in 1887, criticizing his manager and unburdening himself to any reporter who cared to print the story. Anson had become an ogre and did not mellow with age, leading his players to drift away from him to scout out new opportunities where they might make more money and suffer less abuse. The team's unofficial nickname, the Colts, emanated out of Anson's needing to play young players after the studs had left the barn.

For coltish Hugh Duffy in 1888, the time had not yet come to feel too proud, but he had at least broken into the starting lineup and he meant to stay on the field. In a game against Washington on August 11, Sir Hugh repaid his manager's confidence in him by banging out two of the team's five hits, including a double and a home run, as his team won, 4–2.

The Chicago outfielders, which included a forgotten star of the era, George Van Haltren, kept the team in many a game, but the clownish infielders in many cases reversed their work. The *Sporting Life* likened the antics of the Chicago infielders to a bunch of Comanche Indians in the midst of a war dance, indicating that political correctness had not yet seeped into the pages of that venerable publication.

Chicago's days of dominance in the National League had set. Heading into the fall, the club had no realistic bid to catch league-leading New York, and needed to play nearly flawless baseball to finish in second place. Pitching did them in as they tried to transform a natural hitter and outfielder George Van Haltren into a hurler, and second pitcher Mark Baldwin had trouble winning games. Only one-year wonder Gus Krock (a teammate of Tommy McCarthy the year before in Oshkosh) proved a stopper, as he enjoyed a 25-14 campaign, on his way to only 32 career wins and eventual oblivion.

As the team struggled, Duffy became a favorite of both Spalding's and Anson's, partly in reaction no doubt to the ornery nature of other team star hitters Jimmy Ryan and Van Haltren, two ballplayers who were very difficult to like. The fans fell in love with the feisty, good-natured Duff, too, as his ebullience in the field ingratiated himself with his growing cadre of followers. While he had achieved much since the previous season when his teams kept folding, an added treat awaited the poor boy from River Point, Rhode Island, as the team steamed into Washington, D.C., for a late-season series.

Cap Anson was rarely at a loss for words, but when he and the Colts met President Grover Cleveland toward the end of the 1888 season, Anse choked. In one short year, Hugh Duffy had come from playing in a field with three-foot ponds to schmoozing in the White House.

Although the Chicago team did not win a championship in 1888, it did end the season in October in auspicious fashion by gaining an audience in the White House with President Grover Cleveland.

In a rare departure from his natural bluster, Anson stood in the East Room speechless, blushing a deep crimson as the president entered the area to greet the team. Two of the ballplayers had to yank the coattails of Anse's suit to prompt him to utter his prepared spiel. Briefly and awkwardly Anson requested that the president give his blessing to Spalding's planned All-American teams' tour of Australia, adding that although the teams would be away for the presidential election, the men were all loyal Democrats and planned to vote for him.

Cleveland replied that since the team consisted wholly of Democrats, they hardly needed his blessing, which he gave ultimately to the venture, at which time the awkward meeting in the White House concluded and Anson's club departed to defeat Washington in their game. Cleveland probably begrudged the players leaving the country and not voting for him as he was in the midst of a heated race with Benjamin Harrison, a race Cleveland lost despite obtaining a majority of the popular vote. Harrison was apparently a uniter and not a divider.

For his part, Duffy probably relished seeing the normally bullish Anson rendered near mute and socially maladroit during the presidential audience. Or perhaps he briefly considered that last year he had bounced from Springfield to Salem to Lowell as his old clubs folded under him, and now he had met the president and shaken his hand. Duffy did not accompany the team on its Australian tour (which actually became a world tour), and undoubtedly he did vote for Cleveland. Otherwise, he returned to the East and began to work out for the next season. Chicago had not won this year, but with a few tweaks, the club had every reason to expect a return to prominence in 1889.

Even before the spring of 1889 arrived, Tim Murnane gushed in a column about Duffy as "the greatest find of the season of 1888 ... he today ranks as one of the leading ball players of the league." Of course, Murnane did not come to praise Duffy as much as honor himself for being the one who "discovered" him and ensured that Chicago signed him. With his pipeline to the Windy City intact, Murnane communicated with Chicago owner Al Spalding, who confirmed that he would not trade Duffy to another club for even $8,000, and that he had tried to enlist him in the World Tour to help spread baseball to other continents, but that Duff had declined, deciding to return to Rhode Island in the off-season to pursue his "studies."

More likely, Duffy had already tired of Spalding and the prospect of taking interminable boat rides across the Pacific Ocean and around the world held little appeal for him. No spendthrift, Spalding would have watched every nickel expended by the players, and Duffy did not need any further evidence or experience of operating under this penurious boss.

While Duffy ostensibly spent his off-season in the library poring through weighty tomes and thinking solemn thoughts, one would not know it by his demeanor on the field. By late May of 1889, the *Sporting Life* commented on his act, noting that "Hugh Duffy, as a coach, with Anson on bases, is far more amusing than either Latham or Kelly ever were. Listen to him." Latham, of course, was Arlie Latham from the Browns, already the "Clown Prince of Baseball" and Kelly was King Kelly, the reigning superstar and an entertainer in his own right; Sir Hugh had entered the pantheon.

Feeling particularly courageous coaching first base with Anson at bat on one occasion, Duff might have pushed the envelope a bit too far. Anson hit the ball pitched to him weakly to an opposing infielder and had no chance at legging out a single. Yet Duff screamed at him good naturedly and to the delight of the fans, "Run Cap, run! You aren't half-running!" Anson was thrown out by at least ten feet, and when he finished huffing and puffing, he had a quick talk with Duffy, who immediately terminated his coaching for the afternoon.

This seemingly innocuous incident demonstrated that Duff liked a good joke, but also that he did not cower before bullies. Anson may have frightened other people, but not Duffy. This attitude always served him well in life because while other players might exhibit poor attitudes that shortened their careers or ensured they did not have a future in baseball after their retirement, the young Chicago outfielder had the talent to take the mickey out of someone without planting the seeds of a grudge.

While Duffy's hijinks earned raves, his hitting and fielding kept Chicago in the running in the games. In a mid–June game against Pittsburgh, "Little Duffy made a great dive among the carriage wheels for Miller's long hit in the eighth. He bruised his face badly against a hub but gamely held onto the ball, and by a good throw held Miller to third." He also had two hits in the game and his team won, 9–8, after which his mates capitalized on the momentum created by this stirring victory by losing four out of the next five games. Mere days later Chicago defeated a team from Elkhart, Indiana, in an exhibition and the *Chicago Tribune* deadpanned in a headline, "Found A Club They Can Beat."

The demoralized play of his fellows did not deter our hero as he drove in the game-winning runs in another contest against Pittsburgh. He even improved his hitting as the *Sporting Life* noted that "Duffy is not the largest man in the Chicago team, but is doing the tallest kind of hitting." On August 19 he hit a double and a home run to pace his team to a victory over Indianapolis. The next day, batting lead-off, he lead his team to another victory with his three timely hits.

Although Chicago had finished in second place in the National League the previous season, the team had barely hung onto third place in 1889, winning only two more games than it lost. Pitching fell apart and offset a number of fine performances on the field and at the plate as Duffy, for one, hit .312. Sir Hugh also placed second in the National League in runs scored, third in hits and fifth in home runs. Cap Anson admitted that perhaps he had not spent enough time putting together a team in the midst of his touring and his hobnobbing with the likes of Mark Twain.

As the team faded, some comments from talking heads exonerated the peerless Chicago outfielders, one expert commenting that "...if there is or ever has been an outfield in the League that combines batting, fielding, base-running ability, reliability and good habits to the degree possessed by the old man's [Anson's] present 'big three,' I am open to correction." The big three in question, Duffy and sourpusses Van Haltren and Jimmy Ryan, all three batted over .300 during the course of their productive careers.

The most significant threat to Chicago did not come from eventual pennant-winner New York, but rather by the second-place Boston team. A triumvirate of owners named Arthur Soden, William Conant and James Billings had purchased the team in 1887, and recognizing the club as an aging and overrated assemblage, they began to aggressively change scenery. After 1888, they axed Honest John Morrill, the manager who had let Tommy McCarthy slip through his hands, and replaced him at least temporarily with Jim Hart.

They aggressively pursued Chicago star King Kelly, paying Al Spalding $10,000 for him, and then repeated the process at the same price for pitcher John Clarkson. All Clarkson did was win 82 games combined in 1888 and 1889. Spalding had mistakenly assumed when he sold Clarkson to Boston that he was at the twilight of his career. The Boston club had also pruned star hitter Dan Brouthers and catchers Charlie Bennett and Charlie Ganzel off the powerhouse 1887 Detroit team to join a steady talent named Billy Nash to form the nucleus of a championship club.

The surprises did not end there. Before the 1890 season, most of the professional ballplayers worth anything ditched their allegiance to the American Association or the National League to form a new Players' League. Anson stayed with Chicago, and apparently he and Spalding initiated a whispering campaign that Duffy meant to turn tail on his fellow players and stick with Chicago. Duffy angrily composed a letter and fumed the whole way up from Rhode Island to Boston to deliver the missive to Tim Murnane. In his letter to the editor of the *Boston Globe*, Sir Hugh stated:

> There is a story going the rounds to the effect that I was dissatisfied with the Chicago club of the players' league. I wish to say that there is no foundation for any such rumor. I have signed with the players' league for three years and will be the last one to go back on my agreement. The Chicago club treated not only myself but several other men, unfairly last season and I have no earthly use for them. I am with the players to stick, and Mr. Spalding has not money enough to make me turn deserter and go back to the men who classified me last season.

The classification system referred to in this open letter was a temporary system whereby team owners essentially graded players, and once slotted, a player could not make more money than the maximum allowed for someone in that particular class, or pay scale, if you will. The system may theoretically have been designed as a crude type of salary cap, but folks like Anson and Spalding manipulated it to pay a star like Hugh Duffy the same amount as rank mediocrities in the league.

As a postscript to this bridge-burning, as much as Anson drove Duffy crazy, he did not stay mad at his old manager forever. In 1916, Anson came to Boston and visited its Mayor Curley, who took Old Anse for a car ride around Boston. When they returned for a lunch at the Carter House, a few special guests greeted Cap Anson, Hugh Duffy being one of them. By that time, Spalding had also mistreated the loyal Anson, so perhaps Cap and Sir Hugh had a few things in common to chat about.

But in 1890, Hugh Duffy excoriated Anson and Spalding, and as an added shot at them, he decided to stay in Chicago but would play for the Players' League entry, nicknamed the "Pirates." His new skipper, Charlie Comiskey, had ditched Chris Von der Ahe's St. Louis team, and he came over with some other Browns stars such as Tip O'Neill, Arlie Latham and Silver King. Many of Duffy's Colts teammates from the previous year joined him in what became largely an amalgamation of players from the Chicago National League club and the St. Louis Browns of the American Association. Despite his professed zeal for union politics, St. Louis star outfielder Tommy McCarthy did not join Duffy, choosing to succeed Comiskey as manager for owner Von der Ahe. Most scribes and fans conceded the Players' League title to Chicago before the season began since it consisted of such a constellation of stars.

No team wins a pennant without playing a game, and so it transpired for the Chicago Players' League entry. On a personal level, though, Duffy decided to cast his fate with the team, as his batting average ended up second on the team behind only Jimmy Ryan, and he finished first in the league in at-bats and hits and third in stolen bases. He also paced his team in home runs.

As an extra perk, he displayed his leadership abilities for Manager Comiskey, a person who in the future owned the Chicago White Sox and hired Duffy as the team manager for two campaigns. Comiskey, a fairly tranquil man under most circumstances, appreciated Duffy's demeanor, and did not like Jimmy Ryan much. As the season progressed, Comiskey suspended Ryan for "big-headedness." Wisely, Duffy outwardly practiced humility.

His modesty was misplaced. In early July, the *Sporting Life* dubbed Duffy a "great run-getter," and one recent game in particular demonstrated his prowess. On July 1, 1890, Duffy scored four runs, had three hits and stole two bases in a game against Philadelphia. He also excelled on defense, specializing in throwing men out at first base on what appeared to be certain singles. By the middle of the year, he had firmly established himself as the greatest all-around baseball player in the country.

Although Duffy prospered, the all-star Chicago team underperformed while running into many of the woes of an unsuccessful squad. The *Sporting*

News quoted a poem from the *Chicago Post* that stated in part, "Comiskey's men are daisies, And the way that his club plays is Quite enough to prove his men are dandies, one and all." It did not rhyme, but one gets the picture, sort of.

After an increasingly rare victory, one local paper commented icily that it was "due to Comiskey, Pfeffer, and Duffy, who did about all the playing...." In corroboration, the *Sporting Life* concluded that the team had too many stars, too many factions and too many injuries to obtain greatness, but other problems persisted. On July 27, 1890, the *Chicago Tribune* ran a headline "Comiskey Wins At Last" and then reported that before the game, infuriating third baseman Arlie Latham "was backed up in a corner of the clubhouse and told that he needed rest...."

In September, Comiskey finally disciplined Jimmy Ryan for his selfish attitude. Around this time Comiskey also tried to jump from the Chicago team to the Philadelphia team. Ego issues raged throughout the clubhouse. Ryan claimed that "there have been days when games have been played by a team in which five men were not on speaking terms with each other," a statement backed by Ed (also known as Ned) Williamson, who chirped, "Players were quarreling among themselves and that it had affected their work." Ryan and Tip O'Neill had thrown punches at each other, and rumors circulated that Ryan refused to play squarely while Silver King pitched. Heavy drinking by Pirate players also did not help matters.

Had Duffy received sufficient support from all of his teammates, he may have carried them to the Players' League pennant. In a game against Pittsburgh, Duffy "turned the tide" for his team as he lofted a ball to "left center for a home run." Similarly, he hit two singles, a double and a triple on another occasion in which Chicago edged Cleveland. But the great Duffy discovered his limitations after clubbing two singles, a triple and a home run in a 12–10 loss to Philadelphia. He never gave up.

The Chicago team did not fail because it had too many stars, a ridiculous concept on its face. Rather, too many people performed poorly, such as third baseman Ned Williamson and shortstop Charlie Bastian, neither of whom batted above what we now term the Mendoza line (a .200 average). The right side of the infield did not hit much better, leaving most of the offense to outfielders Duffy, Ryan and Tip O'Neill. Mark Baldwin and Silver King each won thirty games or more but also lost over 20 games, a galling fact given that King led the league in earned run average. For a pitcher to lead the league in ERA but also lose more than twenty games demonstrates that Chicago did not have too many stars, but rather possessed an infield that collectively did not hit the ball and had an outfielder like Ryan who actively worked against him. The club was a mess.

At times, Chicago manager Charles Comiskey probably felt that his untenable situation did not markably differ from the insanity that he encountered trying to skipper the St. Louis club under Chris Von der Ahe. As for Hugh Duffy, he thrived. All season, Al Spalding and Cap Anson read the Chicago newspapers that lauded their former outfielder for feats in the field and at the plate, knowing in the deep recesses of their consciousness that losing him was pretty much all of their fault, as their team finished in second position in the National League. For all of Duffy's heroics, his new Chicago team limped to fourth place in the Players' League, with its team of superstars losing more games than it won.

Boston player-manager King Kelly led his team to the title, an achievement which meant little because before season's end, the players had commenced negotiating their way back into the graces of the established major leagues. Although Chris Von der Ahe is often written off as a buffoon, he actually quite presciently suggested that the American Association and Players' League combine for a post-season series, a step that might have led to greater cooperation between the leagues at the expense of the National League. The series never took place; the Players' League ceased to exist after 1890, and the American Association lasted only another year after that.

The players' failed attempt to enhance their earning potential and to better their lives had crashed. The owners became even more powerful, arrogant and wealthy. The players? They drank.

Chapter 7

Swan Song for the American Association

Before the death knell sounded for the American Association after the 1891 campaign, its owners welcomed back prodigal sons and tried to recruit former National Leaguers to augment their rosters. In their zeal to beckon former National Leaguers, the American Association magnates entered into a war with some very calculating customers like Al Spalding, a contest they had no chance of winning.

In St. Louis, Charlie Comiskey, Honest Jack Boyle and Tip O'Neill returned to the Browns from the Chicago Players' League team and Von der Ahe stumbled into common sense, designating Commy his manager again. The Browns also picked up outfielder Dummy Hoy from the Buffalo club, and he teamed again with old Oshkosh friend Tommy McCarthy. With Tip O'Neill, these three formed one of the strongest outfields in the nineteenth century, as the Browns stood poised to recapture the pennant and perhaps become world champions again.

Unfortunately, other American Association teams restocked and had similar ambitions, primarily the Boston Reds, a new entry to the association composed largely of emigrants from various Players' League rosters, chiefly hard-hitting future Hall of Famer Dan Brouthers and two down-on-their-luck pitchers, Gentleman George Haddock and Charlie Buffinton.

And maybe Hugh Duffy. Everyone wanted Duffy because he was young, fast and an unusually talented hitter who hit for average and, by the standards of the day, power. He had improved significantly as a player every year in his major league career and showed no signs of his progress abating. His major suitors consisted of the Chicago and Boston National League clubs and the new American Association Reds.

In the bleak midwinter, Cap Anson and Al Spalding flirted with their former outfielder, but their blandishments had little effect other than to annoy.

Duffy positively loathed them both, particularly Spalding, whom he believed owed him money from two years back. Said Duffy, "I didn't get along very well with Anson the last season I was with him. On seeing in the papers that Anson would release me if I didn't care to play with him, I wrote him that I would consider it a big favor if I got my release. Last Saturday I got a telegram from the 'old man,' saying that Chicago would not release me under any circumstances and they were ready to do business with me at once. I suppose they will try to keep me out there but if I don't get the salary I am entitled to I might lay off."

The *Boston Globe's* Tim Murnane seemed to know what Duffy planned to do before Duffy did. In perhaps the first direct communication between the future Heavenly Twins, Tommy McCarthy initiated negotiations on behalf of the Browns to secure Duffy and catcher/infielder Charley "Duke" Farrell, a fact Mac must have leaked to his old manager and mentor Murnane, as the news littered the papers. It should be noted that Mac did not recruit these players for their welfare or because he liked Von der Ahe, but because he received money to perform this service.

While McCarthy pursued Duffy, Al Spalding maintained his ambivalence towards matters by agreeing that Arthur Soden, owner of the Boston National League team, could sign Sir Hugh but only on condition that they had to return him to Chicago upon demand, a provision not likely to win friends and influence a disgruntled former star. Still based in Rhode Island, Duffy visited Boston where Frank Selee, the Boston Nationals manager, desperately sought to sign him. However, Owner Soden sealed his fate not by responding to the overtures coming from Chicago, but rather by counting on the player's ill-feelings for Spalding and Anson, thus capping his offer to Duffy at $3,000. Duffy did not prevaricate by demanding respect, as he candidly admitted that he was "out for the stuff." And $3,000 a year was at least a thousand dollars short of the stuff he felt he deserved.

In cloak-and-dagger fash-

Arthur Soden was one of the triumvirate of owners of the Boston National League team. He is credited with instituting the notorious "Reserve Clause" which bound players to their clubs for decades thereafter. Collection of Donald Hubbard.

ion, McCarthy continued to beat the ancient brick streets of Boston for Duffy and Farrell. His problem, of course, was that he worked for an unstable owner who enjoyed arbitrarily fining his players and reneging on fiscal promises as a means to punish his players and maximize his profits. Von der Ahe had already established an unsavory reputation, but Mac continued his recruiting efforts on his behalf to ensure he received pay for his services, win or lose.

By this point, a sportswriter, in commenting upon the conflicts between the American Association clubs and the National League teams, rhetorically asked, "If it isn't war, what is it?" Al Spalding lamented that Duffy was "out for the coin," and loyalty meant little since Sir Hugh hated Anson and Spalding. Informed sources had Cap Anson simultaneously at this time in Marlboro, Massachusetts, wooing Farrell, and in Cincinnati, causing Tim Murnane to deadpan that "[t]he old man is a noted hustler, but there is some doubt about his making this jump in such a short time. It is easy to distinguish him from the ordinary man, as he is large, wears a hot Scotch moustache and has the color of early dawn on his face and his neck."

By February 27, 1891, Duffy received a substantial offer from the Boston Reds of the American Association and had returned to Boston on his way down to Hot Springs. Anson and Spalding made one last pitch to him, but they expressed no willingness to match the Reds' offer, or pay him for his claims against them. Having no leverage against an American Association franchise, they reconciled themselves to parting with their former golden boy.

At this point the Boston National League team, led by Soden and Frank Selee, reentered the fray and agreed to pay Duffy a $1,000 signing bonus and $4,000 a year. With $2,000 more a year being offered by the Boston National squad over its cross-town American Association counterpart, Duffy ran for the pen to sign the proposed contract, but as a last spiteful gesture, Spalding blocked the transaction, something he had every right to do as a fellow National League owner. That left it up to Duffy to either return for short money to Chicago to play for people he despised or remain back East and play for somewhat higher wages with the Boston Reds of the American Association. By early March, both he and Charley Farrell signed with Charley Prince, owner of the Boston Reds, and Duffy made arrangements to come up from Hot Springs to meet his new team in Baltimore. The Boston Reds sweetened the pot by making Duffy the team captain.

And to think there was a season of baseball still to play.

On March 28, 1891, Duffy traipsed to St. Louis to visit his friend and former manager Charlie Comiskey. While there, he reiterated his hostility toward Spalding and intimated that some of his friends who signed with Chicago now regretted their decision. He also felt that the Boston Reds could take the pennant, a bold claim to make while in St. Louis.

St. Louis, of course, had other intentions as the team prepared for its opening game at Sportsman's Park against King Kelly's Cincinnati club. As was his custom, Kelly pontificated before the game and claimed that his "boys will remain straight, as they are a well behaved lot of young fellows." The chances of King refraining from drink were negligible, but on April 8, 1891, the two teams marched behind a band to the ball field where a concert preceded the game, won by the Browns.

A different but equally spright band led a parade from Boston's United States Hotel on the afternoon of April 18, 1891, to the Congress Street Grounds for the Reds' home opener against the Philadelphia Quakers. Carriages transported both teams behind the band to the park, where the Massachusetts governor and Boston mayor arrived with various other dignitaries amongst the estimated 5,000 fans. A banner waved in the breeze, celebrating the Reds as the 1890 Players' League champions, although that incarnation of the Reds bore little resemblance to the team on this field to open its American Association season.

Boston has always loved parades for its teams and when they win the last game of the season, millions of people flood the downtown area to see their heroes and perhaps catch a glimpse of a championship trophy. The typical preseason marches to the park may not have attracted anywhere near the current crowds, but that allowed boys and girls more room to run around, and a fan might yell out to Hugh Duffy and get a friendly wave in return and feel transcendentally happy.

Once the festivities stopped and the games began, Duffy distinguished himself from the start. In the fourth inning he attempted a bunt off Quakers pitcher Gus Weyhing, and then on the next pitch took a different tack as he hit the ball over the left-field fence, driving in two runs. The Quakers promptly lit Boston pitcher George Haddock up for two runs of their own when they came to bat, but Duffy drove in another run the next inning with a sharp hit and by the end of the sixth inning Boston led, 6–2. Local yahoo, General Dixwell, sat in front with a tall stovepipe hat and stood up and yelled "Hi, Hi, Hi," at times, both opportune and inopportune. Seeing the game no longer in doubt in the late innings, Reds manager Arthur Irwin left his dugout to walk into the stands and pay his·respects to the governor as the game continued and the band presumably played on in his team's opening-game win.

In Kentucky on the same day, the Browns did not have the same type of fortune as they lost to Louisville, 5–2, wasting a good pitching effort by Stivetts. Louisville pitcher Doran actually gave up many more hits, but St. Louis did not capitalize on its opportunities. Frustratingly, McCarthy only went 1-for-5 batting in the critical second spot in the order, after Dummy Hoy and before Tip O'Neill.

Two days later, both the Reds and the Browns were shellacked. The Quakers defeated Boston by a 9–3 score and Captain Duffy was tossed from the game and fined $65 by umpire Charley Snider after Duffy protested a call on a double play in the seventh inning where he had forced out Bill Joyce at second.

Snyder apparently had his back turned to the bag and held out that Joyce had interfered with the Quaker second baseman by knocking the ball out of his hand, although that same fielder held the ball aloft when Snyder turned around. The *Globe* commented on the umpire's "outlandish" decisions, "which would make a saint turn green with disgust." After the game, Snyder visited the Boston clubhouse, leveling threats to whomever would listen.

Fireworks went off that same day but in a different fashion as Louisville pummeled St. Louis, 14–3. Rain interrupted play for half an hour in the second inning and the wet field and ball caused a sloppy game to ensue. McCarthy hit well in the second spot but he could not make up for his pitcher's performance. The newspapers lamented, "St. Louis is Now Fourth in the Association Race." The Browns hoped to reverse their fortunes by signing star pitcher Silver King, but they lost out when King demanded that team owner Von der Ahe return to him the money he fined him in 1889 for allegedly "indifferent play." McCarthy helped reverse his team's maladies by his hitting, none so timely as on May 4 when he "secured" four hits for his team en route to an 11–1 victory over Cincinnati.

On May 6, 1891, former Boston superstar, Cincinnati leader and living legend King Kelly came to Boston with his club on an unseasonably cold day. Again, the teams paraded to the park, this time led by the Coast Guard band, with one exception. Kelly came alone; he rode in by a coach given to him by local friends, carried along regally by a dapple gray mare. Once on the field, he continued to radiate attention to himself by receiving a large horseshoe-shaped floral arrangement as the band struck up "For He's a Jolly Good Fellow." Kelly, either mistakenly or for effect, sat down on the Boston bench and not his own.

It did no good, though, because Boston soundly beat his Cincinnatis behind the strong pitching of George Haddock, who also went 4-for-4 at the plate. Duffy manufactured a run early in the game after he singled. He stole second and ran home on a single from Dan Brouthers, in some way perhaps showing Kelly that there was a new superstar in Boston.

On an equally cold day in Washington, St. Louis eked out a 4–3 win, which helped reverse its fortunes, showing the team could win a close, well-played game. At this juncture of the season, Boston stood first in the association standings at 15–6, followed in order by Baltimore, Louisville, St. Louis (14–10), Columbus, Cincinnati, Philadelphia and Washington.

Theatrically, Kelly wreaked his revenge on Boston on May 7, when, with the scored tied 9–9 in the 14th inning, he yelled out to Boston pitcher Bill Daley, "a thousand dollars to a cent it's over the garden wall." At which point Daley tried to blow him away, and Kelly drilled him for a walk-off home run, executing a perfect cartwheel and backward somersault in exultation. Kelly doused the Boston hopes that day, though the setback proved to have no long-term consequences, as the Reds soon embarked on a nine-game winning streak.

Meanwhile in D.C., the Browns clobbered the hapless Nationals, 14–2, behind the forceful hitting of Tommy McCarthy, who just missed hitting for the cycle with a single, double and home run. They followed this game with a 20–4 drubbing of the Nationals, as the Browns humiliated pitcher Jersey Bakely. Having succeeded against largely inferior opposition, the Boston and St. Louis clubs needed to face each other.

On May 20, St. Louis made its first appearance in Boston that year to play the red-hot Reds, currently riding their wining streak. In an article printed before the first game of that series, a local St. Louis scribe excoriated Boston captain "Little Hugh Duffy" because "[t]here was a terrible howl in Philadelphia the other day over Capt. Duffy's actions, and a demand was made that such conduct be punished by suspension. This little man played in several games here last fall, and he proved conclusively that he is not one of the angelic order. Once Al Jennings made a decision he did not like, and when he turned his back to his position Duffy grabbed the ball and threw it with all his might at the knight of the indicator [i.e., Umpire Jennings]. The ball missed Jennings by a bare foot and the crowd hissed the young tough, who deserved the rebuke he got." Substitute Duffy's name for McCarthy's and one has almost a carbon-copy description of McCarthy's alleged explosion against Umpire Ferguson three years earlier.

To the game. In a pitcher's duel, Happy Jack Stivetts barely out-pitched Haddock, 2–1, ending Boston's eight-game wining streak. The next day, St. Louis won again, this time by a score of 5–2 as Boston pitcher Daley flailed all over the plate with his pitches. Offensively, McCarthy hit three singles and Denny Lyons hit a homer to continue to place the Reds on a streak of a different type than they recently had experienced.

Boston finally turned the tables on the Browns on May 22 in a 9–7 slugfest. Native son Tommy McCarthy was roundly "hissed" by the crowd when he interfered with catcher Duke Farrell, who was trying to tag out at home St. Louis second baseman Bad Bill Eagan. McCarthy's efforts to guide this run home proved unsuccessful as he earned the scorn of his once and future neighbors.

Boston evened the series the next day behind the blue eyes of pitcher Gentleman George Haddock. Having gone 9-26 the year before and having led the Players' League in losses, Haddock pitched like a man revived as he just missed a shutout, winning this game, 7–1. McCarthy accounted for half of his team's six hits with a double and two singles.

Nevertheless, at this point in the season, McCarthy stood tied for 43rd in the association batting standings at .276 while Duffy checked in at a scarier .258 average, tied at 54th in the order with someone named McGuire. Happily, Duffy led the league in sacrifice hits, while still trailing by a considerable margin Dan Brouthers, who led the association in hitting with an even .400. Licking its wounds, Boston traveled down to Cincinnati to visit old friend Kelly while St. Louis departed for the edge of the then-known baseball world for a series against the Nationals, as owner Von der Ahe predicted a Browns pennant.

Unfortunately for Boston, the Reds only won one of their next six games as their trip to Cincinnati took 28 hours, and when they arrived, they had no place to stay as the hotels were packed by Baptist ministers on a convention and the Knights of Pythias. After finally finding accommodations, the Reds promptly lost the first game of the series, 21–16. In that game, Reds left fielder John Irwin's fielding gave the game away, and as captain, Duffy switched spots with him to stave off the bleeding. Rather than incurring the wrath of John Irwin's brother, team manager Arthur Irwin, this event foretold the quick demise of the former's career. Nepotism could take him no further.

Concurrently, St. Louis thrived on its next segment of the road trip, sparking a seven-game winning streak against the likes of the weak Washington and Philadelphia teams.

By June 6, the American Association enjoyed a tight three-way race between Boston in first at 29-16, St. Louis in second at 32-18, and Baltimore fading at 25-18. Decimals separated the two leaders, and in the midst of this excitement, Boston visited St. Louis for a three-game series, commencing on June 6.

The Reds promptly relinquished their lead by losing, 11-10, on a sacrifice fly hit by McCarthy to Duffy, bringing in Bad Bill Eagan to score. Over 17,000 fans came out for the next game, a huge crowd by American Association standards, but Reds pitcher Charlie Buffinton held a one-run lead to the end to even the series on a rainy day.

The rains postponed the rubber match a day later, as many of the players went off to the race track to gamble on the horses, the astute ones picking the ponies who were "mudders." The next day the Reds won, 8–6, in a bitterly fought contest, with Duffy hitting soundly and leading his team, with one exception. In the third inning, he sprayed a single over first baseman/ manager Comiskey's head and began to "prance" off of first base, at which time Tommy McCarthy in right field heaved the ball to Comiskey, who tagged out the taunting Duffy. The Reds left with their meager lead in the pennant race intact.

The two association leaders continued to play excellent ball after they good-riddanced each other. The Reds had a scare when Duffy had to return to Rhode Island with an injured ankle, but he returned to see his team go on another terrific run from mid–June through early July, a skein matched by St. Louis. During that time, Duffy's aggressive enthusiasm as captain had reached its apex.

In modern baseball parlance, Hugh Duffy would be known as a "red ass," a player that simply hated to lose and did not care how he acted or who witnessed his behavior in the furtherance of his goals. He did not perform acrobatics or otherwise hog the stage like King Kelly, but as a perfectionist, he expected himself, his teammates and the umpire to strive for flawlessness with equal fervor. He took his captaincy very seriously, and at this stage of his life bore faint resemblance to the kindly soul that Ted Williams held so much affection for a half-century later.

By June 26, 1891, at least one of the Boston dailies memorialized this in its "Baseball Notes" section by teasing, "Come Duffy; be good natured, old man; you will play just as good ball and have more friends, even the umpire will enjoy the change." The estimable *Sporting Life* also weighed in, claiming, "Hugh Duffy is too noisy and offensive to spectators. Continual chinning is not necessarily an indication or evidence of captaining ability." It was a good thing that Hugh Duffy was such a winner because he certainly made for a poor loser.

If the Boston papers criticized the home team, at least one of the St. Louis dailies had all but capitulated with their club. In a column headlined "Why Boston Has a Better Chance to Win the Association," the *St. Louis Post Dispatch* on July 6 delineated all the ways that their team was inferior to its rival. The writer marveled at the Reds hitters and pitchers, claiming in defense of the Browns that only Stivetts could compete and that the Browns were going to have to resort to "some unknown Eastern college man whom President Von der Ahe says will be signed." The paper wrongly claimed that twirler Clark Griffith was "unskilled," although it did draw the correct bead on fellow pitcher McGill, who in so many ways was "second class."

The Browns then made the *Post Dispatch* look terrible by beating the legendary Reds two games out of three in a series which started two days later. In the first game, the Reds led the Browns, 7–1, in the fifth inning when Comiskey shook up his lineup by placing pitcher Happy Jack Stivetts in right field (Stivetts often played outfield when he did not pitch as he was one of the greatest hitting pitchers in baseball history), moving McCarthy to third base and planting Clark Griffith on the mound. The new combination worked as the Browns rallied to win, 8–7, due in large part to some "wretched" fielding by Boston third baseman (and old McCarthy sandlot friend) John Irwin.

St. Louis vaulted into first place past its hosts in the next game as Stivetts returned to pitch for St. Louis and earned the win behind some "heavy stick work" from Tommy McCarthy. Two days later, Boston regained the first position behind the pitching of Charley Buffinton and a three-run home run from third baseman Duke Farrell, whose daughter was born the previous evening. Comiskey received a giant horseshoe-shaped floral arrangement from his Boston friends, and he and his team trained down to Washington to feast on the Capital City's team, the association's doormat organization.

After this series, St. Louis played .700 ball for the next couple of weeks, and Boston went on an even more impressive tear, going 12–2. McCarthy won a game against Columbus by driving in the winning run with a double, and he also won props for his fielding at second base, proving his versatility for a team experiencing injuries and other maladies in this stretch.

In order to remain in the pennant race, St. Louis had to derail the Boston

Reds in a four-game series in Sportsman's Park at the very beginning of August. The Browns accomplished the task, taking three games out of four from the league leaders. In the first game on August 1, 1891, Duffy killed a Brown rally by making a daring running catch off of Tip O'Neill in the fourth inning, and when he came to the plate, he "batted and ran the bases magnificently."

After that loss, St. Louis went on a tear of its own. The next day, despite wet weather and the constant threat of showers, Comiskey tinkered with his lineup, starting Stivetts in right field, McCarthy at second base and journeyman Jack Easton at pitcher. McCarthy had a particularly good day at the plate with a double that knocked in two runs in the fifth and another timely hit later in

Back in the 1890s no one sang about wanting to be on the cover of the *Rolling Stone*, but every red-blooded American boy did want to make the cover of the *Sporting Life*, and in the last year of the association, Tommy McCarthy achieved this feat. However McCarthy's accomplishments are viewed today, in his era he was a star. Collection of Donald Hubbard.

the game. To accommodate the approximately 15,000 fans with far too few seats, ropes were installed to rein the standees along the perimeters of the field, and as agreed before the game, any hit into that "enclosure" counted for at most a double.

On August 3, the enigmatic southpaw McGill pitched a three-hitter to down Boston, as McCarthy and O'Neill paced the Browns with their hitting. Although St. Louis supposedly did not have a surfeit of pitching, the Browns had previously released future Hall of Famer Clark Griffith, who started for Boston on this day. Boston endured its first shutout of the campaign in its final game of the series as the Reds usually reliable lefty Darby O'Brien got hammered, particularly by Tip O'Neill, and the race tightened up nicely after this game.

As was so often the case in this race, after playing so well against Boston, St. Louis lost ground, in this instance losing five out of their next six games in a pair of series with Philadelphia and Baltimore. Conversely, Boston proceeded to win 11 out of its next 12 contests.

If matters seemed favorable for the Reds heading into the second half of

August, King Kelly came out of nowhere to potentially foil the situation. On August 18, 1891, the *Boston Globe* announced that Kelly aimed to join the team as a player, and it was assumed, its team captain. The papers reacted rapturously at their star attraction returning to the Hub, and one writer mused that Duffy would have responsibilities removed from his shoulders, which would help both him and the team. The scribe sagely did not solicit the thoughts of Duffy on this issue.

Essentially what occurred was that the Cincinnati club had moved to Milwaukee and this freed Kelly from any obligations he owed to the defunct club and its successor. By this point Kelly had little left to offer a club as a very old 34-year-old catcher, weighed down by too many games caught and too many beers hoisted. Disturbingly, while he could add little to a successful and harmonious club, he had replaced a catcher more skilled than he and promised to further disrupt the team. He no longer was the straw that stirred the drink.

Fortunately, he stayed less than a handful of games with the Reds, choosing to bolt leagues and teams as he joined the National League's Boston Beaneaters, who also had a pennant race to conclude. The development temporarily stalled peace negotiations between the American Association and the National League, but otherwise created a tempest in a teapot for a player who loved the spotlight.

It did give Duffy the occasion, however, to display the diplomatic skills that ultimately guaranteed him a lifelong career in baseball and financial reward throughout life. Sensing his employer's betrayal at Kelly's about-face, Duffy marched himself and seven other players into Reds owner Charles Prince's office and signed a contract for the next year. In an interview around this time, Duffy downplayed the effect that Kelly's actions had on his team and otherwise demonstrated that while Kelly was an attention-grabber, Duffy always knew how to parlay his star power into access with influential people. He never kept his eye off the prize.

On his way out the door, Kelly mused, "Well, boys, you don't need me; you have the pennant won, and I have signed with the Boston league team." His opinion was shared not too secretly by others, including Charlie Comiskey, who did not express glee at the Boston Reds losing Kelly as he reasoned, "[t]he Reds, if anything are stronger without Kelly." Thus, the sideshow shifted across town, as the Reds continued their pursuit of the association pennant.

While St. Louis never completely lost hope, the Reds made matters academic by hammering away at their other association opponents. Still, the Browns had one more chance to gain ground in the standings as they played the Reds for the last time in a four-games series in Sportsman's Park beginning on September 8, but they only managed a split of the series, which all but clinched the race for Boston.

In the final game of that series, Boston displayed its supreme confidence by walking off the field in protest of the umpire's play calling. The *Post Dis-*

patch dubbed the incident "a glaring case of baby act, Boston's refusing to complete the game." It had no effect on the pennant race and the Reds probably figured as much at that time as Hugh Duffy carried on his long-standing feud with umpires. He would not always be so lucky in this pursuit.

Shortly thereafter the wheels fell off the cart for St. Louis as McGill's drunkenness brought him into unfortunate "contact with Barleycorn and Comiskey." This fell on the heels of similar incidents involving Browns players Denny Lyons and Yank Robinson, who also experienced shortcomings in meeting minimal club behavioral expectations.

Never one to be outdone, Hugh Duffy's face graced the cover of the *Sporting Life* as he became known as being one of the game's stars.

Surreally, the battles between the American Association and the National League continued against the backdrop of the possible demise of the association. Always stirring the pot, King Kelly, now catching for the Boston National League team, attempted to persuade Chicago's Al Spalding to relinquish his rights to Hugh Duffy, so that Sir Hugh (under contract to play not only the rest of 1891 but also the 1892 season with the association's Boston franchise) could sign with the Boston Nationals. The *Post Dispatch*, by now a firm supporter of the Reds captain, opined that "Hugh Duffy is not made of the material such as Kelly came from, and is not apt to sell his honor for gold."

On September 25, 1891, the Reds clinched the pennant in a game against the Orioles, marked by the fine pitching and the sharp hitting of Brown and Duffy. Against this backdrop, the rumors continued to fly about the fate of the two baseball leagues and their players as Von der Ahe in particular attempted to dampen rumors of the association folding or merging into the National League.

The Browns could have won the pennant, and it is difficult to fathom why they were not even close at the end on a pure analysis of statistics, as the teams matched up very well together. Indeed, St. Louis won its season series against Boston. The Browns had a skilled field leader in Comiskey, good pitchers, and if anything, a much better third outfielder than the Reds had. The Bostons did get lucky with a pitcher like George Haddock, who only had two good years in his career and 1891 happened to be one of them. Likewise, 28-game winner Charlie Buffinton fell apart after that season and promising righty Darby O'Brien, who won 19 games, never won another ball game. Tragically, the popular handle-bar mustachioed young man died after a short bout of pneumonia, to which a stunned Gentleman George Haddock could only say upon hearing the news, "Poor Darby."

Statistically speaking, the outcome of this race came down to the fact that St. Louis had many more unreliable players and habitual drunkards than did Boston. The *St. Louis Post Dispatch* flattered Duffy for leading such a reliable group of players, and the *Boston Globe* famously said in July that there was not a "lush" on the home team. In contrast, McGill acted like a spoiled superstar and Comiskey never knew when he was going to show, or when he did, if he was intoxicated. McGill only had one decent season as a pitcher, and that occurred in the 1891 race; after that he was useless and even during that year, he failed to post all too often.

Other Browns players such as Robinson and Lyons also let the team down at inopportune times. Because Von der Ahe had arbitrarily fined such players as Charles "Silver" King in the past, he could not recruit former players with proven abilities to perform in a pennant race and strike out major league batters. On black and white, St. Louis and Boston should have finished in a virtual dead heat, but unpopular ownership and unreliable sots in essence sabotaged their own cause.

It mattered little to Duffy and McCarthy. The American Association collapsed at the end of the year, its players parceled out to the National League teams, so that the Boston Nationals obtained both players and instantly became the favorite to win the pennant. Each week the *Sporting Life* contained exactly one sketch of a ballplayer or magnate on its front page, and in 1891, for the first time, both Duffy and McCarthy's images graced the front page of that venerable publication.

Clearly they had arrived.

Chapter 8

The Heavenly Twins Lead Boston to a Title in 1892

On March 22, 1892, a crowd of well wishers saw manager Frank Selee and players King Kelly, John Clarkson, Tommy Tucker, Hugh Duffy, Tommy McCarthy and Harry Stovey off on an afternoon train to Charlottesville, Virginia, for their spring training session. Among the crowd stood two of the three Triumvirate of Boston Beaneater club owners (a.k.a. the "Triumvirs"), William Conant and James Billings. Historian Robert Smith referred to these owners as "grasping, mean-spirited, and suspicious men who valued money far above anything it might bring."

Billings was not a bad guy, but those other two, Conant and Arthur Soden, were the type of blackguards that even Charles Dickens would have rejected as character models for his novels as too one-dimensionally bad. No one knew how Billings got involved with them; it was like Ebenezer Scrooge and Jacob Marley had seen a platoon of ghosts or gotten drunk one night and declared that Bob Cratchit would henceforth join them as their partner.

In America's Gilded Age, Conant and Soden cheaped out on their players' salaries, and Soden has historically received credit, or discredit, for formulating the reserve clause that kept ballplayers in a state of exploitation for approximately 80 years before free agency finally emerged. Conant and Soden crassly engineered (some would say colluded) plans with other owners to keep salaries capped, while bragging of significantly increased revenues from one year to the next.

Universal darkness did not cover all, as some good guys populated the train platform. Tim Murnane scurried around sniffing out stories for the *Boston Globe* and picked up the scoop that management had designated Billy Nash for the team captaincy for the upcoming year. It must have vexed the Triumvirs to make the choice since the team roster contained five players who had served at one time or the other as a captain of a major league team, but they had wisely curtailed controversy by ending any speculation on the matter before spring training began.

Hugh Duffy always made an effort to deny that he wanted to serve as a team's captain, and yet on the occasions that he earned that honor, he never turned it down. As news of the Triumvirs' and Selee's selection filtered down the train platform, Tommy McCarthy busied himself by carrying the great King Kelly's bags onto the train as the King thanked him in his own fashion by bellowing, "That's right my boy: You look out for me." Weird pitcher John Clarkson sat silent, oblivious to the hubbub surrounding him, as last good-byes resounded and the team journeyed south.

At the moment they arrived in Virginia, a number of their other teammates met them at the station, including shortstop Herman Long. A young midwesterner nicknamed "Germany," Long was a good hitter, but a spectacular fielder. In his 1897 *History of the Boston Base Ball Club*, author George V. Tuohey tries to convey what a terrific gloveman Long was, and in the midst of heaping superlatives upon the player, he somehow makes the spectacular somewhat dullish, until he wisely provides the reader with an example of just how acrobatic Long could be.

> It was during 1892 that Long made one of the most remarkable catches ever seen on the diamond. With a runner on first the batsman hit a hard ground ball to the left of Long, directly over second base. Long made a great effort, but seeing that he could not catch the ball he threw out his left foot and caught the ball on the point of his shoe with force enough to bring the ball in the air, and by a great left-hand catch he was able to get the sphere to Joe Quinn at second in time to nail the runner there. All this while Long was moving at top speed, and the audience went wild over the phenomenal play.

Virtually identical accounts and descriptive language exist elsewhere of this remarkable fielding feat, which demonstrates how deeply the event, real or imagined, became baseball folklore before the end of the nineteenth century. One can imagine what this play looked like and how often it would end up on a sports show if it happened in the twenty-first century.

While many of the Beaneater players of this era eventually received recognition through induction into the Baseball Hall of Fame — some deservedly and some not — Herman Long quietly and efficiently provided the heart and the backbone to the fine Boston teams of the turn of the century. While he never achieved baseball immortality at Cooperstown, his teams did, and much credit must be given to their marvelous middle infielder.

Hugh Duffy in particular had spent a memorable off-season, as he married the Belle of the Pawtuxet Valley, Katie Gilland, in Sts. Peter and Paul Church in Phenix, Rhode Island, in late October and then commenced a two-week honeymoon in California. Like McCarthy, who had dropped twenty pounds in weight, he reportedly had devoted at least two months in the off-season at a gymnasium to condition himself for the upcoming season.

The 1892 Boston Beaneaters included six eventual Hall of Famers, including manager Frank Selee. Two of them, King Kelly and John Clarkson, were about spent when this photograph was taken, but several other star players distinguished themselves during this pennant winning year. Boston Public Library, Print Department.

Cap Anson continued to haunt Duffy, as Al Spalding and Cap wanted him to play for Chicago now that the American Association had ended its existence and players were being assigned to new National League teams. Fortunately for Duffy, Boston seized him (as part of the consolidation settlement) along with Tommy McCarthy, who wanted to play for Chris Von der Ahe again as much as Duffy wished to toil for Al and Cap. Merrily, Duffy and another former teammate went about suing Chicago for the $1,200 they claimed Spalding owed them from past years.

Gaudy resumes aside, Hugh Duffy and Tommy McCarthy did not stride into the Boston Beaneaters' clubhouse as saviors because the team had won the National League championship the year before without them. Future Hall of Fame pitchers Kid Nichols and John Clarkson had both won 30 games or more that year under the stewardship of manager Frank Selee, another Hall of Famer in the making.

Like McCarthy, Kid Nichols had been managed as a minor leaguer out west by Selee, and was not going to be picked up by another team. The Boston dynasty in the 1890s rested on the peerless performance of Nichols. In the late nineteenth century, most baseball teams carried three pitchers on their rosters, thus magnifying the strength of an individual hurler to a team's fortunes. The 1890s Boston teams had many stars on their clubs each year, but if one indispensable person had to be named, it was Kid Nichols.

Never a flashy player, Nichols swallowed up innings for his teams, never seeming to tire. His sinker ball, in particular, proved elusive to league batters. Arguably, he was the finest pitcher in the nineteenth century, and Selee built his staff each year around this most trusty of aces.

Clarkson, whose best days had passed, was a fish of a different kettle. He had excelled in Chicago, with King Kelly as his battery mate, because manager Cap Anson knew how to motivate him. Anson felt that if one berated Clarkson, he would simply brood ineffectively, but with constant praise and support he excelled. The handsome but peculiar Clarkson, who hailed from nearby Cambridge, where he and his brothers all played baseball, had won more than 30 games the year before for Boston.

While Nichols steadily accumulated peerless records each year, Clarkson figuratively bled every season. Almost always described as high-strung, he did not act out so much as react to the slightest bit of criticism or bad news in a manner that plunged him into the depths of depression. He could only sit and envy Nichols for his seemingly effortless approach to excelling on the baseball diamond. Clarkson fretted while Kid Nichols quietly dominated.

The team hosted a strong infield with Tommy Tucker at first base, Long at shortstop and Billy Nash, the team captain at third base. Only second baseman Joe Quinn lacked the credentials of the other infielders, and was suited best for a role as a utility infielder rather than as a starter. As the year wore on, he grew increasingly fat and marginal to the team's success.

Tommy Tucker had a loud voice and often coached for the Beaneaters, with coaching back then consisting of mainly annoying the opposing team's pitcher and fans. Tucker came from Holyoke, a small city at the other end of Massachusetts, a locus that once produced a disproportionate number of quality major league baseball players. Holyoke is one of the region's poorest communities today, much like a century ago, although at least when Tucker grew up there, it held the promise of sitting in a growing industrial area.

An Australian by birth and upbringing, Joe Quinn attended church regularly, and like Duffy possessed an acute sense of how to save and invest money wisely. Due to his weak hitting, he justifiably felt pressure that he might lose his job to the emerging Bobby Lowe, a hard-hitting batter who squandered his considerable talents on the field simply as a spare outfielder. Since Harry Stovey (a power hitter as well as a clever base-stealer) joined McCarthy and Duffy in the outfield, this temporarily at least left the considerably talented Lowe the odd man out on the team.

Changes lurked in the outfield, with Harry Stovey at the end of a fine career and Bobby Lowe at a crossroads. Born Harry Duffield Stow in Philadelphia in 1856, Stovey had played mainly in his hometown until 1890 when he joined the Boston entry in the Players' League, where he stole close to a hundred bases. Now in his late thirties, he had clearly lost a step on the bases as well as the ability to get around on the ball as a batsman. Young Bobby Lowe spied his position enviously even as he must have surely known that he had more of a future as an infielder than an outfielder. For Harry Stovey, on the other hand, the future was now.

Poor Charlie Bennett and Charlie Ganzel caught for the team, but even their futures appeared clouded by the arrival of the flashiest superstar of the day. By the time he returned to the Boston National League team, Mike "King" Kelly had experienced his best years, and one suspects his best beers, in the past. Equal parts Buffalo Bill and St. Patrick, he dominated baseball in the 1880s in a manner that far outreached his talents on the ball field. He thrived as a catcher and outfielder in Chicago, even though he always threatened to outshine fellow blowhard Cap Anson. The Chicago owner sold Kelly to the Triumvirs just as Kelly's usefulness, always overrated, had begun to ebb.

The baseball season of 1892 was peculiar because the league magnates had decided to split the season into two halves, with a winner in the first half either winning the second half or facing the winner of the second half to determine the champion. It confused fans and diluted from the excitement of a true pennant race, and nothing like it was tried again until labor troubles caused a similar set-up to be adopted nearly a century later. Tim Murnane deadpanned that a champion be declared for each month of the season and the team that won the most months be crowned the grand champion. The suggestion proved only slightly less absurd than reality, but for 1892, this ridiculous format existed to the dismay of many.

Making matters murkier, Billy Nash had been tabbed as team captain from a host of four other players on the club who had served in that capacity elsewhere, despite Kelly claiming his contract stipulated that he must serve as captain. Born in Richmond, Virginia, in 1865, just as the Union forces had captured the Confederate in the Civil War, Nash has intermittently received credit as one of the first Jewish baseball players in history.

Nash's Jewish roots are dubious, as a Congregational minister directed his funeral service several years later. Current accounts differ concerning his faith, with some sites claiming him as one of baseball's Jewish ballplayers and other accounts deleting his name altogether. Nash's religion, or lack thereof, aside, Selee trusted him and knew that players respected him.

While the Boston National champions of 1892 retained some of their veterans, they also benefited disproportionately in their ability to land players from the disbanded American Association. In many cases such as Duffy's, the player had some influence over his choice of a new club. Those team owners who abused or patronized their men in the past did have cause to regret their past practices, at least in private.

But Boston had no cause to complain about the players that it received as a result of the American Association's termination, as the blend of new and old players scrambled out to a 10-2 record to commence the new campaign before they boarded a train for a series with the Chicago Colts.

His team having lost 10 of the previous 11 games, Cap Anson did not disguise his feelings well as his team hosted Boston on May 2. Striding despondently into the Beaneaters' dressing room to ask his old star, King Kelly, for some advice, Anse remarked, "Kel, this would be a nice day to be hanged." Taking what Anson said literally, John Clarkson actually worried about whether the Chicago manager meant to commit suicide, to which the completely unsympathetic Hugh Duffy sarcastically queried about the distance to the "detention hospital for the insane" that might be available upon Anson's arrival for treatment.

If Duffy had any apprehension about playing against Anson again, it paled in comparison to what Tommy McCarthy experienced in returning to St. Louis and old owner Von der Ahe. At the end of the 1891 season, McCarthy had supposedly been paid $300 by St. Louis to try to recruit East Coast players to the team. Of course, McCarthy jumped to Boston in the off-season and did not overexert himself in securing new recruits to the Browns. Further, McCarthy purportedly returned to Von der Ahe a $500 advance, but did so in an envelope which contained a letter so "hot" in its condemnation of his old owner that Von der Ahe threatened to sue for interest.

Like anything emanating out of Von der Ahe, one had to warily eye his claims, but being a man of impulsive action, he plotted his revenge against his former player. In early May, when Boston came west to play the Browns, McCarthy was rudely roused from his hotel room when Von der Ahe's goons extracted $19 from his pockets and a watch and chain. Von der Ahe never understood that when one pushes another person, quite often one gets pushed back, and what seemed like a brilliant plan did return to haunt him in the future. Chris Von der Ahe did not treat people well on his way up, and he was on the verge of seeing all of them on his way down. Around this time a rumor circulated that Von der Ahe had committed suicide. In a figurative sense, he had been doing so for several years.

In late April and early May of 1892, the *Sporting Life* lauded the efforts of McCarthy and Duffy, who had "no superiors and few equals," chiefly due to their being easy to coach, never sick, and ballplayers through and through. Duffy deserved the plaudits as his overall game continued to improve, but Mac did not approach the exalted plane, and by late May, he batted well under .200 and ranked 103rd in batting out of 128 batsmen. For the latter Heavenly Twin, heaven could and did wait.

During the season, Selee exhibited a willingness to jettison unproductive or disruptive ballplayers. With Nichols, Stivetts and Harry Staley (a newcomer from Pittsburgh, where he never posted a winning record despite winning 21 games twice) thriving, the quiet and less effective John Clarkson no longer fit in with the team. Since four starters constituted a luxury for the day, as the first half of the season ebbed, the club cut Clarkson loose. Unfortunately, Selee cut the wrong person at the wrong time, as King Kelly had grown old overnight. He could not hit for power or average and frequently did not play due to claimed rheumatism (rheumatism being a euphemism in the day for inebriation) in one of his arms and legs. Cleveland manager Patsy Tebeau picked Clarkson right up, thus giving the pitcher the opportunity to wreak havoc on his old team and former hometown.

With embarrassing ease, Boston captured the first-half National League championship, as Hugh Duffy paced the team in batting average, walks and stolen bases. But ominously, almost everyone began to predict that they would not repeat the feat in the season's second half. King Kelly bounded onto the bandwagon, dubbing Brooklyn as the likely new winner, while Tim

Mercurial St. Louis Browns owner Chris Von der Ahe. He hired goons to raid McCarthy's hotel room and obtained $19 and a watch and chain for the efforts. When Von der Ahe traveled to Boston at a later date, McCarthy returned the favor by having his old boss incarcerated.

Murnane presciently predicted that Boston players would play more as individuals and less as a team as the season progressed.

Not only did King Kelly lose faith in his team, he also undermined team captain Nash, who resigned as the King took over the job. Conspiracy theorists from late 1892 have since alleged that the Boston team collectively laid down to permit more excitement in the National League and allow another champion to emerge in the second half, creating a final world series to unite the two crowns.

While anything is possible, the theory ignores the absolute knack that King Kelly had to blow open his own team if he so desired. Frequently hurt and useless as a catcher and a hitter when he did play, Kelly became captain not out of merit, but due to a misplaced assumption by Selee or the Triumvirs that Kelly might prove less of a hindrance if the team appeased him with a title that he had not earned. Rather than neutralize him, it only convinced him of the boundless love that the fans and the press possessed in their hearts for him and he became even more disruptive to the team once he gained some authority. Often, Duffy served as captain when Kelly got a hangnail or had a hangover and did not play, while Kelly publicly pined to return to his old Chicago club as a first baseman.

While Kelly staggered around, Happy Jack Stivetts immortalized himself on August 6, 1892, by pitching a no-hitter against a formidable Brooklyn team. He aided his cause by hitting a triple when he came to bat in the fourth inning. Duffy also tripled, and he and McCarthy helped lead the team to 11 runs against Brooklyn to punctuate their dominance in this contest.

Nevertheless, neither Stivetts' no-no nor his crisp batting ingratiated him to his teammates, as he went AWOL less than three weeks later. His behavior had alarmed the Boston management to such a degree that they had worked out a trade a few days after his no-show with Cincinnati, straight up for their star pitcher, Tony Mullane. It is not clear why Boston never consummated the deal, but Happy Jack remained a Beaneater. Still, the pitching staff gave out toward the end of the season as Nichols suffered from a sore right hand, Staley developed a lame arm, and Stivetts had "no more speed than an old-fashioned cider-mill."

Although the Beaneaters' fortunes seemed to wane, the team's management took some long overdue steps by formally firing Kelly as team captain, replacing him with Tommy McCarthy, and handing the starting catching job to Charley Ganzell, also at the expense of Kelly. The moves came upon the heels of some strategic criticism by Tim Murnane of Kelly, whom he claimed had "pout[ed] like a three year old boy," and the almost overnight desertion of the superstar by the fans, other press scribes and the team management. Not until Nomar Garciaparra's experience over a century later had a Boston baseball idol fallen so swiftly in the eyes of so many in such a short period of time. The King had left the ballpark.

Long live the new King, and Tommy McCarthy responded with what the *Sporting Life* called the single best offensive display of the season in one game as Mac went 4-for-5 with a double, triple and two home runs. The team responded to Mac's revival, and although they did not come in first in the second half, the Beaneaters entered the playoff with the other fractional winner, Cleveland, with renewed enthusiasm.

The split-season format pleased no one, and yet it did promise some level of excitement at the end of the season when Boston faced Patsy Tebeau's Cleveland squad. The eighteenth-century version of trash talk commenced almost immediately upon the games being arranged, as Boston had to travel out to the Midwest for the first two contests.

The first game, oddly enough, ended in an 11-inning, 0–0 tie, as darkness terminated a strong duel between Happy Jack Stivetts and Cy Young. The Cleveland fans cheered the spectacular plays of both nines and the owners sat together and enjoyed the game. Of the six hits for the Bostons, Duffy accounted for two and McCarthy contributed another.

The next day, Cleveland trotted out John Clarkson, and Hugh Duffy nearly ripped him apart with two triples and a double, knocking in two runs and later scoring a third run in a narrow 4–2 victory for Boston. Young Staley pitched well for Boston and Tommy McCarthy had a base stolen until he was called back by the umpire after it was ruled that King Kelly interfered by kicking the ball.

In the second official game of the series, Stivetts again faced Cy Young, and they stalemated each other again after seven innings to a 2–2 tie. In the eighth, though, Stivetts did nothing to detract from his reputation as one of the best hitting pitchers of all-time by stinging Young for a double. Although Tommy McCarthy had struggled in 1892, particularly at the beginning of the campaign, he proved to be Mr. October as he shot a pitch over second base and Stivetts chugged around third and slid home, just avoiding the tag from the Cleveland fielder for the game-winning run. Mac also distinguished himself earlier in the game by stealing second base with two outs and then scoring on a hit by catcher Ganzell.

The trains rolled the teams and their entourages from Lake Erie to Boston Harbor for the third game, scheduled at the South End Grounds. The Beaneaters marched onto the field to thunderous applause from their fans and surprised many by wearing brand new blue socks to replace their traditional red hose.

Nig Cuppy, a mainstay for several strong Cleveland teams in the 1890s, pitched for Cleveland and never had a chance. Kid Nichols made his first appearance in this series for Boston and shut Cleveland out on seven hits. In the third inning, Tommy McCarthy walked with two outs and then scored when Hugh Duffy drove the first pitch to him over the friendly right-field fence for the game-winning RBI.

Although the Boston cranks, all 2,400 of them, again cheered their ballplayers wildly, Cleveland came out with a vengeance in the second inning of game four and pasted Happy Jack Stivetts with six runs, including a home run by Cleveland pitcher Clarkson. That was almost all the runs they scored in the game as the Beaneaters methodically chipped away at the impressive lead.

Again, Tommy McCarthy sparked a rally by opening the fourth inning with a single and by some skillful manufacturing of runs, including a sacrifice by Hugh Duffy. McCarthy scored, as did two of his teammates. In the next time up, Mac again earned batting honors by doubling home Germany Long with a "screaming double to right," and later scored a run himself. Duff doubled home Mac in the next inning, a four-run sixth, as Boston went on to clobber Cleveland, 12–7. Duffy and McCarthy began to become closely associated with each other in this series as they continuously found ways to set the plate so that the other batter could drive him in. They were cute, short, fast guys who acted as interchangeable parts.

By now a thoroughly demoralized Cleveland squad plodded out to the fifth and potentially decisive contest. Two of the greatest pitchers in history, Cy Young and Kid Nichols, faced each other, but the Cy Young Award winner that day was Nichols. Young was slow and wild as his team lost, 8–3, to the champion Beaneaters. With the last out, the Boston fans streamed onto the fields to cheer and slap the backs of their heroes, and old retired ballplayers and friends crowded into the dressing room to cap off the celebration.

The Boston players disbanded for the season to pursue their various careers outside of baseball. Tommy McCarthy pursued an apprenticeship in the pajama game and learned how to manufacture a pair of pants in addition to refereeing polo matches with King Kelly around Boston's suburbs. Duffy began looking around the Hub's many local colleges to coach a baseball team after the Christmas holidays. Bobby Lowe gave up his usual winter job at a billiard hall to look for work playing winter baseball.

Almost every player had to find work as the league owners convened after the 1892 season to enact a $30,000 team spending cap on personnel. For teams such as Boston, the cap necessitated spending cuts and the forsaking of certain expensive players like King Kelly.

The magnates also agreed to lengthen the distance between the pitcher and home plate to sixty feet, six inches.

Chapter 9

Repeat for the Beaneaters in 1893

While Duffy and McCarthy congregated with their friends and new teammates as the Beaneaters departed by train for spring training the previous year, as late as April Fool's Day in 1893, McCarthy sat for an interview at an event at Wright and Ditson's sporting goods store in downtown Boston and reiterated his demand for higher pay. Rather than working off the winter fat, an increasingly difficult chore for Mac, he tried to shill some new baseball invention by his short-lived Boston manager in 1885, Honest John Morrill. If McCarthy still bore a grudge against his old skipper for releasing him that year, he hid it well, and earning an endorsement fee for Morrill's product probably helped ease any hard feelings.

Duffy and McCarthy's friendship had progressed so rapidly and had grown so strong in the past year that they presented a united front to management in holding out for higher salaries, as Sandy Koufax and Don Drysdale did seven decades later in Los Angeles. Their two personalities matched up well. Duffy could talk the leg off a chair and always had a quip or a one-liner for every occasion. More reserved, McCarthy still possessed an outwardly friendly nature, and when he spoke, he generally spoke in a very well-crafted and thoughtful manner, often at length.

They liked the same type of friends, typically other ballplayers or superfans, mostly Irish Catholic in background. Their spare time generally consisted in playing all types of sports, training or playing cards. In this period, they often frequented bars, with Mac always being the more dedicated drinker.

Philosophically, Duffy was a much more religious person than Mac, the latter whom observed the religious practices of his day, which generally consisted of weekly attendance at Mass and at periodic Holy Days of Obligation. But Duffy absolutely wore his faith on his sleeve, and had he not played major league baseball, it is likely that he would have escaped a life of carrying around heavy blue-dyed fabrics by joining the priesthood. Red Sox legend Johnny Pesky, who met Duffy in the 1940s, always wondered why Duffy did not make that life his vocation.

The answer, of course, is that Sir Hugh had a higher calling, that of knocking baseballs out of stadiums and stealing bases, and he enjoyed making money.

Those who focused on Hugh Duffy's height missed the point. One of the secrets to his success was his powerfully built body. He was arguably the finest power hitter in the nineteenth century. Boston Public Library, Print Department.

Which is why he and McCarthy were on strike in the early spring of 1893. Unlike the future ace Dodger twirlers Drysdale and Koufax, Duffy and Mac faced owners who did not respond well to pressure from their employees, and the ballplayers' situation grew more grim by the nanosecond.

Turning to their old mentor, Tim Murnane, Duffy and McCarthy asked for his advice on their contract demands as they planned to meet three days later with the Beaneaters management. Their great mentor duly went up to the team offices and the Triumvirs prohibited any raises for his protégés, but if he could get them to sign, the team would buy Murnane a free hat.

Murnane passed along the owners' hard-line stance and advised, perhaps even wheedled and cajoled, Duffy and McCarthy to sign for what management had offered, which they immediately did. A half-century later, Duffy still remembered the experience and noted that the only good that came out of the holdout was that Tim Murnane received a new hat.

While McCarthy had forgotten any bruised feelings he might have had with John Morrill, neither he nor Sir Hugh quite forgot how the Triumvirs stiffed them in their contract negotiations. And while it took another eight years, they crafted a scheme which hurt their old bosses very hard indeed. Revenge, however, would have to get ice cold before they played their cards.

With Duffy and McCarthy aboard, Selee facilitated important changes that he had planned in the off-season by shifting Bobby Lowe from the outfield to second base, supplanting the weak-hitting and hefty Joe Quinn. To fill the third outfield spot alongside Duffy and McCarthy, the Beaneaters obtained veteran Cliff Carroll, a man who had once been shot and lived to talk about it. And the club bid farewell to King Kelly, who transported his massive ego and diminishing skills to New York.

The management of the Beaneaters also reinstalled Billy Nash as their team captain — a sound decision not only because Nash possessed the requisite leadership abilities for the position, but also because he had tenure as a player for the Boston club. In fact, he had served with one brief interruption (in 1890, when he jumped to the Players' League Boston club) continuously with the Boston Nationals since 1885, just as then-manager John Morrill kicked Tommy McCarthy off of it. While issues concerning which former captain amongst the Beaneaters would be appointed captain remained, Nash got along very well with *uber*-Catholic Hugh Duffy, so it was hoped that fact might pacify McCarthy, who had served with distinction at the tail end of last year after King Kelly fell derelict in his duties.

While the re-appointment of Nash cleared up many of the uncertainties that had existed under bozo captain King Kelly, Bobby Lowe did not immediately master playing second base, much to the consternation of his teammates. Fortunately his double-play mate Herman Long continued to star at short and assisted in the transition. In an early series in Baltimore, Long participated in three successful double plays in the game. Unfortunately, Boston lost two of three in that series and in the course Tommy McCarthy was caught swearing in front of the grandstands.

Mac had more to curse about in the days ahead as Boston stalled out of the gate, winning only six of its first 13 games. Murnane commented upon his protégé's temper by noting that Mac was "not at all slow in calling umpires down." In a bit of one-upmanship, Hugh Duffy in the course of his life-long crusade against umpires riled up an arbiter named Gaffney, who fined him $25, upon which "the pugnacious little centerfielder offered to whip him at any time and place."

Although Boston initially struggled, the team seemed to have broken out by early June after sweeping two three-game series, one with Louisville and one with the Chicago Colts. On June 3, they faced the Cleveland team for the first time since the season-ending games of last year, for a few games in Boston's South End Grounds. Substituting classlessness for skilled direction of his team, Patsy Tebeau threw sand into Herman Long's eyes. It did little good as Boston defeated Cleveland in two of the three games.

While the Beaneaters continued their attempt to win another title, another form of entertainment mesmerized most Bay Staters that summer.

On June 20, 1893, in one of the most sensational trials in American jurisprudential history, a jury sitting in Fall River, Massachusetts, after deliberating for only one hour, found Lizzie Borden not guilty of the murders of her father and her stepmother. More than ten months had elapsed since a deadly hot August day when Lizzie's stepmother and father had been bludgeoned to death with an ax, and many more people followed the investigation and subsequent legal proceedings than attended on the travails of the Boston Beaneaters.

Although Lizzie Borden was acquitted, history has not treated her kindly. This childhood nursery rhyme has been passed down to the centuries: "Lizzie Borden took an axe and gave her mother forty whacks, when she saw what she had done, she gave her father forty-one." Due to the circumstances under which Borden walked at the end of her trial, most people believe today that she was guilty. Opinions differ.

It was too bad. The Beaneaters before the date of acquittal had won three straight games and looked poised and prepared to return to first place. Then on June 20, as if the entire world had temporarily spun off its axis with the hard-to-fathom Borden acquittal, the Beaneaters meandered into the odd karmic flow with a bizarre loss to the Brooklyn Bridegrooms by an 11–4 score. In the midst of slaughter, the normally heady Boston fielders committed nine errors as the team dropped to third place in the standings. Fortunately, the Lizzie Borden nonsense only plagued the Beaneaters that one day, as thereafter they went on another modest winning streak, taking four straight.

As the Beaneaters began to play better, the mood of the clubhouse relaxed a bit, a trend not unnoticed by Cap Anson when his Chicagoans came to the

South End Grounds. Of course, Hugh Duffy had not developed the love for Cap Anson since the time he first played for him in Chicago, and time had not softened his enmity for him. By 1893, Anson was at least a couple of years past his 40th birthday, and jokes began to circulate that he had been around since Christopher Columbus had sailed the ocean blue in 1492.

In an August 31 game, Duffy strode up to the plate with a bat inscribed "1492," which caused Anson to go nuts. He quickly sought to have Duffy thrown out, and when that proved unsuccessful, he searched for a new umpire to do his bidding. The outspoken white Anglo-Saxon Protestant and the sometimes cantankerous Irish-Catholic loved to clash, but this did not stop Cap Anson from later naming Hugh Duffy to his all-time team.

Playing professional baseball in the late nineteenth century in many ways was comparatively sweet. That's right, sweet, for there is no better word for it. Ballplayers escaped 60-hour workweeks of hard labor in factories and farms and earned more money than most of their peers. They traveled across America and even sometimes ventured on goodwill trips to foreign lands, and they often stayed in nice hotels and the best lodgings in trains.

Players did not have to eat in their hotel rooms or shun their fans, and indeed the closeness between the players and fans may have been one of the nicest elements of the dynamic of ballplaying in that era. The Boston cranks in many instances personally knew their heroes, who were in many cases their friends.

The press sanitized much about the baseball players' lives on the road — no surprise since most teams paid for the sports writers to travel with the clubs. Most of a player's personal life stayed private, the sole exceptions seeming to occur when a man became a skid row type of alcoholic or missed games repeatedly without excuse. Most sports notes tended to describe a ballplayer spending time on the road at either an Elks Club or a religious-sponsored event. Often a home team went to the theater with the opposing team as its guest, but little else was revealed about where the players went before or after the show.

Gambling was not considered so bad a vice that it could not be mentioned in a good-natured baseball bit in a paper. Players often bet on their own team with opposing ballplayers or managers, and very few people looked askance. Duffy won considerable money on team trips from his teammates in pinochle games, and McCarthy took most of the remaining teammates for considerable sums of their earnings in the game of poker. The one exception was Duffy, who almost always bested McCarthy.

Still, a baseball career did not constitute an ideal way to lead a life, as ballplayers were exploited. While the Triumvirate in Boston begrudged Duffy a raise in 1893, they possessed between themselves conservatively at least $2,000,000. The death of the Union Association and the Players' League set back the cause of players being treated anywhere near equitably by management for eight decades.

Some ex-players like Al Spalding and Charlie Comiskey reached greater financial heights once they stopped playing baseball, and some like Harry Stovey entered into estimable careers in police work and the like. But so many other ballplayers, short on education and training in anything but baseball, had bleak financial futures awaiting them at the eclipse of their careers.

Back to the action. To Cap Anson's credit, not only did he shy from alcohol and many other temptations of the flesh, he never stopped playing hard, a fact punctuated a couple of weeks later in Chicago, when he tried to stretch out the game to force a tie in a contest that his Colts had by any other measure hopelessly lost. Equally determined to win, Boston played the game seriously, and Tommy McCarthy even dashed for third to steal a base and add another run to the slaughter. Perhaps because of the impending darkness, McCarthy did not see the bag correctly or misread the distance between second and third, but for whatever reason, he struck third base awkwardly and broke two of his toes.

To this point, he arguably was the Beaneaters' most valuable player, batting fourth and driving in and scoring several runs with his clutch hitting, base stealing and occasional power. He continued to try to catch every ball near to him and often got to those otherwise certain hits for outs; at the least he entertained everyone. Without him, his team stopped winning.

As his team traveled onto Pittsburgh for a three-game series, Mac stayed behind to nurse his sore toes. Despite rosy medical reports, his season had ended. While McCarthy's injury may have started his team's tailspin, it continued in large part because his teammates already saw that they had won the pennant in a walk. Their previous winning streaks had provided them with enough insurance to coast into the end of the season, and that is just how events transpired.

The team's success obscured many of the internal problems affecting the players. Nevertheless, the Triumvirs blissfully ignored foreshadowings of dissent as they saw their profits increase. By August, Soden boasted that revenues for the league had increased by one-third since the previous campaign, begging the rhetorical question of how much of these profits trickled down to the players. Of course, since only one professional league existed and the team owners all cried poverty as they colluded to keep salaries down, even the most outwardly harmonious of clubhouses kept up the appearances with extreme forbearance.

The Beaneaters had begun to split off into factions. Bobby Lowe, nicknamed the "Poor Indian" for reasons lost to memory, began to develop a strong dislike for first baseman Tommy Tucker. Although they had played with St. Louis together, Tommy McCarthy did not like Happy Jack Stivetts very much, and at times some of the Catholic players took exception at some of the comments made to them by the Protestant boys. Duffy and McCarthy did not have much respect for the abilities of their outfield comrade, Cliff Carroll. Something had to give.

In Cincinnati on September 21, some of the Boston Beaneaters went on a bit of a toot to the local saloon before their afternoon baseball game and came to the park intoxicated. At the least, Tommy Tucker, Hugh Duffy, Happy Jack Stivetts, and perhaps Harry Staley had gotten drunk before the game, quite a high proportion of players for a team that typically carried three or four pitchers and 10–11 position players. It is unclear if they had started drinking the night before the game or the day of the game, but by the time they had arrived at the park, they constituted a spectacle.

Once on the field warming up, Tucker was hysterical, missing easy catches and falling all over himself in a decidedly uninspired effort to conceal his inebriation. He could not catch the ball and threw balls all over the place, causing the fans at the park who witnessed the display to begin laughing at him. Tucker then decided to address the matter by throwing a ball out of the park's pavilion. Manager Selee perceived the situation fairly quickly and benched Tucker for the afternoon game.

Rather than accept his punishment stoically, Tucker, a loud and somewhat obnoxious individual in the presence of an audience, let the liquor do the talking for him, and he abusively started screaming at his manager. "I'll show you up in Boston as the figurehead you are!" thundered Tucker at Selee, who held his ground and insisted that Tucker sit out the game. The vast majority of the invectives that Tucker spit at Selee could not be printed in a family paper, never mind a Victorian family paper.

At this point, Hugh Duffy's old sandlot buddy, Morgan Murphy (who had played on Duffy's squad with the old Lowells and the Boston Reds and currently caught for the Cincinnati team), ran over and told Duffy about the incident and warned him that matters looked quite serious. Upon learning this news, Duffy flew off the handle and staggered down to where Selee was gathering his composure after his unpleasant meeting with Tucker.

Acting as an accelerant, Duffy blasted Selee loudly, all the time exhibiting "maneuvers that were painfully suggestive of a high time." Holding up to this abuse, Selee walked from his office to the team bench as Tucker followed him so menacingly that Judge Hart ordered him arrested, an action prevented only by Cincinnati manager Charlie Comiskey, who interceded on Tucker's behalf and led him to his bench.

At some point in the proceedings, Happy Jack Stivetts became belligerent, and he, Duffy and Tucker grabbed baseball bats to go after each other until their teammates separated them.

Somewhat anticlimactically, a game did take place that day, and Boston lost to Cincy, 7–5. The ill feelings of the morning did not dissipate as someone told Beaneater outfielder Cliff Carroll that Duffy had badmouthed him behind his back. Carroll bounded up to Duffy's hotel room that evening and confronted him angrily.

"What is that you've been saying about me?" quizzed Carroll.

"All that I said," responded the angel-faced child [Duffy], "was that you have been playing in luck in the latter part of the season."

Of course, this constituted a left-handed compliment at best, and Carroll had every cause to feel insulted, although he failed to pursue the matter. For one thing, Carroll had never batted well for Boston, and Duffy was a superstar. Furthermore, Duffy, a very strong and coordinated man, probably could have boxed in Carroll's ears. Marginal ballplayers who take a swing at superstars do not get the benefit of the doubt.

Selee pleaded with the press for understanding, believing that some of his players had bad tempers and that Tucker did not usually act in such a belligerent manner. Having embarrassed himself, Tucker the next day solemnly declared, "Either Selee or I will have to leave Boston for this."

Eventually, both Tucker and Duffy apologized for their behavior, and Tucker apparently cried and cried on the bench. Diplomatically, Selee proclaimed, "'Tis said that both Duffy and Tucker have vowed that never again will they look upon the lager as it foameth." Selee then stood up for his players, saying that their recent behavior contrasted with their normal routine and that they were neither loafers nor drinkers.

Matters got curiouser and curiouser. Happy Jack Stivetts was seen in the Cincinnati team uniform, and rumors circulated that Cincy had purchased his contract and that of Tommy McCarthy for $6,000. The McCarthy rumor proved untrue, but Stivetts began to express his pleasure at joining his new team and stated that Tucker and Duffy were "disturbers and mischief makers."

Stivetts offered to allow Tucker to try on his new uniform, to which Tucker began to berate him and challenged him to a fight, a clash that never occurred as Tucker began to appreciate the dire nature of his predicament. Stivetts waited for Tucker to come out for a further round of fisticuffs, and when the appointed hour for their bout had passed, he put away his watch and breezily deadpanned, "Quarter past and the duel is off."

While King Kelly's captaincy of the previous season was an ill-conceived attempt to appease a washed up egomaniac, the King served one useful purpose in keeping the team loose. Although King Kelly was a Catholic, he did not outwardly show much devotion to faith, and only sought to have the spotlight directed toward him. In this way, religious differences on the team did not play much of a part, and everyone looked toward King, for better or for worse. Without its lightning rod, the team broke off into factions.

The season sighed to a conclusion as the Beaneaters simply did not have any enthusiasm for playing games meaningless to the final standings. Someone organized a barnstorming tour of the Midwest and some talk circulated about having a trip to California arranged.

Once the season concluded, the *Globe* interviewed Duffy about the Cincinnati incident, and his version of the events lacked the solid ring of truth. He claimed to have visited two priest friends of his, which may have occurred, but does not explain his condition the next morning before the game. He argued that he acted to tamp down the tension between Selee and Tucker but failed to explain why he lost his temper and exacerbated matters. Both he and Tucker received $50 fines for their disturbances. Duffy was a great ballplayer but one of the least accomplished liars of his age.

He did express disdain for some of his teammates who he claimed enjoyed to drink, impliedly omitting Tucker and himself from the ranks of the indiscreet, and claimed that it influenced him not to barnstorm with his teammates at the season's end.

He also intimated that one reason for his reluctance to travel across the Midwest in October was due to the declining health of his wife. He anticipated a trip to California with her in order to play ball and help restore his wife to health in the much warmer weather on the other coast.

Instead of barnstorming across the Midwest with a number of teammates he did not cotton to, Duffy did depart with his very ill bride to California. They had recently honeymooned there and now ventured forth in a desperate attempt to restore her to heath. He did not want for good company: Joining him there was the event's organizer, Billy Nash, along with teammates Tommy McCarthy,

Herman Long and Kid Nichols. Mac's wife and three young daughters took a train trip from Boston to Chicago to meet him, at which time they boarded another train for California and a nice family extended vacation away from the harsh New England winter.

Hugh Duffy was no fool and he did not want people to think he was. From his the time of the incident in Cincy until the end of his life, he did not permit himself to be compromised in such a way that his drunken antics made the front page of newspapers.

Probably the most effective catcher on the early Beaneater championship teams, Charlie Bennett's career was tragically cut short after he lost his legs before the 1894 season. Returning to Detroit, where he had played eight seasons for the Wolverines, Bennett was so loved that a ball park was named after him. Collection of Richard A. Johnson.

He may or may not have been a teetotaler, but he at the least learned to control his appetites when it came to imbibing.

And so the Beaneaters ended their season as three-peat champions and should have rightfully enjoyed their success in the ensuing months. But very few of them did so, enduring more often winters of discontent. For instance, on January 10, 1894, the Beaneaters popular catcher, Charlie Bennett, had left a train in Kansas to say goodbye to a friend, and when he went to get back onto the train, it had begun to travel out of the station. He tried to jump on the train, and in the process he fell between the wheels of the train and the platform and lost both of his legs. That quickly, a man who prided himself on his conditioning and who walked sometimes between eight and 15 miles a day lost his livelihood in this ghastly accident.

His friends rallied to him, and former teammate John Clarkson visited Bennett, as did current teammate Kid Nichols. Everyone in Boston expressed shock and sadness at the tragedy that befell this popular and skillful veteran catcher. A benefit was planned for a date once the season began, as Frank Selee and the Triumvirs went about finding themselves a new catcher.

As much as a kind-hearted man like Hugh Duffy must have fretted about what befell Charlie Bennett, he had personal problems of his own. On March 31, 1894, his wife died from tuberculosis while returning from the health-seeking trip to California. She had to be taken off the train in Blackstone, Massachusetts, due to her extremely sick condition, and she died a few hours later.

Across the Atlantic Ocean, an author with the rather haughty pen name of Madame Sarah Grand wrote a book entitled *The Heavenly Twins*.

Chapter 10

Hugh Duffy Sets a Record as His Ball Park Burns Down

Baseball scribes have attributed Charlie Bennett's tragic train accident in large part to the reason that the Boston Beaneaters' 1894 club failed to win the pennant. In a purely baseball sense, he had not hit effectively for almost a decade and had largely stopped drawing walks after 1890. His most significant contribution came in managing the pitching staff and in not acting as a clubhouse lawyer in a tempestuous clubhouse, and Kid Nichols, for one, greatly missed him.

The excuse largely ignores the huge strides that Ned Hanlon had made in a brief time in assembling a powerhouse of a team, centered on an Irish-Catholic core of Hall of Famers in John McGraw, Joe Kelley, Hughie Jennings and Wee Willie Keeler. Boston no longer stood as the lone superpower in major league baseball and had to adjust accordingly.

In addition to assembling a squad of stars, Hanlon imbued the players with a nasty attitude, one which came naturally to John McGraw, and one that he fostered in his teammates. McGraw once explained it as "all done for its psychologic effect on the ballgame.... But to make it good we'd go tearing into a bag with flying spikes as though with murderous intent." The *Sporting Life* took a somewhat less sanguine view of McGraw, whom they accused of "always looking for trouble at the ball field, and frequently find[ing] it." Some of it was show, and certainly Hanlon did not tolerate drunks or out of control men, as did Patsy Tebeau and the underperforming Cleveland club. But some of the meanness came naturally and some of it came to Oriole players with little encouragement as they projected an image of grit and orneriness. They cared little about the lofty reputation of the champion Beaneaters.

Some changes in addition to the need to replace Bennett had occurred in the Boston clubhouse. Weak-hitting Cliff Carroll, Duffy's nemesis, retired, and in his stead the Beaneaters brought in good-hit, no-field Jimmy Bannon from

Saugus, Massachusetts. Known as Foxy Grandpa, the 22-year-old Bannon earned his nickname due to the liberal dusting of gray hairs on his head, a condition he attributed to his family's proclivity to lose their natural lustrous hair color early.

With the 5' 5" Bannon joining the 5' 6" (or at best 5' 7") Duffy and McCarthy, the Beaneaters had the major leagues' shortest outfield and quite possibly the only outfield in history where the total of the three fielders' heights did not exceed 200 inches. Still, Bannon hit better than Carroll and he got along better with Duffy, so at least an addition by subtraction had occurred in the Boston roster.

More tangible evidence of trouble came out when the *Boston Globe* reported that star outfielder Tommy McCarthy "had been threatened with some awful fate" by the Triumvirs when they called him in for a summit meeting to address rumblings of team dissension. This incident coincided with the raising of the 1894 championship flag over the South End Grounds to the tune of "The Star Spangled Banner" (not yet the national anthem) for hopefully another enjoyable race at the old ballpark. It was not the best time to confront Mac, as he had recently sustained a big black eye after being hit by a wild pitch; in the age of no batting helmets, he got off relatively easy.

Actually, McCarthy only met with Conant, who asked him if he had been discussing team finances on a recent road trip, to which Mac replied that he and every other Beaneater had. Vintage McCarthy. He had an opportunity to lie or fudge or tactfully find a way to conclude the meeting on a diplomatic note, and opted instead to take control of the meeting and its agenda.

Conant merely accelerated the simmering discontent on the team and soon reporters accosted every Beaneater in sight, seeking to ascertain whether a strike for higher wages was afoot. Conant tried to pooh-pooh the whole business, as team Captain Nash danced around the whole strike possibility with the very interested sports writers.

More ominously, an unnamed prominent player volunteered, "Put it down as a lie that any of the Boston players have been drinking to excess, but I will admit there is some dissatisfaction in the team, owing to the pauper-like style of financial management pursued by Soden and Conant. Yes, you can say that the players of the Boston team after being cut down two seasons in succession are dissatisfied, and do not care whether we win the pennant this season or not."

More likely than not, by the tone and manner of speaking, the anonymous statement emanated from Mac, with Duffy an outside candidate for the speaking honors. Lending credence to this theory, the *Sporting Life* reported that both of the Heavenly Twins wanted out of Boston at the end of the season. And this year everyone referred to Duffy and McCarthy as the Heavenly Twins, even though privately the Triumvirs and some of their teammates thought them more appropriately to be at best angels with dirty faces. Of far more import, the sentiments contained in the quote amount to mutiny, and while no one specifically threatened to throw games, the possibility presented itself that the Beaneaters would practice hippodroming, the art of deliberately trying not to win.

That last possibility seems remote, since so many of the Boston players bet so heavily on their repeating as champions. Nevertheless, the possibility existed that a team might gather together a few players to deliberately lose one game, figuring that it may have little impact on the pennant race. Or other players who did not bet on their team may bet against their team, as just desserts for the Triumvirate not paying them adequately. Most likely, the fact that key Beaneater players resented their owners and felt exploited, at least subconsciously, had an effect on their willingness to give their all. And against an opponent such as the hard-charging Orioles, no room for error existed.

Where there is smoke, there is fire. Disaster struck on May 11, 1894, when a conflagration started at the South End Grounds during a Beaneaters game with Baltimore, which ultimately not only burned down the Boston team's stadium, but also obliterated as many as 20 acres of surrounding neighborhoods. The accepted version of how the fire began is a purported 14-year-old eyewitness who had snuck into the park with his friends that day. Young James Laskey claimed that a gentleman with a "sandy mustache, dark hair ... a brown derby [hat] ... a dark checked coat, with a grease spot on the sleeve, and a pair of dark striped trousers" carelessly let a lit match fall between some boards in the seats, which landed on a pile of dry wood. After the fire erupted, Laskey disappeared for a couple of days before emerging to tell his tale, which the authorities apparently bought hook, line and sinker. The extraordinarily detailed description that Laskey gave of the alleged pyromaniac apparently never produced a suspect, and at least one publication figured the culprit was Laskey himself.

In any event, fans started noticing some smoke curling up from behind the 25-cent seats and initially thought nothing of it as right fielder Jimmy Bannon apparently stamped out the fire with his shoes. One popular account has the crowd diverted by a fight between John McGraw and Foghorn Tucker, but the fire seemed to take off during a routine at-bat by Baltimore's Brodie in the third inning.

Moments later, however, a plume of fire leapt straight into the atmosphere. The fire spread rapidly, causing the fans and players to rush out, with at least some effort made to save baseballs and the like. Surrounding neighbors tumbled out of their tenements in horror and many saw their neighborhoods consumed by flames. The papers did note that Sullivan's Tower fell in the blaze. Parenthetically, fans had constructed this monstrosity outside of the park to get a free view of the game, and as the Triumvirs tried to build up around it to obstruct the view, the fans built Sullivan's Tower higher, to the point that at one juncture as many as 500 fans climbed it to see a game at no charge.

Before the fire department finally contained and doused the blaze, the fire had destroyed the South End Grounds. A rumor circulated around this time that the slow pace of controlling the fire was caused in large part by the Triumvirs failing to pay money they owed to the City of Boston. True or not, the greedy Beaneater Triumvirate had failed to take even the most basic precautions like running a hose nearby or leaving water buckets around.

Sketches of the scene after the accident depict an absolute holocaust. Parents spent days seeking out missing children, and hundreds became homeless and had to relocate to shelters in churches or bunk with relatives and friends. Miraculously, no one perished. Still, it developed into the worst fire in Boston since the Great Fire of 1872, which destroyed much of downtown Boston, stopping mercifully short at the historic Old South Church. The Boston club had to temporarily relocate to the old Congress Street Grounds, upon which Herman Long deadpanned that he had played on many a prairie but Congress Street was in much worse shape.

The dark cloud seemed to stalk the Beaneaters on their next road trip, just days later in Philadelphia. Foghorn Tucker did not start for the Beaneaters but coached first base, where he spent considerable time berating the umpire, Tim Hurst, in addition to the fans and members of the press with his "unearthly howling." After five innings of this diatribe, Hurst ordered Tucker to the bench. In that same inning, Hugh Duffy had a right to feel ruffled after Hurst called him out on a close play while running to first base.

"You're on the level — not!" screamed Duffy.

Hurst shot back, "That'll cost you ten dollars!"

"I will see you in Boston," threatened Duffy.

"I will see you here and you will now sit on the bench for the rest of the game," shouted Hurst. Oddly enough, since Tucker had only been thrown out as a coach and had not played in the game, he replaced Duffy in the field, and uncharacteristically was "as meek as a little lamb" for the remainder of the contest. The outburst foreshadowed much more trouble in Philly for the Beaneaters.

McCarthy did his best to support his benched Heavenly Twin by tripling, stealing third base in another inning, and stealing a home run off the bat of a Philadelphia batter, but Boston lost, 5–4, in ten innings. The most disturbing event in the game might have occurred when Duffy screamed "NOT" after making a sarcastic statement that he did not believe about Hurst, as this overused type of phrase became extremely popular a century later. It is sad to contemplate that this boring piece of etymology might have originated with the great Hugh Duffy.

On a more joyous note, Beaneaters second baseman Bobby Lowe at the end of May did something only fourteen other batters have accomplished in major league history by hitting four home runs in one game. In doing so, he helped bail Kid Nichols out of an uncharacteristically poor pitching performance against Cincinnati as the Beaneaters rode out a 20–11 victory.

The home run barrage fell in an era not marked by home run hitting by a player who did not have a reputation in his career as a power hitter, although in fairness, he did hit quite a few in relation to his peers. Lowe's historic performance occurred in the second game of a doubleheader (both games won by Boston), in juxtaposition to his efforts in the first game, during which only he and captain Billy Nash failed to scratch out a hit on the team. In the second game, though, Lowe hit his four home runs in succession and banged out two of them in the same inning against a hapless pitcher who stayed in the entire game without relief, as was the custom of the day. To top it off, Lowe hit a single after he had fired off his final home run.

In appreciation, the Boston fans at the Congress Street Grounds went wild and reportedly lavished a total of 150 silver dollars on Lowe. Afterwards, the team repaired to Duffy and McCarthy's newly opened bowling alley to celebrate. While it seems that players on the Boston club in the 1890s either made the Hall of Fame or were forgotten, Bobby Lowe found a niche in the middle, forever commemorated each time a new player hits four homers.

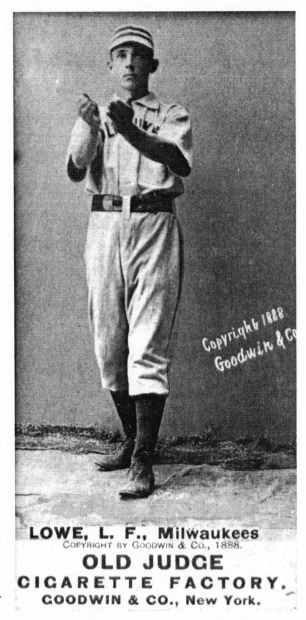

LOWE, L. F., Milwaukees
COPYRIGHT BY GOODWIN & CO., 1888.
OLD JUDGE
CIGARETTE FACTORY.
GOODWIN & CO., New York.

Bobby Lowe, shown here in his Milwaukee Brewers (Western Association) uniform, was the first batter in history to hit four home runs in a ball game, a feat he accomplished in 1894. Like Jimmy Collins, he found his true calling as an infielder after breaking into the major leagues as an outfielder. Library of Congress.

Historically, the feats of Lowe are diminished because of the mistaken belief that the South End Grounds had notoriously short porches, which means Lowe's shots had to travel only about 250 feet to reach the fences. There is one problem with this belief and that is the South End Grounds burned to the ground two weeks earlier.

The Congress Street Grounds might not have been that much more challenging than the torched park, but to maintain perspective, before 1900 only Lowe and Ed Delahanty hit four homers in one contest and few home runs were hit in relative terms before the advent of Babe Ruth due to the deadness of the baseballs. Had the Bambino had to hit the awful baseball of that era, his home run totals would have suffered. Viewed through this prism, receiving credit for this milestone is warranted. It should not obscure, however, where Lowe's true strength lay, which is in being part of a terrific keystone combination with Herman Long in those great Boston infields.

In addition to Lowe's heroics, Duffy and McCarthy continued to crush the ball. While their contributions certainly kept Boston in the fray, the pitchers weighed down the squad. Selee expressed a frustration that filtered down to the *Sporting Life* scribes when he stated that Boston would be in first place if not for the struggles on the mound. Specifically, Selee chastised Happy Jack Stivetts, who did not keep himself in sufficient shape to please the manager.

To stem the tide, Selee auditioned numerous promising pitchers, but none of them had the talent or the training to supplant the current starters, causing the Beaneaters to continue to founder a bit. A rumor floated around that Cy Young was Boston-bound but it proved premature by several years; Young helped deliver world championships to Boston in the early 1900s, but not for the Triumvirs. Meanwhile, misfortune continued to stalk the Beaneaters.

For one thing, not only had Charlie Bennett met with tragedy, but the remaining catchers kept getting hurt. Late one night in mid–June, Frank Selee called up a Brown University senior, Fred Tenney, and offered him a spot on the Beaneaters' roster that day. Tenney had partied all night after a senior dinner, but needed money and wanted dearly to play professional baseball. He signed with the team and caught, apparently plagued by an overbearing hangover. In his zeal, he promptly broke a finger that disabled him, only to return a month later in an away game in Philadelphia.

On July 17, 1894, by which time Tenney had fully mended, more than 6,000 Philadelphia fans passed through the turnstiles to attend a riot between their team and Boston, but for almost eight innings a baseball game took place. As the game progressed the skies darkened and thunder rumbled in the distance. Then in the eighth the Phillies scored seven runs, putting the game seemingly out of reach. Boston conceded the game in all but name because they calculated that a rain storm might break out, which would hopefully cause the umpire to call the contest. Unlike today, the game did not have to go only five innings to make it official, so the Beaneaters resorted to every dilatory tactic in the book to try to elongate the game into the path of a storm and a reversion to the seventh inning, at which time they led, 2–1.

For more than twenty minutes the Beaneaters allowed hits to go through with no effort to put the opposing batters out, which angered the spectators, who commenced hissing and groaning at the masquerade played out before them. Tommy McCarthy saw one hit coming to him and instead of fielding it, stepped aside like a toreador and let the ball roll past him. At other times, Boston players tossed the ball back and forth to each other and rolled the ball into the infield like a bowling ball. Finally, a Phillies runner deliberately failed to stop at second base on his way from first to third base, thus outing himself in an effort to mercifully terminate the inning.

The Phillies players ran out into the field, but Boston infielders Nash, Lowe and first baseman Tommy Tucker stood around the umpire, arguing that basically they should be allowed to continue to joke around or have the game called for them. Tucker particularly made a loud fuss, apparently not only abusing the umpire but also the Phillies players and the fans in his loud and resonating voice. They did not call him Foghorn Tucker for nothing.

Hugh Duffy did not help matters by running around the outfield with the game ball and refusing to relinquish it, a lesson Duffy first learned when the Waterbury team employed it against his old Springfield club in the spring of 1887. Apparently he had earlier angered the crowd by deliberately holding a Phillies infielder to prevent him from forcing out Duffy's teammate at second base to complete a double play.

Losing patience, the umpire warned Boston to play the game for real, and gave them one minute to take matters seriously, but eventually he called a forfeit in favor of Philadelphia. The players left for the dressing rooms but angry Phillies fans sprinted onto the field in dissatisfaction. Unfortunately, first baseman Tommy Tucker left his glove on the field, and when he ran back onto the field to retrieve it, pandemonium ensued. After a youngster handed him his glove, Tucker directed a number of sarcastic comments to the cranks, at which point someone in the maddening crowd threw a shoulder at him. Swiftly, another rowdy fan threw a punch that connected with Tucker's left cheek, and he failed to topple over only because the crowd had gathered so close to him that it broke his fall.

A detachment of police formed on the diamond, and with the help of some Phillies players, broke through and rescued Tucker, injured cheekbone and all. In the midst of the chaos, Duffy almost did not get out of the park, and Tommy McCarthy, only partially clothed, barely escaped. Upwards of two thousand fans continued to mill around the field. Police reinforcements were called in, and after a cooling off period, they escorted the Beaneaters through the throng. One policeman was hit in the face with a mud ball thrown by a street urchin, who in turn was smacked in the face by a cop. Two people were arrested for assaulting and battering Tucker and, of course, they denied everything.

The Beaneaters would rather have been anywhere else than in Philadelphia, but when they actually played baseball rather than carp about the umpire, great things happened. In their last home game in June, the Beaneaters hosted the league-leading Orioles in theatric fashion.

In one match, down 7–5 in the eighth inning, the Beaneaters loaded the bases and McCarthy cleared them with a towering double that kept the crowd cheering in a frenzy for several minutes thereafter.

In the next inning, however, the Orioles came rushing back by loading the bases. Boston pitcher Jack Stivetts then drilled the next batter in the ribs before walking Hughie Jennings, bringing in two runs. Tom Lovett then relieved Stivetts and was so wild with one pitch that it caromed all over the place, scoring all three runs. After choking, Lovett then prompted the next three batters to fly out harmlessly. But now Baltimore led, 12–10, heading into the bottom of the ninth.

With two men on and one out, Hugh Duffy came to bat. The Baltimore pitcher, Sadie McMahon, had already derisively tipped his cap to the crowd, which already had developed a hatred for their opposition and its perceived dirty play. All Hugh Duffy did was crack a pitch over the left-field fence for a walk-off home run, sending home Herman Long and Bobby Lowe. Duffy did not even trot around the bases, but veered off toward his team after rounding second as fans pounded him on the back in glee while directing their catcalls for the departing Orioles.

The worst insults came in the next day's edition of the *Globe*, in which Tim Murnane detailed the perceived sins of the Orioles. "Visions of the pennant have so worked on the revolving machinery of the Oriole's brain that to maime [*sic*] a fellow-player for life seem to them, apparently, just retribution for trying to stop them in their temporary flight. Diving into the first baseman long after he has caught the ball, throwing masks in front of the runner in front of the home plate, catching men by the clothes at the third base, and interfering with base runners, and gathering around the home plate to interfere with the catcher performed by these young men from the south."

Not to be outdone by the theatrics of Duffy and Bobby Lowe, Tommy McCarthy had a terrific day in the field on August 15 in Pittsburgh. With runners on first and second and none out, Pitt's Bill Merritt hit a blooper to short left-center field, with Mac and infielders Connaughton and Tenney all converging on the ball. "Let me have it!" shouted Mac as he waved his teammates away. As part of the show he made a grand stab at catching it but then let it deliberately drop at his footsteps.

Correctly feeling that the fly ball constituted no challenge to such a fine outfielder as McCarthy, the Pittsburgh runners cradled their bases. When the ball plopped in front of him, Mac seized it and whipped it to second baseman Bobby Lowe, who tagged the stunned runner off second base and then stepped on the bag for the force.

Lowe then tossed the ball to third baseman Nash, who tagged the Pittsburgh runner for the second time off second, the baseball equivalent of beating a dead horse. Inexplicably, Merritt, the batter had run to first and then walked back to home plate. Nash ran to first to touch the base, but since Merritt had successfully singled, he was not yet out. At that point, Mac yelled, "Give me that ball," then ran to tag Merritt for the third out. Boston went on to win the game in eleven innings, no small part due to the heady play of one of the Heavenly Twins.

Heading into the last week of August, the Beaneaters had every reason to feel confident of repeating as champions. They had beaten their toughest rival, the Orioles, in their season series eight games to four, and that they did not have any more games against them. In that statistical fact came opportunity for the Orioles, though. By contrast, they did not have to go against a Boston club that clearly had their number, allowing the Orioles to feast on inferior competition until the end of the campaign.

The plan got off to a poor start for Baltimore on August 23, when the Orioles lost to the Browns by a score of 10–6. And then something rather remarkable happened. Licking their wounds from their last game, the Orioles went on a 17-game winning streak, beating up on the western clubs in the circuit.

Inexcusably, Boston lost two out of three at home to the breathtakingly bad St. Louis Browns. Owner Chris Von der Ahe had dragged his franchise down by his bizarre behavior and mistreatment of players. One former player, Tommy McCarthy, decided to commemorate Von der Ahe using his goons to steal Mac's watch and money in St. Louis from two years back by swearing out a writ and having Von der Ahe placed in a Boston jail. Two of the Boston Triumvirs, Soden and Conant, bailed out Von der Ahe from prison, but McCarthy had exacted his revenge.

The only respite for the team came in its exhibition game with a picked team for the benefit of their former catcher, Charlie Bennett. For all the faults that one can find with baseball at the turn of the century, a lack of generosity to the unfortunate in its ranks is not one of them. Heavyweight boxing champion Gentleman Jim Corbett came out for the event and played, rather poorly, for one of the teams. Still, the event raised $6,000 for Bennett, or about three times what he would have been paid by the Triumvirate had he not been injured. He went on to run a successful business in Detroit, where his neighbors named Bennett Park after this very popular ballplayer.

As fall beckoned, Boston not only had to contend with the Orioles, they now had to compete for the pennant with the New York squad. In a pivotal one-game makeup in the Polo Grounds, New York, behind the hard throwing of pitcher Amos Rusie, defeated Boston and their ace Kid Nichols, 5–1. Taken with the recent poor home series with the lowly Browns, this game demoralized Boston greatly. Duffy and McCarthy played their hearts out and McCarthy in particular played the field with élan. With a New York runner on second base, the batter hit the ball to McCarthy in the outfield. Decoying a throw home (knowing he could not throw him out at the plate), he rifled the ball to first base and caught the batter off base, stealing an out for his team.

As the season ended, most of the star Beaneater players refused to sign new contracts for the next year, pending news of whether a new proposed league, the National Association, would come to fruition. With a new league came the possibility of jumping from the Beaneaters to a new franchise, with expected bumps in pay to the deserting players. Opined captain Billy Nash, "I am in no hurry to sign a contract for next season. The present season has not been as pleasant as I should like to have seen it. Several of the boys claim that they have grievances against the owners of the club, and continual talk of this kind has handicapped our chances for the pennant." Hugh Duffy, Charley Ganzell, Tommy Tucker and Bobby Lowe joined Nash in the public condemnation of the stingy Triumvirate as the last games of a frustrating year played out.

Despite the inspired play of the Heavenly Twins, the Beaneaters could not catch the Orioles, and in the end, they even fell behind the New York team for a humbling third-place finish for the campaign. There would be no four-peat for the Beaneaters.

Boston may have gotten marginally better as a team since the end of 1893, but Baltimore and New York had improved dramatically, leading the Beaneaters to a disappointing third-place finish. Boston's downfall came with the surge of the Baltimore Orioles, who stockpiled more stars each year until by 1894, six of their position players eventually earned plaques in the Baseball Hall of Fame as did their manager, the shrewd Ned Hanlon. In one year they finally had enough pieces to vault over the Beaneaters, who continued to play excellent ball.

On a more sublunary note, Kid Nichols had a bit of an off-year, as did most pitchers who tried to cope with the new distance to the plate. Very few pitchers had decent earned run averages in 1894. Some of the youngsters the Beaneaters brought on to replace Bennett proved unqualified, but veteran Charley Ganzell stepped in and performed his usual competent work at catcher. The replacement of Cliff Carroll by young Jimmy Bannon proved a net improvement to the team.

In mid–October, a banquet was held for Hugh Duffy in the United States Hotel, consisting primarily of McCarthy's Southie friends and the local cranks, politicians and scribes. Mac had played with a "large bump on his shin" caused by being hit by a batted ball in 1893, and had set up an appointment to have it operated on as soon as the 1894 season ended. Whether he had the operation or not, he attended Duffy's ceremony.

State congressman Michael Moore of Boston, the brother of a very eligible young woman named Nora Moore, stopped by. Old friend Tim Murnane broadcast some pithy remarks to the crowd and Duffy received a gold Howard watch. By then, his bowling alley venture with McCarthy had proven quite successful, and around this time he announced his permanent relocation from Rhode Island to Boston.

Tim Murnane told the assembled guests about how he discovered Duffy, a man that he termed the "most loyal man he had ever met," a sentiment echoed by the other Heavenly Twin when he came up to speak. Edmund McHugh serenaded the crowd in his baritone voice with two popular songs of the day, "Send for Mother, Birdie's Dying," and "I'm Sitting on the Stile, Marie." "Wreaths of perfectos" cigars filled the atmosphere as Duffy received his gold Howard watch with a gold and platinum chain.

Lost in the din of the loud music and smoky banquet hall, Hugh Duffy had hit .440 for the year, and though no one in attendance knew it, that mark remained unchallenged into the twenty-first century as the all-time mark for a single campaign. Much has been written about how the mark is inflated because pitchers still had not accustomed themselves to the longer distance between the pitcher and home plate, but these analyses do not give Duffy his due credit, particularly since he labored the entire year in grief over the death of his young wife Katie.

The loss of Hugh Duffy's young wife was unimaginably heartbreaking to him, but he channeled his grief into the highest single-season batting average of all-time and arguably, the major league's first triple crown. This does not mean that he did not feel the loss of his wife deeply, but the specter of an early death was more of a fact of life, and if people seemed callous at times, it was because the calluses were built up over time by personal tragedy. True grace under pressure.

Fittingly enough for Irish Catholic Boston of the day, a letter from Father Doherty to Duffy was read as a benediction for the evening. The priest used the gold watch as a metaphor for the golden reward of heaven, which he hoped awaited Hugh Duffy after a life well led. And there the evening ended.

Sadly, King Kelly died soon thereafter. King Kelly quite literally came to Boston one last time in early November, 1894. He had ventured from New York on a boat to take part in some theatrical event at the Palace Theater, but a pre-existing cold soon turned into pneumonia. An old friend at his hotel made arrangements for him at a local emergency room where he gravitated between life and death for a few days. So serious was his condition that a Fr. Hickey administered the Last Rites of the Catholic Church and his wife rushed up from New Jersey to sit with him, but he died before she arrived in Boston.

Mike Kelly received a hero's funeral in Boston, and Duffy and McCarthy seemed particularly saddened by the death of their old teammate, who once said of the Heavenly Twins, "the first in the profession, all things considered...." They buried Kelly at Mount Hope Cemetery in Boston, which is forever associated as his town. Like Carlton Fisk who played more time in Chicago, the Windy City lost out on his legacy to the scene of his most memorable triumphs.

Thousands visited his final resting place for years after, but today his stone is largely ignored.

The failure of the hard-hitting 1894 Beaneaters to win their fourth pennant in a row is shrouded in foreshadowing and omens, like Charlie Bennett's accident bookended with the death of King Kelly and a burned down stadium and surrounding neighborhood sandwiched in between. Thus ended an annus horibilis for Boston sports fans, only to usher in a period of acrimony and open breach between the Heavenly Twins in the coming year.

Chapter 11

Where Everybody
Knows Your Name

Long before the mythical retired Red Sox relief pitcher Sam Malone piloted his Cheers bar in Boston, Tommy McCarthy and Hugh Duffy established their own saloon and bowling alley at 603 Washington Street. By the holiday season of 1894–1895, the "baseball fraternity [met] regularly at Duffy and McCarthy's bowling emporium on Washington to play over old games." It sat in the middle of what became fourscore years later Boston's notorious adult pornographic Combat Zone.

As expected, the Heavenly Twins' star power created a considerable draw for the new enterprise, and unlike today when sports stars generally go out only to extremely expensive restaurants, they availed themselves to fellow baseballists and wannabes alike in their efforts to ensure crowds. Also, they had tapped into an emerging bowling craze that spawned 80 alleys in the greater Boston area in a very short interval of time.

Underlying these trends lay more important sociological and demographic changes. For at least a decade, General Dixwell was *the* fan in Boston baseball. A trust fund baby, Dixwell had little to do besides follow his favorite ball club around, maintain scrupulous box scores of each game, and ejaculate a very loud and vocal "Hi, Hi" cheer when the mood struck him during a game. The players either liked him or thought him harmless as he showered them with attention and gifts.

Dixwell may have linked the Boston baseball teams with the traditional Yankee/Brahmin local establishment, yet his background clashed with the largely Irish-Catholic local population and fan base.

Concurrent with Boston becoming an overwhelmingly Irish city, its Celtic citizenry grew less tolerant of meek obeisance and deference to the Yankee elite. New politicians such as John "Honey Fitz" Fitzgerald and Mayor Curley, the latter of whom railed against the "overlords" who trampled upon the aspirations of the Irish, flexed their political muscle and demanded power for themselves and their constituencies. By the mid–1890s, a verbal and visible group of mainly Irish cranks, soon to constitute the core of the Royal Rooters, emerged at the South End Grounds. They had musical instruments as well as numbers and soon drowned out Dixwell while beginning to really get on the nerves of opposing teams' ball players.

Duffy and McCarthy loved these guys, probably because they reminded them of themselves; perhaps born into poor families, the new fans ascended economically from their roots, loved baseball and loved to drink, but went to church on Sundays and invited the presiding priest of their parish to their homes for a pot roast and a blessing. Many of these fans, such as Jack Dooley, Charles Lavis and Bernie Lennon, became their life-long friends. Since they liked hanging around these guys so much at the ballpark, Duffy and McCarthy kept the party going by opening up a bowling alley and inviting their friends over to knock down some pins and spend a few dollars at their joint.

Although Duffy and McCarthy's emporium originally opened as a bowling alley and billiard room in the late summer and early fall of 1894, plans quickly changed. By September 1895, they had applied for and obtained a liquor license from the City of Boston, making their concept complete. Although liquor may have found its way into the building before the license had been granted, the outfielders now had the ability to add another legitimate stream of income by charging patrons for potent potables.

One can imagine their friends from the Beaneaters and other major league teams congregating with some of the lesser lights of McCarthy's South Boston sandlot days. Stars from other teams, like the Orioles outfielder and future Hall of Famer Joe Kelley, often stopped by. As their mentor (and a former saloon owner himself), Tim Murnane from the *Boston Globe* inevitably must have dropped by with his fellow sports writers to rest their bowler hats and boaters and put down some bowling pins and beer. Boston, like many American cities of the age, abounded in breweries, all eager to deliver their product to the new saloon and its patrons.

Unfortunately, cracks began to show in this business very quickly. By the late summer of 1885, the *Boston Globe* noted that "bowling is passé," and the trendsetters rapidly removed themselves to the nearest maypole or torchlight parade to regroup and take advantage of the next big thing.

Demonstrating early evidence of his astute business sense, Duffy decided to bail on the partnership around this time. Noting that saloon owners often proved their best customers, Harold Seymour exempted ballplayers such as Duffy and Dummy Hoy, who actually made money through shrewd investments outside of ball fields and bar rooms. By logical extension, folks like Tommy McCarthy, who wished to stay in the business, curried temptation every day they showed up at work and a crank or fellow ballplayer offered to buy them a drink.

JAMES B. McALOON & CO.

= Merchant Tailors, =

125 TREMONT, OPPOSITE PARK STREET,

BOSTON.

HOTEL SAVOY,

Washington Street, Boston.

EUROPEAN PLAN. LADIES' AND GENTLEMEN'S CAFÉS.

An advertisement for Tommy McCarthy's saloon in Boston, shortly after he terminated his partnership with Duffy. The saloon is long gone, and in its place is a modern day high-rise. Collection of Richard A. Johnson.

The death knell officially came when Tim Murnane noted in his column on November 10, 1895, that the partnership had ended and Duffy was getting out of the business, leaving matters to McCarthy. Concurrently, Duffy attributed his decision to a desire to devote himself full-time to baseball, something the bar business evidently precluded.

Or did it? Perhaps he noted the declining interest in bowling and his keen instincts instructed him to get out of the business immediately. After losing his first wife, his new bride, Norah Moore, may have wanted her husband at home and not in a bar all night. It may also be he saw that running the saloon required his constant presence there and it may have contributed to his drinking more than he or others preferred. Most likely, he saw McCarthy's own career careen at about the same time they started their business together and he simply did not want the same outcome for himself.

Interestingly enough, while the split in financial interests affected the underlying friendship for about a year, it did not destroy it in the long term. Thereafter, it appears that McCarthy took on a new partner, namely Bernard Lennon, almost certainly the minor politico of the era, who served as a member of the Ward 17 Committee. This partnership too proved fleeting, and a number of years later a Bernard Lennon served as a member of the Archdiocese of Boston's Temperance Society's Decoration Committee, which may provide some insight into why Lennon should have stayed far away from the gin joints, either as a proprietor or customer, or both.

Supposedly McCarthy decided to play another year of baseball in 1896, mainly to keep his name in the papers and continue to draw a crowd at his bar. This suggests that at the turn of the century, these saloons turned on the popularity of the players much more so than any entertainment or atmosphere offered, and also that McCarthy had essentially subordinated his baseball career to his pursuit of his bar business. Baltimore Orioles stars John McGraw and Wilbert Robinson also ran a bar around this time. Manager Selee perhaps saw through this and sent McCarthy packing to the Brooklyn team during the off-season.

After 1896, and for about the next 17 years, McCarthy ran the saloon and bowling alley alone. He employed at least three bartenders at any given time and liked to decorate his bar with sports photos and sketches of Boston. At one point he added the pictures of the Harvard varsity and the Lowell minor league baseball teams as well as a sketch or portrait depicting a part of Boston in the year 1808, which is about all we know about the inside decor. A photo or a sketch of the joint is the Holy Grail of Boston sports bars.

Intriguingly, as Duffy's own baseball playing career declined around 1900, he returned to the saloon business, this time with a new partner named Charles Lavis. While Bernie Lennon subsisted mainly in obscurity, Lavis scrupulously courted controversy. While later scribes and Red Sox of the 1940s and 1950s remembered Duffy mostly as a harmless and friendly grandfather figure, in his youth he traveled with some very Runyonesque characters.

Charles Lavis might have been the shadiest of the bunch, and in no way did Duffy not know of his friend's renown. In June 1885, for instance, Boston police raided the three most lucrative illegal baseball pool-betting parlors in the city and arrested and imprisoned the ring leaders, among them young Charles Lavis. Within a half-hour of the raids, the joints all resumed conducting their activities, but the appearance of action placated the local Society for the Suppression of Vice. Two hours after the raids, Lavis bailed out and lawyered himself up to contest the sweeps.

Lavis at least publicly kept his nose clean for another twenty years until he stood trial for serving alcohol to a young damsel in distress named Bessie Dutton, who played her role to the full post–Victorian hilt. It seems that Lavis again dodged trouble and it is not difficult to see why, as the society pages of the day were littered with notices of Lavis' appearances at prominent social functions, sporting events, funerals or matters important to the very popular Archdiocese of Boston. Lavis, in a bad sense, was untouchable.

And Duffy did not conceal his association with Lavis as they opened up a bar at 1 Harvard Street in what now borders the old Combat Zone and present-day Chinatown in Boston. As if to punctuate matters, Lavis openly took caravans of people down to Providence in the 1900s to see Duffy once he secured an ownership interest in that minor league team.

While not as overtly corrupt as Boston's notorious Sport Sullivan of the 1919 Black Sox scandal, Lavis nevertheless skirted the fine line between being a respected community pillar and pushing every legal nicety in the advancement of his financial interests. While Duffy could choose his friends, his partnership with Lavis manifested a refreshingly brief lapse in his usual sound financial judgment, and no trace of their establishment is found either before or after 1900.

Folks like Lavis should not have associated with professional athletes, but in turn-of-the-century Boston, the downtrodden Irish had emerged as the majority of the citizenry and began to flex their new-found political muscle. Indeed, in the early twentieth century, Boston Cardinal O'Connell had defiantly proclaimed, "The Puritan has passed, the Catholic remains!" Many Irish in the new Boston chafed at the perceived interference of their white Anglo-Saxon overlords and rejected their good government initiatives.

If the Society for the Suppression of Vice targeted sharpies like Lavis, many of his co-religionists either turned the other eye or actively condoned his behavior because he was one of them. He attended Mass and funerals of prominent Irish-Catholics, he was a loyal and devoted son of the church, and he prospered.

If official and semi-official Boston let Lavis operate freely, organized baseball had an obligation to intercede and keep him and his minions away, but for different reasons, no one took effective action in the pre–Kenesaw Mountain Landis days. Baseball was still decades away from its Black Sox scandal, and it cared as little about gambling as it did about steroids or amphetamines.

Duffy and McCarthy were Heavenly Twins, but they were no angels. They lived better and more productive and moral lives than most of their peers, but they too flirted with temptation. Their saloon-operating days did not show them in their best lights, and ultimately proved a dead end for both of them.

Sam Malone had his Cheers where "everybody knows your name" and later Boston sports hero Sammy White operated a successful bowling alley in Boston's Brighton neighborhood for several years, but Duffy and McCarthy's bar lives in the memory of no one. Until 1913, McCarthy proudly listed his business in the Boston city directory at 603 Washington Street, and then any reference to it disappears.

In its stead stood a new hotel, dubbed the Avery, built by wealthy William Gaston. Befitting Boston's transformation into a modern city, Gaston funded a thirteen-story building with offices, parlors, stores and a café on the first two floors. The remaining floors housed guests in walls of mahogany with a bath, shower and modern plumbing.

The Avery Hotel did not long maintain its status as a luxurious destination as more elegant establishments sprouted up around more fashionable areas of town, such as downtown, abutting the Boston Common and Public Garden and the Back Bay. The Avery Hotel soon rented out mainly to theater folk, folks who either did not know better (or could not afford better) and transients.

In the 1970s, a young woman built a snowman on the roof of the Avery Hotel and then plunged to her death, either by accident, foul play or suicide. By this time the neighborhood had long since passed into a dilapidated seediness as hundreds of thousands of Bostonians escaped to the suburbs and the local theaters lost their patrons. In a desperate gasp, the city of Boston redlined an adult entertainment district in this area, the notorious Combat Zone, and the Avery became a whorehouse. Long before the Combat Zone faded away, the Avery Hotel had been shuttered up, waiting to be razed out of existence.

While Duffy and McCarthy's joint may have been demolished to make room for the Avery Hotel, there is some reason to believe that part of the bar remained off to the side of the hotel. Perhaps the most reliable information concerning what eventually happened to the bar came from a Boston cop, who believes that it survived until very recently as a gay bar, after which it was finally knocked down to accommodate the construction of the current luxury high-rise building. If you try to stroll into Duffy and McCarthy's saloon today, you will walk directly into a Roche-Bobois furniture store, a place where no one knows Duffy and McCarthy's names.

Chapter 12

Tommy McCarthy
Takes a Bow in Boston

As Tommy McCarthy catapulted from his team "bus" down to the pavement, and the horses' hooves thundered heavily around his head, he may have speedily uttered the beginnings of an act of contrition or mused that there had to be a better way of making a living. The incident occurred after a tough loss to Baltimore in late September of 1895, when his team's equine-driven "bus" collided with a trolley car and Mac, sitting next to the driver, flew out onto the street and under the horses by the force of the impact. Joining him underneath the pounding of the horses' panicked gaits were teammates Kid Nichols and Charley Ganzel, as outfielder Jimmy Bannon swung in midair, clinging to a railing on top of the "bus." Miraculously no one sustained a serious injury and the campaign continued for the Beaneaters into its final weeks.

The season had begun in much more mundane fashion. Although Hugh Duffy hit for the highest batting average in baseball history, before or since, the Boston owners did not offer him a raise for the 1894 season. Many youngsters in the 1950s and 1960s read Bill Stern's books, one of which had Duffy becoming the team captain after 1894. With this honor, he supposedly did not receive a raise, yet had to pick up baseballs and did not have any other real duties. He later received only a $12.50 a month raise once he made a stink of things.

Like many of Stern's stories, it contains only a grain of truth and the reality is much more interesting than the tall tale. For one thing, Duffy did not serve as captain in 1895 because Billy Nash still held that position, and Duffy did not have to pick up balls and bats unless he felt like it. He did hold out for money and refused to sign, leading manager Frank Selee to pay him a visit at Duffy and McCarthy's emporium just before spring training to try to negotiate a truce between the player and management.

Duffy did make another attempt at settling matters by walking over to Owner Soden's offices on Water Street in Boston and meeting with him.

Matters went so well that Duffy left with a wide smile on his face and a $200 raise. That amount was not a whole lot, but then again, many of the Boston players were already at the maximum salary allowed, meaning Duffy had bargained for his top dollar. A bit more satisfied, he packed his bags and prepared to join his team on the train ride south to spring training.

While Duffy cooled down and honed his considerable leadership skills, Tommy McCarthy chose a different path, unburdening himself to friend Tim Murnane at the *Boston Globe* at the expense of Manager Selee and Billy Nash. Offered McCarthy, "We ain't playing the ball we should be, especially in team batting. Neither Capt. Nash nor manager Selee ever coaches the men how to work. We ought to have it down so fine that the man on base should know what to do as the batsman walks to the plate. The way a player holds a bat should be a cue. The Baltimore team and others are going ahead of Boston in team work and this means the loss of a great many games."

Ouch!

Murnane endorsed these comments by quoting McCarthy and by also calling him one of the "brainiest players in the game," which he was on one level, but not in the realm of self-preservation, having just publicly dressed down the manager and team captain. Murnane also believed that the team's past successes caused them to engage in careless play, and that individual goals had replaced the team concept, a common lament at the time for any team that had gone bad. Either that or the players were not in shape. Then, as now, the statements by McCarthy impress the reader as a very bold affront to authority, one which he got away with so long as he enjoyed star status.

Early in the season, Tommy McCarthy still possessed the implicit right to make controversial statements without fear of retribution, as he maintained a very high level of performance. Shortly after embarrassing his manager and captain in print, McCarthy found himself coming to bat with the bases loaded in the second inning in a game at the South End Grounds against Washington. The Washington pitcher, Win Mercer, had just granted Hugh Duffy a deliberate walk to face the supposedly less dangerous other Heavenly Twin. Resoundingly, McCarthy crushed the second pitch from Mercer, sending it clear over the left-field fence. As he jogged around the bases, he "sang" to the dejected pitcher, "Now will you be good?" Life had generally been quite good for a star player in Boston.

Brimming with confidence, after an early series in Chicago ended, Duffy and McCarthy reportedly bet Cap Anson at least $150 each that Boston would outpace his team at season's end. For baseball purists, it is unknowable if the bet actually occurred or resulted in a pay out, but if true, this allegation does not substantially differ from those leveled against (and subsequently admitted by) Pete Rose. At that time, no one investigated this report nor would anyone have acted upon the story, but the Black Sox scandal of 1919 did not operate in a vacuum. A long tradition of gambling and hippodroming led inevitably to a suspicious product that needed, and later received, draconian reform. That development had to wait another quarter-century, and clearly Hugh Duffy saw no harm in the wager, as he simply thought he had a sure thing and wanted to screw Anson out of some money.

While Duffy's major issues seem to have dissipated with his raise in salary, not every member of his team shared his enthusiasm. As losses mounted in mid–May and the club hovered between third and fifth place in the league standings, the team divided, as it so often had in very good and very bad times. In a Louisville hotel one evening, antagonists Tommy McCarthy and Jack Stivetts sat at two different tables with their respective friends on the team. Apparently Stivetts either said or did something not to Mac's liking before dinner, because after Mac had finished his meal, he strode up behind Happy Jack and soundly socked him on his right jaw.

Women screamed and men rose from their tables as McCarthy calmly walked out of the dining area and into the street outside. To his credit, Stivetts refused to retaliate, but to make sure the much-taller Stivetts (by at least six inches in height) did not change his mind, McCarthy stayed out of the team hotel that evening. Selee quelled the clash, feeling that both men shared the blame equally for the incident, and he did not fine them.

Fissures in team unity had existed at least since Tommy Tucker and Hugh Duffy rebelled against Frank Selee at the end of the 1893 season, and Stivetts had injected himself into that controversy, a portent of future troubles. McCarthy had played with Stivetts in St. Louis and had missed the conflagration at the end of 1893, due to his broken toes. Nevertheless, he had read and been told about matters since that time and probably regretted not being with the team when tensions mounted and broke on that occasion. In 1895, McCarthy spoiled to fight.

A Cincinnati paper reported that religious differences on the team spurred the outburst, with Catholic players McCarthy, Duffy and Tommy Tucker arrayed against Protestant ballplayers Lowe, Long and Stivetts. Religious bigotry obviously played roles in disputes on several major league teams, famously on the 1910–1916 Boston Red Sox, where Catholic outfielders Duffy Lewis and Harry Hooper despised Tris Speaker, whom they regarded as a bigot and a member of the Ku Klux Klan.

It is difficult to believe that manager Frank Selee had any anti–Catholic biases, and he certainly liked and respected both Duffy and McCarthy very much. Selee only possessed deep-seated hatred of ballplayers who were fat, lazy, out of shape or over the hill. Most of the ballplayers on the team were probably Protestants, but they had played together as a team for so long that this factor alone generally did not cause friction between the players.

The *Boston Globe*, perhaps in a note contributed to in whole or in part by Tim Murnane, dismissed the religious slant of the Cincinnati paper piece. As he had demonstrated by having Chris Von der Ahe imprisoned in Boston in retaliation for Von der Ahe raiding his hotel room in St. Louis, Tommy McCarthy bore grudges and settled scores. He probably had never liked Stivetts, particularly after Happy Jack blasted his friends in the press.

After the fact, McCarthy ruminated about the incident and felt that team disharmony in 1895 on the Beaneater squad existed, but that he had helped reduce tensions among the players. It is difficult to determine how attempting to break someone's jaw contributes to easing tensions, but they were violent times. It certainly cleared the air, or at the least, the hotel dining room.

While Mac and Stivetts cooled down, the Triumvirs quietly began to make overtures to other clubs to move McCarthy out of Boston. In late July, a trade between Boston and Philadelphia, Tommy McCarthy straight up for Billy Hamilton, was widely rumored and publicized without consummation. At the time, each player carried a reputation for being a malcontent, and the deal certainly would have cleared out negative clubhouse influences from their respective teams, but it made little sense for Philadelphia because Hamilton was at the top of his game and Tommy McCarthy had greased his skids for oblivion. The Phillies wisely declined to make the deal; they would not possess this acuity forever.

Nevertheless, McCarthy never escaped being cast in trade rumors throughout the campaign. A couple of months after the aborted discussions with Philadelphia, Arthur Soden spent an entire evening with Giants owner Andrew Freedman, trying to hash out a cash deal for McCarthy. Despite Mac's protestations that he meant to retire at the conclusion of the 1895 season, Freedman wanted to place him in left field and install him as team captain, but those trade talks did not materialize, either. They did demonstrate the urgency under which Boston wanted to rid itself of Tommy McCarthy, whose reputation as a clubhouse lawyer had reached such a level that he should have hung out a shingle over his door and gone into practice. He had to go.

Mac had to go not simply because he got on peoples' nerves, but mainly because Selee began to perceive a decline in the star outfielder's skills. Mac had battled his weight problems for several years and recently conceded defeat in his personal battle of the bulge. A slow outfielder who did not steal bases or hit the ball particularly well did not stay long in Selee's clubhouse. It is a credit to Selee that he perceived Mac's decline long before anyone else did and also suspected a point of no return had been breached.

Perhaps out of loyalty, Selee tried to provide McCarthy with some last chances to change. In an attempt to prod his old Oshkosh player to improve his game, he inserted McCarthy in the second place in the batting order, but this not only failed to propel his batting average upward, it also apparently caused him to take foolish chances on the base paths. Still, in July, Boston remained a factor in the pennant race, and the team tried very hard this month to overcome their shortcomings and the dreadful karma surrounding them.

On July 11, they held off Louisville for 16 innings in a crucial away game.

In the fourth inning, Duffy contributed to the eventual stalemate by blooping a ball behind third base, and as the ball tailed left away from the fielders, he sprinted to second base, eventually coming home on a hit by Billy Nash. In the next inning Sir Hugh proved brilliant by leaping and catching a shot from opposing batter McDermott that interrupted the game for several minutes while the Louisville fans expressed their appreciation for this effort.

In the fourteenth inning, Tommy McCarthy almost won and lost the game for his team with his antics. While batting, an umpire called a strike that sent Mac into a fit, which took considerable time to subside. When he settled down, he swatted a liner to the outfield, and then for no good reason while he was rounding second base, he pushed the Louisville fielder, Harry Spies, and smacked him in the eye. Not appreciating a sucker punch, Spies raced after McCarthy and around third base returned the favor by pummeling Mac. The umpire ultimately kicked both players out of the game and fined them $25, with Fred Tenney permitted to replace Mac and stand on third base, hoping for a hit to bring him home and bring victory to the Beaneaters.

The hit never came and darkness necessitated that the umpire call the game in the sixteenth inning, culminating in a 2–2 tie and a little less money in McCarthy's pay check. Despite this valiant battling, the Beaneaters only won 40 percent of their games in July and assumed pretender status in the pennant race.

In early September, Tim Murnane wrote a curious column in which he gently chastised Frank Selee for protecting the feelings of veterans and not using his bench enough. Contextually, the Triumvirate had just extended Selee another year, but the Silver King did not believe wholesale changes needed to occur. He contended that Tommy McCarthy and a couple of other players had labored with injuries and sickness all season and only had to rehabilitate over the winter and come back in fine shape for the next year. While supportive of old friends, Murnane had no use for the third Beaneater outfielder, Jimmy Bannon, who looked lost on the field in the sportswriter's opinion.

Although sharply critical of others in his columns, Tim Murnane was too nice a man to successfully manage a baseball team. A manager must make difficult decisions, and even though he went back almost as far with McCarthy as did the Silver King, Frank Selee had reached a point where sentimentality and a fierce inner desire to win began to diverge. Tim Murnane could never have disposed of Mac. Selee would.

Parenthetically, Mac sustained the minor injury that Murnane referred to when Billy Nash mistakenly hit his leg with a bat during warm-ups. Either that or Nash remembered being ripped by McCarthy in Murnane's column back in the beginning of the season. In any event, Mac does not show up in the box score two days later, apparently due to the boo-boo.

Selee did not agree with the Silver King, as he saw other teams in the National League grow faster while the Boston team sluggishly ran the bases and patrolled the field. He definitely intended to remold the team into a younger and faster unit and eyed at least two veterans for release or trade. He did err by retaining Jimmy Bannon for the next year, as that player came apart very quickly, just as Murnane prophesied. After old Tim's article appeared, the Beaneaters fell apart, staggering to an under-.500 record for the remainder of the month.

Tommy McCarthy, for one, mailed it in in September. Two days after the Murnane article, he sat out a game due to a bruise, and an unnamed *Boston Globe* note writer commented that "[s]everal of the Boston players look fat and out of condition." Duffy, for his part, remained trim, making a crucial catch in center field after covering an "immense amount of ground" while banging out four hits.

On September 10, Fred Tenney subbed for Mac during a game due to Mac's "injury." The former Brown University standout had largely failed as a catcher but had caught on with the team as a spare outfielder, and more importantly ran fast and hit very well. A little over a week later, McCarthy received the day off to tend to business at his bowling emporium, an event that Hugh Duffy wisely missed in favor of playing baseball. The day after that he failed to play again and enjoyed a nice game viewing his teammates from the bleachers. The bowling alley had become a cash cow, and McCarthy increasingly saw himself as an entrepreneur and less as a baseball player. Duffy, a natural businessman, never forgot that he knew baseball best and that it provided him with joy and a foundation for financial success; accordingly, he treated his career with respect. Fred Tenney just wanted to play ball.

Another eager young outfielder, Jimmy Collins, emerged this year with the Beaneaters. Purchased from the minor league club in his hometown of Buffalo, Collins initially underwhelmed Frank Selee, who after auditioning him in the outfield, "loaned" him to the woeful Louisville team, basically for seasoning. The unusual transaction proved beneficial to all parties as Louisville shifted him to third base, where his confidence and his batting average shot up (from .211 to .279). Judging from afar and occasionally from the opposite dugout, Selee pondered returning Collins to the team in 1896, to join or replace Billy Nash as a third baseman.

While Tenney and Collins showed promise and McCarthy's skills eroded, Hugh Duffy overcame an early slump to again rise to the levels of the league's elite in batting. Not only that, he received kudos from the press for his improved quality of play in the field. While he certainly popped off more than advisable in 1893, two years later he had assumed the mantel of a team statesman, and any frustration he exhibited almost always focused on his own performance on a given day. Still, he had not fully learned how to get along with umpires, but no one liked umpires in that day.

Much of the credit for smoothing some of his rough edges rested with a young woman named Nora Moore from South Boston. While Duffy grieved

One of the greatest infields in the nineteenth century. Clockwise from the left are shortstop Herman Long, first baseman Fred Tenney, second baseman Bobby Lowe and Hall of Fame third baseman Jimmy Collins. Boston Public Library, Print Department.

for his first wife and drank and carried a chip on his shoulder in 1894, in 1895 he experienced his personal summer of love and began to look at his own future through the prism of this remarkable woman. She taught him gentleness and he learned to transmit positive reinforcement to his grateful teammates. The beloved and patient teacher that ballplayers at Boston College and the Boston Red Sox later revered had begun to emerge through this most joyous of unions.

As Nora Moore's influence over Duffy ascended, that of McCarthy began to drop precipitously. Prompted by Selee, Duffy doubted that he could play major league ball effectively and operate a bowling alley at the same time. Inevitably, differences in opinion arose between Tommy and Duffy, and he no longer felt that his older friend held a monopoly on good judgment. Repeatedly, Tommy McCarthy invited stupid fights and the ire of teammates as he grew fatter and more slothful. With stronger athletes such as Cy Young emerging, one could no longer rely on an old set of skills, and Duffy wanted to stay ahead of the curve rather than rest on his laurels as Mac increasingly did.

At the end, even old friend Murnane began to lampoon McCarthy. The Silver King never hesitated to support friends or advance their careers when he could, but he loved organized baseball more and never learned to tolerate lax or disinterested play. On a day that Boston earned a rare win versus Baltimore, Mac's alleged sore leg looked pretty fit when he raced after a ball hit by his friend Joe Kelley. And yet he dogged it trotting to first base after forcing Herman Long out at second, for "[a]s usual, Mac only ran a part of the way to the base." In the last week of September, he went on safari to stay as his DNPs stacked up and younger players filled in for him. During this interim, Soden had his meeting with Freedman in which he tried to unload the Heavenly Twin that was no longer so revered. Meanwhile, Mac ventured boldly on in his quest to commit career suicide.

Eventually, Boston's holes sunk them and the team staggered to a 71-60 record and a sixth-place finish in the National League, as Baltimore waltzed to another pennant. Much was lacking in the 1895 edition of the Beaneaters as big Tommy Tucker had trouble hitting anything. Perhaps Selee itched to replace him with young Fred Tenney, but Tenney was a college kid in an age where few ballplayers attended high school, and Selee may have feared that permanently inserting Tenney at first base might exacerbate already tense clubhouse relations. Plus, Tenney could catch and spell Mac in the outfield, so he stayed as a role player for the time being, much like Bobby Lowe had done years earlier.

While some of the players suffered at bat, the true weakness of the Beaneaters lay with their pitching. Kid Nichols suffered through an off-year by his standards and Happy Jack Stivetts marginalized himself not only with teammates, but by posting .500 numbers in wins and losses. His ultimate record of 17-17 seems a model of consistency, or at the least consistent mediocrity, but maddeningly he looked like a world-beater on some occasions and got knocked out of the box rather roughly on other starts.

In his *History of the Boston Base Ball Club* written in the very late nineteenth century, author George Tuohey had had little regard for the pitchers beyond Nichols and Dolan, observing that "[i]n the season of 1895 Boston used eight pitchers.... Stocksdale, Wilson, Yerrick and Sexton were more or less frosts, and were pitched in but few games. Of the two games won from the Orioles, Nichols and Dolan are each credited with one."

The season over, Hugh Duffy got hitched again to Miss Nora Moore of

South Boston in October 1895, in South Boston's Gate of Heaven Church. Naturally, fellow Heavenly Twin Tommy McCarthy served as his best man. The new couple then embarked on a honeymoon to Montreal and Niagara Falls.

The union between Duffy and Nora was simply blissful. She knew little about baseball before she met Hugh but promptly became an expert. Similarly, she was very close to her family, so Duffy lived with his in-laws virtually the rest of his life to please her. She supplanted Tommy McCarthy as her husband's best friend.

When he returned from his honeymoon, Hugh Duffy had had time to reflect on his career and concluded that running a business and keeping one's skills sharp clashed. Once a bar business gets established, it largely becomes a boring venture as the business essentially runs itself. The bartenders come in and pour drinks and the day proceeds with a central sameness until closing time. Plus, for the most part Duffy did not like to drink, so he had little tolerance for sitting around the joint all day, passing the time and guzzling his own liquor. McCarthy did not seem to mind this lifestyle, and it bothered Duffy that his partner and best friend felt that way.

Chapter 13

Always a Bridegroom

Tommy McCarthy began his long winter of discontent almost as soon as the 1895 season ended. Feeling unappreciated and insulted by his long-time mentor and manager Selee, Mac pondered retirement as he threw his Boston uniform onto the floor, apparently for the final time. Selee did not regard his old protégé as an old or slow person, but rather as a lazy and out of shape one as he searched for new answers for his squad.

By all outward appearances, Mac's partnership with Duffy remained solid, as they obtained from the City of Boston the right to serve liquor at their establishment in the middle of September 1895, an event that probably coincided with McCarthy getting the day off toward the end of the season. However, even there Duffy chafed at the thought of continuing to run a bowling alley and saloon, if not by his own feelings, at least through the influence of his new wife Nora and perhaps even Manager Selee.

After Duffy married Nora Moore and became quite close to her family, McCarthy not only had to run their business by himself for two weeks during the honeymoon, but he also had to contend with Duffy's wife and in-laws, whom Duffy began to reside with after the honeymoon and lived with for the next five decades. Furthermore, while McCarthy was clearly in Selee's dog house, Duffy fashioned a longer career in baseball and hungered for the captain's position held by Billy Nash.

As events transpired, Duffy did not have to wait long. On November 14, 1895, the Beaneaters traded Billy Nash to the Philadelphia Phillies for Billy Hamilton, a swap that in time would prove to favor Boston as one of the most one-sided in baseball history. Nash petered out ineffectually over the next three years while Hamilton hit .300 consistently and stole dozens of bases a season. Duffy became team captain, and his heavenly twin began to see the handwriting on the wall etched even more ominously with the addition to the team of a young outfielding star in Hamilton.

If his partnership in the bowling alley and saloon did not offend Duffy's wife and extended family, it did not please Manager Selee, who watched McCarthy transform in one season from a superstar to an out of shape mediocrity, and he clearly did not wish to see Duffy follow suit. It may also be that Duffy began to see the business as an unneeded and unwanted intrusion in his life, because in the *Boston Globe's* November 19, 1895, edition, Murnane's column quoted him as saying, "I have discovered that business interferes with a player's work, and next season our men will devote all their time to the game, so Mr. Selee says."

It appears that the two best friends also disagreed on business matters, a pattern that would mark many of the business projects Duffy embarked on with others over the following years. Although Duffy had an innate sense for business and making money, he did not always play well with others and his joint ventures tended to end in acrimony. Murnane held his powder when the split was occurring, but months later he revealed to his readers that Duffy and McCarthy had developed such a distaste for each other that they refused to speak for much of 1896, leaving the Heavenly Twins mired in a very blue heaven indeed. It got bluer in mid–November of 1895, when the ax fell and the Beaneaters sold Mac to the Brooklyn Bridegrooms for $6,000. Supposedly Brooklyn had sweetened the deal by adding pitcher George Harper, but that rumor proved unfounded. Harper proceeded to lose twice as many games as he won in the eventual 1896 campaign and never played in the major leagues again.

In part the transaction demonstrates that Mac had become a spare and useless part since Boston did not wrest a player from Brooklyn. It also reflects his value on the open marketplace because he did not command the $10,000 sales price that Boston paid Al Spalding years earlier to obtain King Kelly and John Clarkson. Hopefully, when he heard the news, the door did not hit McCarthy on the way out.

While Duffy in interviews invariably resorted to clichés to deflect questions, Tommy seemed to enjoy the process and articulated, often at considerable length, whatever dominated his attention. When a scribe from the *Brooklyn Eagle* ventured to Boston and met McCarthy in his establishment, Mac held court in a room crowded with bowlers, drinkers and a couple of ballplayers in the mix.

The writer noted McCarthy's "quiet reserve and dignity," as he assessed his future. "I am pretty substantially located here as you can see," as he scanned his booming business. "I have just secured a liquor license and I can safely say that I can look into the future with little to fear. The work has been confining, however, and I would like at least one more year on the ball field just to get into shape. I have [Brooklyn owner] Mr. Byrne's contract in the safe there now ready for my signature."

With his partnership with Duffy floundering, McCarthy warmed to the idea of returning to baseball, if only to provide a star attraction for the bowling alley. He feverously began to line up a new partner, choosing Bernard Lennon, a minor pol from Roxbury. Lennon could run the shop while Mac continued his sporting career, if he wished to do so.

McCarthy did not break out in smiles when he learned of his sale to the Brooklyn club. Instead, he held out and sought to obtain for himself some of the purchase price of $6,000 that Brooklyn paid for him. Of course, this argument had scant chance of succeeding because with the death of every league but the National League, the players had no leverage other than to sit out.

But to appreciate the utter absurdity of this stance, even after the modern-day Players' Association won huge concessions from management and ballplayers average millions of dollars each year, they did not have the right to garnish a percentage of their sales price to another team. For example, the Seibu Lions in Japan sold the rights to sign pitcher Daisuke Matsuzaka to the Boston Red Sox in 2007 for $51,000,000, but that player did not receive a penny of that amount and had to negotiate his contract with the club independently.

McCarthy never had a chance with that argument, and at the time, Brooklyn President Byrne mused that his reluctant new player had been "badly advised." In a large bar room filled with fawning admirers, McCarthy undoubtedly heard what he wanted to hear, but one of the people who encouraged him to try to extract money from Boston was a bar habitué who also during the season starred as the captain of the Baltimore club, Joe Kelley, a person who surely knew better.

McCarthy kicked up a commotion for awhile but Brooklyn waited him out. He finally agreed to show up in March at the team's spring training site at Charlotte, North Carolina, having succeeded in nothing but alienating his new employer and embarrassing his former one. Once there, he promptly created issues for the team by grumpily expressing his displeasure with Manager Foutz's decision to start him in right field.

This proved a relatively benign concern. Shortly after he arrived in camp, he received a telegram stating that his youngest sister Julia was gravely ill. Mac obtained permission from Foutz to race home to visit her, but before he even got on the train, someone handed him another telegram, this one informing him of her death. Accounts of the day differ concerning whether the news surprised him or whether his sister had suffered from a lengthy illness, but in that era, death often struck suddenly. A broken-hearted McCarthy grabbed another train back to Boston to attend his sister's funeral Mass at St. Augustine's Church in South Boston.

Although McCarthy's winter and spring proved unbearably stressful, noted sports commentator Henry Chadwick predicted great things for the new Bridegrooms outfielder, opining, "The acquisition of McCarthy to the team has strengthened it greatly." Chadwick's opinion in no way reflected a minority sentiment, and certainly the new Bridegroom fit in very well with his new mates. Another talking head felt Brooklyn could win the pennant and proclaimed McCarthy the equal of Billy Hamilton.

By way of a quick digression, Billy Hamilton was a much more accomplished ballplayer than Tommy McCarthy, though not as colorful. Nevertheless, while even the National Baseball Hall of Fame file has a clipping where Hamilton is referred to as a shadowy figure, he actually possessed far more dimension than historically thought.

For one thing, the man was in love with himself and his ability to steal bases. Tom Brown, a contemporary of his, once said about Hamilton that he would "attempt to make steals when a stolen base wasn't necessary. It doesn't make any difference to him how often he is thrown out." Brown then uncorked a good story about playing against Hamilton's Philadelphia team. It seems that after a ball game that Philadelphia had lost largely due to Hamilton's inept play, Hamilton approached Brown's team bus and exclaimed, "What do you think of me Tom? Four stolen bases to-day—That make forty-five this year."

Hamilton knew that he had earned an unsavory reputation as a jackass, and upon learning of his trade to Boston, he admitted to a reporter that "[m]any people have been letting themselves out upon me and have been free to say what a disorganizer and record player I am, always looking out for myself." It was a well-deserved reputation despite Hamilton's protestations to the contrary, but he seemed to want to alter people's perceptions of him with his new team. To his credit, and undoubtedly with Selee's and Duffy's firm insistence that he embrace the team concept, he did develop into a model teammate with the Beaneaters.

The 1896 Boston Beaneater team on a trip to the Southern states. This team would continue to experience growing pains as old stars such as Tommy McCarthy departed and new phenoms worked their way into the lineup. Collection of Richard A. Johnson.

Meanwhile, in Boston, the Beaneaters had ample reason to enthuse about their own pennant fortunes. In addition to the trade for Hamilton paying immediate dividends as the new outfielder injected the team with speed and pure hitting, the departure of Nash opened up third base for last year's rookie phenom and future Hall of Famer Jimmy Collins. Herman Long proclaimed that the young Collins was the greatest third baseman of all time, to which *Sporting Life* quipped, "[t]hat is putting it on pretty thick, Herman." Long proved prescient because by the time Collins finally retired, he had developed into perhaps the greatest third baseman in baseball history. For these and other reasons, the season looked bright for both teams, Boston in particular.

Hope sprung temporarily for McCarthy and the Bridegrooms as they approached their home opener on April 28, having won the majority of their season-opening road swing, culminating in Mac getting three hits to spark his team's victory over Philadelphia. In Brooklyn's home opener, a band played throughout the game, and the cranks cheered McCarthy for a good throw from the outfield and then went berserk when he batted, as he hit a home run over the bicycle track in left field, albeit in a losing cause.

Their home loss set the pace for a poor string of games where the Bridegrooms won only two of seven, exposing their weaknesses of poor pitching and, except for outfielders Fielder Jones and Honest John Anderson, weak hitting. In contrast to Billy Hamilton's sincere desire to use a change of scenery as an incentive to become a better player and teammate, Mac began to dog it early, and in a game in May, "They scolded Tom McCarthy out in Cleveland because he jogged after the ball."

Even when good things happened, bad things also occurred. For instance, on June 13, 1896, Cleveland Spider outfielder Jesse Burkett, exasperated after his team had just been swept in a three-game series at Brooklyn, took the game ball and heaved it over a fence, a serious breach of etiquette in that era. The whole Cleveland team then destroyed the visiting dressing room door with baseball bats after the game, precipitating a ban on their dressing in Eastern Park in future games.

Proving the adage wrong, McCarthy came home again on June 23, 1896, for a series in Boston against his old Beaneater teammates. The cranks in the crowd cheered his every movement, and when he batted in the second, the game recessed while he received a diamond ring "valued at $150" from his many local friends. The crowd chanted "Speech, Speech," to which their old favorite bowed and tipped his cap, blushing a deep crimson the entire time. He also received a giant horseshoe floral tribute in the seventh, as his new team fell hopelessly behind and lost, 9–3, a prelude to being swept in the series.

Boston feasted again on the Bridegrooms when the Beaneaters traveled to Eastern Park for a three-game series, beginning on July 3. Misleadingly, matters started out well for Brooklyn in the opening game when Tommy McCarthy came alive to score the winning run in an exciting 8–7 win. True to form,

Brooklyn lost both ends of a doubleheader on the Fourth of July and then headed reluctantly to an exhibition in Buffalo.

More depressingly, by July 11, having gone 4–7 thus far for the month, the Bridegrooms were seared by the *Brooklyn Eagle*, which showered particular attention on their new outfielder. "It is gradually dawning on the minds of the base ball people in general that Brooklyn secured a gold brick when Tommy McCarthy's release was purchased from Boston. There is a heap of ginger in McCarthy, but his has developed only in spots since the season began. He has gained the reputation for being lazy or indifferent, his work far below what he is capable of."

The *Eagle* got it right. Had a chronic injury or the effects of premature aging contributed to Mac's decline, the criticism might have seemed insensitive and unfair, but he tripled in games in July and August, hardly the sign of a horse who could no longer run. Occasionally, his hitting ripped opposing pitchers, and it seemed as if he had regained his eye at the plate, only to be followed by hitless games and lackluster efforts.

Starting with Selee's remarks during the previous season, Mac had been branded as a dog, an estimation that reporters, cranks and baseball men perpetuated as much as McCarthy did with his generally lackadaisical play. Responding to the press, Manager Foutz began to bench McCarthy for several games in July and the beginning of August, an admission of defeat by Brooklyn, both for its transaction with Boston and its season.

Unfortunately for the Beaneaters, their doubleheader win in Brooklyn did not spark a surge for the pennant as they lost more than twice as often as they won for the remainder of the month, even succumbing to league doormats Louisville and St. Louis, the latter team falling further into the unbalanced whim and caprice of team owner and occasional manager Chris Von der Ahe. Indeed, Boston did not recover again until the Beaneaters returned to Brooklyn in mid–August. By that time, the Bridegrooms had similarly drooped in July, causing Manager Foutz fits as he tried to juggle his mediocre lineup.

Games involving Boston and teams with one or more of its former stars never failed to produce excitement. The August 16 game against Brooklyn proved no exception as Duffy and McCarthy took delight in catching each other's hits and even the normally mellow Billy Hamilton got into the festivities. It is not often that one hears the name Billy Hamilton and flamboyantly in the same sentence, but in one contest, he flamboyantly waved his new and shiny white bat at Brooklyn's pitcher Stein, against whom he sharply smashed a loud double. Later in the game, a more subdued Hamilton homered to further bury the poor Bridegrooms.

Drawing inspiration from even taciturn players such as Billy Hamilton, the Beaneaters began to demonstrate the type of team that many had foreseen at the beginning of the season. When Chris Von der Ahe's hapless Browns crossed them in early September, the Beaneaters swept the five-game series, winning one game by the lopsided margin of 23–7. Oddly enough, Hugh Duffy almost cost Boston its victory in that blowout. Meeting with the Browns captain, they decided to ask the manager to call the mismatch in the seventh inning so they could then start the second game of the doubleheader. Had that plan gone ahead, the first game would have been wiped out, costing Boston its win, since a rule at that time mandated that before a second game began on the same day, the first game had to be completed. Someone caught Duffy before he allowed this to happen and the blowout continued through the ninth inning.

While the rejuvenated Bostons gained ground in the league standings, by September, the Bridegrooms had become completely unglued. Rumors of dissension against Manager Foutz by practically the entire club filtered into the newspapers. The contemporary reports consistently blamed the discord on veteran ballplayers, which given the relatively small squads of the day included Tommy McCarthy within the cadre of the underminers. During the season, he publicly confirmed his desire to retire at the conclusion of the season.

The team tanked at 6-17 for the month, and in a fit of pique for being taken out of a game by Foutz, second baseman Tom Daly, one of their better players, stormed off the field and sat on the opposing team's bench for the remainder of the game. Daly punctuated his insubordination a few days later by staggering onto the field in a game against Washington drunk beyond comprehension. After being removed from the game again, he acted out on the team "bus" and in the hotel lobby, and swore at club President Byrne, who responded by fining him and kicking him off the team for the remainder of the season. Daly did not appear in a major league game again until 1898, when he came up for a cup of coffee.

Brooklyn had very little reason to hope for a significant change in its fortunes as the 1896 season waned. Fielder Jones had an excellent rookie season and Honest John Anderson hit very well. Pitcher Payne held out some promise, but by and large, the upcoming season did not give cranks much occasion to smile. Skillful second baseman Tom Daly sat out the next year, perhaps to dry out and decide what he wished to do in the future.

McCarthy had busted out on them, and in the off-season they offered him a contract with a $700 cut in salary, a massive shift since he did not earn much to begin with. There were rumors of a trade to return Mac to St. Louis, but nothing materialized. At the least, it looked like he would decline Brooklyn's cheapskate offer and sit down for 1897.

As his career vanished, Tommy McCarthy provided the press with an insightful look into a ballplayer at the end of the line. Speaking to a *Sporting Life* scribe, he confessed, "I am accused of being a knocker. These people do not know what they are talking about. Some of them try to sweeten their dose by saying I am a good person socially. How do they know? I do not know some of these writers at all. How do they know what I am socially? Naturally, I would like to say as little as possible about last season, but it would not be fair to myself to allow this thing to pass by unnoticed without a few words."

Despite his avowed reluctance to speak, McCarthy unloaded before the correspondent.

> I have no criticism to make of Manager Foutz. I was treated fairly by him. Of course I was not pleased that I had so little chance to play last season. I think that if I had kept right in the game, I could have given a good account of myself. Had not Lachance been hurt precious little opportunity would I have had to play ball at all. Now I do not like bench-warming. It was the first time in years that I was not right in the game.
>
> I like Brooklyn. I was treated splendidly in that city, and with matters harmonious there isn't a town I would rather play in than in Brooklyn. No club can be successful unless there is entire harmony among all concerned. It is an open secret that such was not the case in Brooklyn. It would ill become me to discuss the matter fuller. The owners of the club have realized that such is the case, for they have made a change in the management.

This valedictory interview of Tommy McCarthy is a fascinating prism through which to view him on so many levels. He professed respect for ex–Manager Foutz and would not have a bad word to say about him, and then he circuitously made the point that he felt that his manger was a schmuck. Clearly, he did not feel that Foutz treated him fairly.

And yet, McCarthy's ego precluded any introspection, any responsibility for his own considerable contribution to the decline of his own baseball career. Selee unloaded him from his Boston team onto Brooklyn because he felt that McCarthy, whom he respected and felt considerable personal fondness for, had permitted himself to waste his talents by not staying in shape. The *Reach Guide* ranks him 123rd in hitting for the league in 1896, a poor statistic for any player, but especially awful for someone so proud and, until recently, so universally esteemed.

What was his manager to do? Start McCarthy in the outfield in place of Fielder Jones, John Anderson and team captain Griffin, all much better hitters than McCarthy and in far better shape than he at this stage in their careers? Particularly in light of McCarthy's oft-stated intention both before and during the 1896 season to retire at campaign's end?

Without doubt, McCarthy had helped to poison the atmosphere in the Brooklyn clubhouse and he contributed mightily to getting Foutz fired. He did not like sitting on the bench or batting low in the order for Tim Murnane for the Boston Unions in 1884, when he was unprepared to play at that level, and he did not take kindly to subbing as his career ebbed due to beer drinking, excessive eating and a couch potato lifestyle.

Nevertheless, McCarthy did not duck the reporter or his questions, and he expressed his hurt and resentment at his situation. While many ballplayers of his era lurked in historical memory as either grotesque Dickensian characters characterized by their central weaknesses or ill-defined ghostly figures lost in time, Tommy McCarthy stood out as a regular guy that one could hang out with and talk to at length over a beer or two. And since McCarthy owned and

One of the most underrated ballplayers in baseball history, Kid Nichols won 361 games in his career and anchored the great Beaneater teams of the 1890s. In this photograph, part of a series, Nichols exhibits his baffling pitching form. Boston Public Library, Print Department.

operated a saloon, the drinks would keep flowing. Still, he did undermine his manager and helped leave his Brooklyn team in a disorganized shambles. Perhaps he even felt a tad guilty less than five months later when he learned that Dave Foutz had died from complications stemming from an asthmatic condition.

In contrast to McCarthy's meanderings, Boston's management had a very productive off-season. Although they won only three more games than they had in 1895, their late momentum had propelled the team to fourth place in the standings. Buoyed by this success, Frank Selee spent the off-season transitioning the team back into pennant contenders.

Disappointed by the almost 100-point loss in batting average posted from 1895 to 1896 by Jimmy "Foxy Grandpa" Bannon, the Beaneaters went elsewhere to replace him, successfully signing another Buffalo minor league sensation, Chick Stahl. Bannon never played in the major leagues again, while Stahl starred immediately in 1897, giving Boston one of the finest outfields of the nineteenth century, joining Hall of Famers Duffy and Billy Hamilton.

Selee did not stop there but continued to scout players everywhere in the off-season. Judging that Happy Jack Stivetts had begun to run low on gas and had become loaded down with excess weight, he placed more responsibility on promising rookie Fred Klobedanz, who responded brilliantly in 1897 to form a solid one-two punch with Kid Nichols. In 1897, it was Nichols and Klobedanz and pray for rain.

Baltimore had alienated many fans with their brash, roughhouse play, and teams like Patsy Tebeau's Clevelanders never seemed serious or sober enough to challenge for league supremacy. It was thus left for the club from the Athens of America, the Boston Beaneaters, to unseat the Orioles as champions. Most cranks could not wait for the 1897 season to begin and the ensuing race disappointed few.

Chapter 14

The Great 1897 Race
With Baltimore

Although Tim Murnane had chronicled the roughhouse tactics of Ned Hanlon's Orioles a number of years earlier, the now-perennial champions had not mellowed with their repeated successes. If anything, they became more arrogant and convinced of the efficacy of intimidating their foes. Dirty and rough baseball had triumphed, and any voice in opposition to this style of play generally resonated with the sounds of grapes souring, as Baltimore envisioned a fairly easy trek to its fourth straight National League title in 1897.

Mild-mannered minister's son Frank Selee thought otherwise. He knew how to assemble championship teams and he had kept the core of the terrific early 1890s squads together while meticulously adding Sliding Billy Hamilton, Fred Tenney, Jimmy Collins, Freddy Klobedanz, Chick Stahl and a young pitcher named Ted Lewis. A native of Wales, Lewis had come up with Boston briefly the previous year and the powerful right-hander, like Tenney, hailed from a local prestigious college, in the former's case, Williams. Selee built up a formidable cast of eight starting fielders to help out his pitchers. Tenney believed that the team's outfielders, infielders and catcher were the best at their positions in baseball.

Much had changed since the Beaneaters met at the train station in 1892, convinced before the season began that their dream team would come in first place. Six years later, with King Kelly dead and Tommy McCarthy probably retired, the mixture of old and newer Boston players gathered more somberly at Wright and Ditson's in downtown Boston, before venturing to the local wharf for their boat south for spring training. Selee had seen his team humbled for three straight years, but he knew that if his pitchers matched the anticipated level of performance of the rest of the team, they might overtake the Orioles. He meant to show that the good guys at times finished first.

At Lewis Wharf, "Tom McCarthy was observed in earnest conversation with Hugh Duffy, and looking as if he would like above all things to be with his old companions." Maybe so, but Selee had passed on him by the end of 1895 and had even less use for a heavy old ballplayer who barely hit .240 the year before. Not when he had two potential young stars in Chick Stahl and Fred Tenney vying for the one vacant outfield spot, the one not occupied by Duffy and Sliding Billy Hamilton. Captain Duffy in particular felt that Stahl was the best right fielder in Boston in several years.

Despite the luxury of having two Hall of Famers and two rising stars in the outfield, by the end of April 1897, the Boston Beaneaters had apparently played themselves out of the National League pennant race, recording an atrocious 1-6-2 record. By a strange scheduling quirk, they opened at home against Philadelphia for one game only and then departed for a road trip against the Orioles, Washington and Philadelphia. Meanwhile, the Baltimore Orioles, more commonly referred to as the "champions," waltzed to a 7–1 skein.

Matches proved tedious and frustrating for the Boston team as it found unique ways to lose and tie ball games, leading Manager Selee to exploit his team's inauspicious start to institute some overdue changes. He immediately supplanted crowd favorite Foghorn Tucker at first in favor of Fred Tenney and put his trust in Chick Stahl as the answer to the third outfielder issue, the latter move strongly endorsed by Captain Duffy. Selee also relied less on Happy Jack Stivetts and pressured Duffy to turn up his game. Feeling defensive, Duffy offered to retire, but Selee knew that his captain only needed the proper affront to his pride as motivation to restore his game to its previous levels of excellence. These changes helped to prompt a mini-winning streak of four games for Boston.

Eventually, Selee sold Tucker to Washington for $2,000, and the player had a pretty good year for his new team before he lost it thereafter. This move dovetailed with Selee's philosophy of emphasizing team speed—a must during this era of poorly constructed baseballs—and ridding the team of a fading player a year early rather than a year late. By the end of 1895, Selee knew that Tommy McCarthy either would not or could not perform to a star level any longer, and he correctly perceived that Tom Tucker was dragging down the team. The early-season skid gave him the reason and opportunity to first bench Tucker and then dump him.

Tim Murnane weighed in with his opinion about this time. He essentially graded each player's performance to date, and he allowed Tommy Tucker to talk himself out of a job by publicly criticizing management. In a rare weak moment, the Silver King failed to either endorse or really oppose Selee's substitution of Tenney for Tucker, perhaps feeling a bit loyal to his old friend Foghorn. Usually he took firm stands, but in this instance he seemed to have waffled so that if Tenney did not succeed, he could editorialize that he never liked the move. Of course, if Tenney flourished, as we now know that he did, the Silver King had an out.

Rebounding by mid–May, the Beaneaters won games as they had done three years earlier, by out-slugging their opposition, but cracks began to materialize in the foundation of the team, particularly with the pitching. Having recently won five of their last six games, on May 18, they trotted out Boston native Mike Mahoney, a 6'4" pitcher patronizingly dubbed by the *Baltimore Sun* as one of Boston's new "giants." The original Moonlight Graham (or Fred Van Dusen), Mahoney gave up five runs in the last two innings, although in fairness, two runs scored on a botched throw from Stahl to Jimmy Collins. In a game that Mahoney's squad seemed to have locked up in the second inning, the Chicago Colts slapped Ted Lewis, Stivetts and him silly en route to an 11–5 win. Until the very end of this campaign, Hugh Duffy pleaded with Selee to stock up on experienced pitching, a point punctuated by the humiliating battering his men received in Chicago.

Pitching did not pose a problem for Boston on May 29, 1897, as the Beaneaters lost a 2–1 squeaker to the Cincinnati squad. Boston bounced back nicely the next day by beating the St. Louis Browns, 25-5, beginning an incredible 17-game winning streak that did not end until June 22, by which time the *Baltimore Sun's* sport headline screamed "Boston In the Lead."

By then, Wee Willie Keeler's 44-game hitting streak had just ended. Hitting on opening day, Keeler did not stop until talented pitcher Frank Killen shut him down on June 19, an incredible string that has been surpassed only by Joe DiMaggio. Although the end of Keeler's mark coincided with a temporary dip in the team's fortunes, Keeler continued to help carry the Orioles past their limitations on the pitching staff to a season-long pursuit of the pennant. Although Duffy to this day possesses the record for highest single-season batting average, Keeler's 1897 batting statistics might actually be more impressive. By 1897, the major league pitchers had adjusted to the increased distance between the mound and home plate, and hitting averages had also dipped.

Back to Boston, the Beaneaters' lead did not hold up for long as the Brooklyn Bridegrooms ended the remarkable skein by a score of 7–4. Seeing the game and the streak fade away in the ninth, Fred Tenney fielded a ball hit by Kennedy of the Brooklyns and tagged him out very forcefully in the ribs, an act that provoked Kennedy to take a swing at the Boston first bagger. The Brooklyn manager prevented the matter from escalating and the game ended otherwise unremarkably. Tellingly, Selee could have started Kid Nichols in this game but wished to save him for the upcoming series with Baltimore, thus sacrificing the streak for the greater goal of winning head-to-head games with the team's main competition.

Baltimore thus held a slender lead in the National League over Boston when the Orioles came to South End Grounds for the first time that season. Champion boxer Gentleman Jim Corbett came to visit his brother Joe, an Oriole pitcher, but his presence did nothing to deter the 5-for-5 hitting of Duffy (including a home run) and the fielding of Herman Long, who led Boston to a 12–5 victory. Anywhere from 12,000–15,000 spectators attended the game in part to unnerve Oriole pitcher Nops; they remained perfectly still until he was prepared to release his pitch, at which time they spontaneously and loudly let out a mass yell. At the end of the game, the crowd rushed the field and cheered loudly for the home team and the visiting Gentleman Jim.

Unable to shake Boston, dissension seeped into the Oriole clubhouse, as Dirty Jack Doyle, Baltimore's excellent second baseman, began to feud with John McGraw, a mistake since McGraw knew how to throw a punch and cultivate a grudge. Also, McGraw got along very well with fellow stars Willie Keeler, Joe Kelley and Hughie Jennings. The latter four might fight amongst themselves, particularly McGraw and Keeler, but they remained friends. Doyle never fit in that group; he was the blackest of Irishmen. Divided clubhouses can win pennants, and not enough time is spent in analyzing the proposition that most often dissension corrodes a team. In order for the Orioles to stay a bit ahead of the hard-charging Boston team, they had no room for error or for bickering. But err and bicker they did.

Heading into the final games of the season, Baltimore seemingly possessed the advantage as the Orioles played all of their last seven games at home, while Boston had to travel for its final six matches. The prognosticators in the day, however, did not factor into their calculations the Royal Rooters, Boston's fanatical fans who took their vacations or had their children hand in sick slips to their bosses so that they could take trains down to Baltimore to cheer on their beloved team.

Like the ancient sports clubs that eventually helped undermine the Byzantine Empire, the Royal Rooters spread rapidly onto the scene, but rather than undermine their own community, these cranks sought merely to become one massive obnoxious coach in their bid to disrupt the opposition clubs. The Beaneaters had improved since the end of 1896 to such an extent that Baltimore had to play nearly flawless ball, and in 1897, they started to display their weaknesses to such an extent that they felt pressured to win two out of three games in their last series against Boston. The Royal Rooters sensed this and migrated en masse down to Baltimore to hone in on the kill.

Tim Murnane joined them as a

Not enough can be said about legendary barkeep and Royal Rooter Nuf Ced McGreevey. He famously ended arguments by pounding his bar and shouting "Nuf Ced." Boston Public Library, Print Department.

reporter for the *Globe*, but in his heart, as one of their own. On September 24, the Royal Rooters made their idols feel at home as they accompanied them into the Union Grounds. Once inside, they sat behind their team's bench and serenaded the crowd with moving renditions of "My Maryland, My Maryland" and "Yankee Doodle." The Rooters also had an unofficial band of fans who came armed with horns and whistles to negate any crowd noise that might otherwise intimidate the Bostons.

Having to listen to General Dixwell proved annoying enough in the past, but now Boston deployed platoons of noisy and persistent maniacs who got on the nerves of many of the Baltimore cranks and players. For Boston, mission accomplished. In addition, the 12,000 fans at the game also included out-of-town patrons, the vast majority who cheered on Boston for the simple reason that they were not the Orioles. The hometown advantage had dissipated and the contests became more exclusively not the clash of cultures, but the struggle between two excellent ball clubs.

Led by U.S. Congressman Honey Fitz Fitzgerald, the Royal Rooters began cheering even before play commenced, and during the game they bellowed out their favorite cheer repeatedly, "Hit her up, Hit her up, Hit her up again, B-O-S-T-O-N." When one of the Beaneaters made a particularly good play, the Rooters passed a hat and took up a collection, giving the proceeds to Manager Selee.

"Outplayed by Boston" rang out the headline in the *Baltimore Sun* after the first game of the series, won by the visitors, 6–4. Joe Corbett had a very nice year for the Orioles in 1897, but he faced a future Hall of Famer and winner of 362 major league games in Kid Nichols, and Corbett "weaken[ed]" while his adversary continued to manage the ballgame. Doc Pond had to relieve Corbett in the eighth inning.

Despite the best efforts of the Orioles' Boileryard Clarke to rattle Nichols, he did not faze him, but Billy Hamilton almost gave the game up by himself with two errors. In the fourth inning, when the Orioles' Jake Stenzel hit the ball to center field, Sliding Billy let it roll between his legs until it had hit the fence, and only Duffy's swift retrieval of the ball and accurate throw into the infield prevented an inside-the-park home run.

The game almost never made it to a point that Hamilton could potentially lose it for his team. In the first, John McGraw led off by walking and then stealing second base. He scored on Hughey Jennings' single, and then Joe Kelley doubled Jennings home. Bent but not broken, Nichols settled down by causing Stenzel to pop up to catcher Martin Bergen and then striking out Doyle.

Boston rebounded nicely in the fourth and fifth innings to take the lead, 3–2, behind some timely hitting of Bobby Lowe, Herman Long and Bergen. The cerebral Fred Tenney walked in both innings and scored in the fourth. Hugh Duffy boldly hit a double on a 3–0 count to lead off the sixth, but his promising hit came to naught as Jimmy Collins doubled him up on a sharp shot right to the pitcher Corbett.

After an inauspicious start, Nichols cut through the Orioles lineup in the next six innings, allowing just two hitters to reach base, with no runs. In the Beaneaters' seventh, Nichols led off with a single and ran to third when Corbett choked. After fielding a timid grounder by Billy Hamilton, Corbett threw way off the mark to first base, thus starting off the inning with runners on the corners. The Royal Rooters went berserk as Corbett folded his hand. Corbett added to his mess by wild-pitching Nichols home and allowing Billy Hamilton to run over to third, from where he easily scored on Fred Tenney's swat. When the Orioles came up in the eighth, they trailed, 5–2.

Now it was their cranks' turn to spur on their team as a fatigued Kid Nichols came out again. Today, of course, a team's setup man and closing pitcher would emerge from the bullpen fresh to toss fastballs at over ninety miles an hour to help seal the win. But Nichols stood alone that late September day and had to win it with a little help from his mates.

Leading off for the Orioles, Doc Pond hit a ball right to Billy Hamilton, who dropped it like it was a live grenade. While Pond was later called out due to interference, the Orioles later meticulously loaded the bases with two out and Stenzel up. Stenzel lined the ball two feet over Herman Long's head for an apparent bases-clearing hit, but Long leaped up and speared it to end the inning.

Thoroughly unglued, Corbett came out after the seventh inning with a phantom injury. Captain Hugh Duffy manufactured an insurance run in the eighth by walking, stealing second and scoring on Herman Long's double, to increase his club's lead to 6–2. Pond held Boston scoreless in the ninth while the Orioles' first two batters in their half of the inning scored to narrow the contest to a 6–4 margin. The Orioles then placed Robinson and McGraw on first and second with one out with future Hall of Famer Wee Willie Keeler coming to bat as the potential winning run.

The Baltimore fans erupted in applause at their turn of fortunes. If Keeler could hit for forty-four straight games, little stood in his way to eke out one measly single. But Kid Nichols tempted him with a curveball well off the plate and Keeler lined it directly to Herman Long. After Long caught it, he flipped the ball to second baseman Lowe to double Robinson before he returned to second. Game over. Recognizing greatness, the Royal Rooters threw coins directly to Germany Long to celebrate his prowess, a matter noted by Baltimore sports writers both then and in print the next day. The Royal Rooters did not stop cheering with the end of the game as they returned to the hotel where the Beaneaters were staying and made a racket all night long.

Baltimore avenged its loss the next day, 6–3, behind a secret weapon, the Beaneaters' uncharacteristically uncoordinated Billy Hamilton. But it was an accident by third baseman Jimmy Collins that gave the Orioles two runs in the second inning. With men on second and third with two outs, Boston's Fred Klobedanz pitched to John McGraw, who bunted down the third-base line. Although the ball veered foul, Collins attempted to field it, but instead accidentally kicked it off to one side, allowing both runs to score. Having already scratched out another run in the first inning with two outs, as Joe Kelley drove Wee Willie Keeler in from second with a hit, after two innings the scorecards read Baltimore 3, Boston 0.

And that is where matters stood until the seventh when Boston roared back with two runs, paced by Herman Long's double, but the rally stalled when Orioles catcher Wilbert Robinson tagged out Sliding Billy Hamilton at home with what would have been the tying run. In the bottom of the inning, the Orioles got those two runs back with Joe Kelley hitting a double off Freddy Klobedanz, bringing home Wee Willie Keeler and Hughie Jennings. Each team scored one more run as the Orioles' fans frantically ran onto the playing field to celebrate the home team's victory.

The Royal Rooters also had an awful time of it as Tommy McCarthy's old bar partner, Barney Lennon, bought a silver horseshoe to bring the Beaneaters good luck, but it proved a poor investment; he could not give it away to the opposing team's fans who saw the horseshoe as bad luck. Barney had it easy as one of his fellow Rooters got hit in the nose by a foul ball in the fifth inning, causing that poor fan's face to swell like a blowfish.

By clever trickery, Oriole outfielder Joe Kelley restored some semblance of home-field advantage with some sage words to his cranks. Since the second game drew another enormous crowd, fans had to stand in the field. When Boston came to bat, Kelley instructed the fans crowding the outfield to push back 15 feet, which they did, permitting him and his fellow outfielders more room to lazily roam after fly balls. When Boston retired each inning, the hometown crowd walked back to its old positions, thus pushing in the "fences" 15 feet for the Oriole batters.

Boston now stood in second place in the standings, silly centimeters behind the Orioles, who sat perched on top. As much as Murnane loved the Royal Rooters, he mused that staying at the same hotel as the Boston players after the first game did not benefit anyone from New England. Sobered a bit by the loss, the Royal Rooters licked their wounds by allowing Honey Fitz to take them on a tour of historic Washington, D.C., before the third game of the series.

Thirty thousand fans swarmed the Union Grounds for the rubber match between the best teams in baseball on September 27. As the crowd shoved through the turnstiles, it got quite rough as a policeman sustained several broken ribs and a young boy broke his arm. Tim Murnane engaged in some participatory journalism by stating that in order to enter the park, he "was forced to adopt a few Harvard football tactics to get inside the gate."

Hugh Duffy proudly marched his men through the throng and Kid Nichols started for the Beaneaters. Nichols did not bring his best stuff to the game, having surrendered five runs by the end of the fifth inning. The Orioles pitchers proved a bit less competent as they let in eight Boston runs. In the sixth inning, the Beaneaters exploded, making their lead insurmountable. Sir Hugh led off the inning with a single to left field, and then after his team batted through its order, he came back in the same inning with a double. His men scored nine runs before the Orioles could record three outs against them. The Orioles lost, 19–10, and Boston had the league lead.

After the conclusion of the game, the Royal Rooters accompanied the team from the field to the hotel, drawing especially gleeful appreciation from Kid Nichols, Lowe and Tenney. Once ensconced at the Eutaw House, the Beaneaters partied like it was 1899, receiving appreciative handshakes and backslaps from the fans and each other, while being regaled by congratulatory telegrams. At the Eutaw House, Captain Duffy read a telegram from Honey Fitz, who said, "Warmest congratulations to you and the nine on your victory. Newspaper Row never so crowded and all Boston never so pleased as she is tonight over your magnificent victory. Tell the royal rooters that although miles away from them my heart beats just as loyally as their horns blew for Boston's great ball team. Good luck at Brooklyn." The team and its fans then let out three loud cheers for Honey Fitz.

The 1897 Boston Beaneaters with the Royal Rooters outside of Baltimore's Eutaw House on the verge of clinching the pennant. Note the various band members on the balcony. **Boston Public Library, Print Department.**

Having learned from the experience of boarding the team and the Rooters in the same hotel, Selee wisely marched his men to the train station for the ride to Brooklyn (via Newark, where surprisingly they had scheduled an exhibition with a local nine), for their season-concluding three-game series against the Bridegrooms. The players lounged in their cars and the train did not leave until midnight, but they got their crucial sleep for the task ahead. As a sop to the fans, the Royal Rooters and their band played all evening at the hotel and then appeared at the station to wish the team well before their train departed for Brooklyn.

Although the Royal Rooters had cheered their lungs out, the race remained very tight. Boston had three games with Brooklyn at Eastern Field while the Orioles hosted Washington, a team they had dominated by winning seven of eight games, for a four-game series.

Boston wisely rested many of its key regulars for their nuisance exhibition in Newark, starting a pitcher named Mills, who does not show up in any baseball encyclopedia. Preparing for Boston, Duffy clutched clichés when analyzing the last stage of the campaign, stating, "Well, we have a fighting chance as well as Baltimore. Had we lost today it was all off. Our boys will play the string out and win if possible. It's no easy matter to beat Brooklyn on her own grounds, and we must work just as hard as we have in Baltimore, for Baltimore usually finds Washington easy fruit. It may be different this time, however, and I wouldn't be surprised to see the championship come down to the last day before it is settled."

Squeezing sour grapes, John McGraw bemoaned, "The Boston club is a hard club to defeat, but I know their players cannot equal ours. The loss of yesterday's game was a great disappointment to me." More diplomatically, Hughie Jennings chimed, "Well, we are not dead yet, and furthermore they can't kill us. No one feels our defeat more than I do. In the sight of about 25,000 spectators we were defeated and defeated squarely, being outplayed in every point."

Duffy's conservatism served him and his team well as Baltimore won its next game against Washington, necessitating that Boston win to stave them off, which occurred resoundingly with a 12–4 knockdown of the Bridegrooms. Boston clinched the next day with a win by an almost identical score as the day before, and the team ran off the field to follow any and all incoming news about the Baltimore/Washington game. Washington won and Boston celebrated winning the pennant as the *Boston Globe* trumpeted that it was a triumph of clean play over inside baseball.

Then as now, Boston fans often looked at their chief opposition as residing in a league with Satan while their players walked with the angels. The problem, of course, is that the Boston Beaneaters of this era had their share of ruffians and their catcher, Martin Bergen, was short years away from turning into Norman Bates. The Orioles had some players who came up the hard way like McGraw, but he went to college and turned a very tough upbringing into a very successful career as a third baseman and as a manager. Hughie Jennings became a lawyer and Arlie Pond was a doctor. While the Beaneaters had their combative Heavenly Twins, the Orioles fielded many players who overcame adversity and accomplished significant achievements both inside and outside baseball.

Having said that, the Orioles did lack a certain grace, and McGraw might have demonstrated some class at evaluating his opposition in a most charitable light, particularly since Boston won games at an unbelievable clip after the first couple weeks of the season. Later in life he did have to admit in his book that Boston had some excellent men as he named Jimmy Collins and Hugh Duffy onto his "All Time Team" as his third baseman and left fielder, respectfully.

Anticlimactically, Boston and Baltimore played again, as the two top teams in the National League annually got together to vie for the Temple Cup. No one from Boston other than perhaps Kid Nichols seemed to care, and Baltimore went on to win the cup, for what proved to be the last time ever. As the series concluded, the Boston players and the Orioles met at historic Faneuil Hall for a dinner, after which, in the delightfully quirky times they lived in, they planned to play exhibitions in Worcester and Springfield.

The Temple Cup, like the exhibitions in central and western Massachusetts, excited few fans or players. The pennant was won by Boston and the rest constituted a last chance of the year to play ball and perhaps make a bit more money. In a world long ago and far away, the Evil Empire had been vanquished.

Chapter 15

Duffy's Last Years as a Player

The 1897 race proved immensely satisfying to Hugh Duffy. As team captain, he had led the Beaneaters to a thrilling pennant at the expense of the seemingly unbeatable Baltimore Orioles. While Tommy McCarthy continued his retirement, Duffy felt rejuvenated and eager for the 1898 campaign to begin.

Nevertheless, his normally joyous Irish heart must have blended with some melancholy as old friends of his continued to depart from the scene. Of course, Mac would never come back — Selee did not like his performance in 1895 and Mac had turned into Big Mac since having sat out the 1897 season. Tommy Tucker, the Falstaffian figure in Duffy's life, was no longer around to occasionally corrupt the Beaneaters' captain.

Fred Tenney had thoroughly supplanted the Foghorn with greater range and intelligence at first base, and he also had become a very good major league hitter. Although some teammates undoubtedly resented Tenney's Ivy League background, Duffy had always tried to cultivate and refine himself, and would someday even coach in college. As a result, Duffy the team captain posed no threat to the heady Tenney. In fact, they became good friends and were two of the few players on the team with any personality, now that the more colorful characters had departed.

Murnane sensed as much and wrote, "Outside of Duffy, Long, Tenney and Bergen, the Boston players are a quiet lot. Two or three of them are likely to drop off into a trance if they are not jolted continually." It was a businesslike and efficient team, much the reflection of Manager Selee. While he won with idiots like Foghorn Tucker, Happy Jack Stivetts and Tommy McCarthy, he much preferred sober men like Sliding Billy Hamilton, Jimmy Collins and Kid Nichols.

And he had grown to like Duffy in the role of his team captain. Reminiscing years later, Selee positively gushed, "During my connection with the Boston Club I had a good lieutenant in Hughey Duffy, Captain of the Club; our associations were very pleasant. He is a good true friend as I well happen to know from what I heard a certain Boston player, who had been in hard luck, say of him."

Duffy matured into a team leader at about the same point that Tommy McCarthy had become a liability and a malcontent extraordinaire. To advance his own personal and financial goals, Duffy cultivated a high degree of self-control and became a bit of a company man. He had shrewdly decided that despite some financial success his business ventures brought him, he had to rely on the security that baseball afforded him in the event that his investments declined. His adopted persona dovetailed with the way Selee increasingly sought to mold his team.

As Duffy had changed, so too had baseball. At the end of the Gay Nineties, the successful teams had shed their dependency on a trio of pitchers centered on one dominant hurler. Through the entire decade, Kid Nichols had provided the Beaneaters with peerless and yeomanlike service, but now the game had altered in its philosophy, encouraging each team to spread the responsibility to four strong pitchers, thereby vitiating the effect of a single star on a team's fortunes.

Fortunately for the Beaneaters, Selee had selected Ted Lewis and Vic Willis to assist Nichols and Freddy Klobedanz, and the team had every expectation for success in 1898. Unbeknownst to the cranks of the day, this year marked the last gasp of the epic series between Boston and Baltimore. Ned Hanlon switched his allegiance to Brooklyn before the 1899 season, thus breaking up his powerhouse club in the process.

Although the Beaneaters snoozed through the initial stages of the season, they had too many stoppers among their starters to continue such spotty play. Nichols earned more than thirty victories that year, as Willis and Lewis chalked up win totals in the mid-twenties and fourth starter Klobedanz lagged behind with a mere 19 wins. They hit their stride in August with an eleven-game winning streak, and after hitting a bit of a rut, they ran off another skein of nine wins in early September.

No one came close to them as they repeated as champions.

In the off-season, Hanlon became manager of the Brooklyn club, with Orioles stars Wee Willie Keeler, Joe Kelley and Hughie Jennings coming over with him. John McGraw stayed true to Baltimore, earning a spot as the team's player-manager, and thus starting a long and successful career leading teams.

Boston narrowly lost to the Brooklyn Superbas in the pennant race of 1899 and Hugh Duffy contributed to slide with a batting average that dipped to .279. Other batters suffered at the plate as well, including Jimmy Collins, offsetting stellar years from Chick Stahl and Fred Tenney. Kid Nichols won 21 games but lost 19, and although Ted Lewis and Vic Willis continued to pitch well, the Beaneaters never developed a reliable fourth starter after Freddy Klobedanz disappeared, perhaps because he caused rifts with organized labor.

Dissension also rippled through the ranks as catcher Marty Bergen became

As Martin Bergen's mental health deteriorated, he threatened to kill Hugh Duffy and another teammate, James Sullivan (pictured above). Collection of Richard A. Johnson.

increasingly unreliable, retreating for games at a time to his family farm in rural North Brookfield, Massachusetts. In late July, scribe Tim Murnane traveled there to interview Bergen and he heard an earful. Bergen mourned the recent death of his young son and periodically vanished from the team. Selee tried to understand, but he had a very small roster of players and had to have a catcher available at all times. He tried to encourage Bergen to show up, which Bergen resented. No one seemed to get through to Bergen.

Bergen became convinced that four members of the team encouraged a crowd of fans during a road trip to turn against him, and as early as 1897 he threatened to kill Hugh Duffy and another teammate, James Sullivan. This despite the fact that Duffy and Billy Hamilton in particular always tried to understand him and bring him out of his periodic funks. Bergen's retreat from his teammates, his sudden absences and his paranoia contributed to an uncomfortable clubhouse and a very shaky situation at a key position on the field. Ominously, Bergen declared that he would not play again after the conclusion of the season, even if Boston released or traded him to another team.

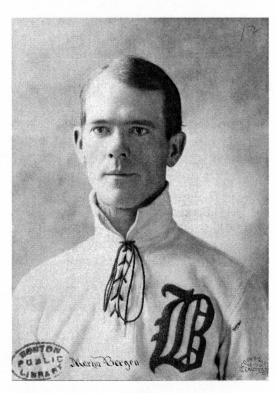

For reasons having nothing to do with baseball, the 1900 season was derailed for the Beaneaters before it began, as catcher Marty Bergen became the Lizzie Borden of the new century after he bludgeoned to death his wife and two young children with an ax before committing suicide. In January, Marty's father walked up to his son's Brookfield, Massachusetts, farm to check on the family because he had not seen nor heard from them in several days. He staggered away from the holocaust in shock.

One might expect the press of the late Victorian era to cast Bergen as an evil and heartless villain, but instead they diagnosed the act as that of a lunatic. The *Boston Globe* ran a headline in black capital letters that read "BERGEN'S INSANE DEED," and in a smaller head-

Martin Bergen, Boston's star catcher in the late 1890s, later killed his wife and two children with an axe. His gaze in this portrait is impenetrable. **Boston Public Library, Print Department.**

line concluded that "Madman's Frenzy Explains Peculiar Conduct of Past Two Seasons." In the course of the article, the writer essentially diagnosed Bergen with every affliction in the spectrum of insanity then known to the psychological community, and really did not attribute it at all to simple spousal or family abuse.

Estimable Boston sports historian Richard Johnson has theorized that Bergen may have suffered from a tumor or experienced some other physical alteration that affected his judgment, as he did not have a long track record of mental illness. This would be consistent with part of what the *Globe* writer wrote at the time, that the "frenzy" somehow explained Bergen's "peculiar conduct of past two seasons." Quite plausibly, alcohol abuse accelerated the madness.

We will never know. It was an unspeakable tragedy then, and unlike the murders of Lizzie Borden's father and step-mother, it has not become a novelty like the Jack the Ripper murders, but retains its horror to this day. It does not take much imagination, however, to contemplate decent men like Frank Selee, Hugh Duffy and Tim Murnane shaking their heads and wondering what got into poor Marty Bergen that he would do such a thing.

As a sensitive person, Duffy felt the loss deeper than many. After the tragedy, Duffy was quoted as musing:

> I have realized for a long while that Bergen has not been "right." His strange personality has been an enigma to me ever since he joined the team, and knowing his melancholy moods, and understanding so thoroughly how false were his ideas that the boys were all against him a more serious outbreak was not altogether unexpected by me. His strange conduct at times while on the road, at hotels, and on the ball field even, caused me to regard him as a fellow never to be contended against, especially when in one of his moody spells. Some times he has threatened violence toward some of us, but that Bergen should finally become crazed while in the bosom of the family he loved so well, and should commit this awful deed, I cannot understand.

The Beaneaters more than adequately replaced Bergen at catcher with Boileryard Clarke (who raised his previous season's average by more than ninety points, to a career-high .315) and Billy Sullivan (who also hit for his highest average in his sixteen-year major league tenure). Still, Boston did not even post a winning record for 1900, despite strong performances from new pitcher Bill Dinneen, third baseman Jimmy Collins and outfielder Billy Hamilton.

Unfortunately, Kid Nichols, Vic Willis and Ted Lewis all had poor years on the mound, and the middle infield continued to age, losing range in the process. In spot duty, Duffy still batted over .300, but with Hamilton, Chick Stahl and Buck Freeman joining him in the outfield, Sir Hugh increasingly scouted new horizons.

The other National League teams in 1900 had improved so dramatically that the Beaneaters could no longer expect to camouflage substandard results from some of their key players. The Brooklyn Superbas under Ned Hanlon had become a dynasty behind Wee Willie Keeler and ace pitcher Iron Man McGinnity. All-time shortstop Honus Wagner led the Pittsburgh Pirates, whose mediocre season from future Hall of Fame pitchers Jack Chesbro and Rube Waddell were more than made up for by the stellar work of true staff aces Jesse Tannehill and Deacon Phillippe. Philadelphia continued to threaten with stars such as Nap Lajoie, Ed Delahanty, Elmer Flick and Roy Thomas.

After the Phillies swept the Beaneaters at the beginning of the season, Boston foundered, limping to a fourth-place finish in the league. Whereas in the past strategic winning streaks guided them past their chief competitors in the pennant race, this year they staggered under the weight of several prolonged losing droughts. Eight-game winless streaks in May, July and October cut them out of the race in decisive fashion. The Beaneaters had suddenly stopped eating the magical fruit and had become quite human.

After the 1900 season, the storied Beaneaters disappeared into myth. The Triumvirate treated Duffy like a horse they had consigned to the glue factory, a decision they would live to rue. Soden injudiciously opined that Duffy was "about through as a player. We'll let him go in peace." For his part, Sir Hugh stated his own issues publicly as he maintained that "I haven't had the full authority as captain, as anybody knows...." In his history of the Boston Braves, Harold Kaese listed other causes for Duffy's disaffection with the team due to his not liking at the South End Grounds and not taking to criticism of his running of the Boston pitching staff.

Since the National League had successively and successfully disposed of the challenges from the Union Association, the Players' League and the American Association, it had grown complacent and owners like the Boston Triumvirate had become increasingly stingy and arrogant with their players. Fortuitously for labor, the monopoly of the National League owners had ended, as a group of sharpies had conspired to create the new American League.

Furtively at first, Connie Mack returned to his Massachusetts home, and his intentions soon became known as he began to beat the bushes in Boston to help create a new American League franchise there. Tommy McCarthy and Hugh Duffy, having never relinquished their grudge against the Beaneaters' management, joined Mack's cabal, and in the act of revenge, played a critical role in the creation of the team that ultimately became the last Boston baseball franchise standing, the Boston Red Sox. Mac and Duffy helped Mack scope out grounds for the planned new Boston franchise, with Sir Hugh showing a particular devotion to the cause. One contemporary scribe, writing under the Dixwellian pseudonym of "Hi, Hi," claimed that "Mack was here on business and business only. He was closeted with Hugh Duffy, and they had several long talks. They went to the theatre together and discussed baseball's troubles. It is now given out that Mack is to have Philadelphia in the new league, but still own Milwaukee, where Hugh Duffy is to be manager."

There is reason to believe that Duffy and McCarthy also used the not-so-gentle art of persuasion to encourage Beaneater stars to jump to the new American League team. For his part, Jimmy Collins deflected Sir Hugh's influence, claiming, "Hughey is looking out for his welfare and sees a good opportunity in managing the American League club in Milwaukee, and I am looking out for James J. Collins." True or not, James J. deserted to become the new team's player-manager and Ted Lewis, Buck Freeman and Chick Stahl followed suit. And Connie Mack and Hugh Duffy approached most if not all of these players and enticed them to jump from the Beaneaters.

The efforts of the Heavenly Twins proved to be a boon to the nascent Red Sox. Few local fans had any inkling of the exploits of the Beaneaters stars after a generation or two had passed, but when the Red Sox won the World Series in 2004, the memory of the Red Sox Royal Rooters were revived in a hit remake of the century-old song "Tessie" by the band the Dropkick Murphys, who celebrated the memory of Cy Young, Bill Dinneen, and Chick Stahl. Fittingly, three Red Sox players—Johnny Damon, Lenny Dinardo and Bronson Arroyo—joined in the song.

The work of the Heavenly Twins haunted the Boston National League franchise from 1901 until 1952, when fed up with low attendance and permanent second-class status in the Boston baseball hierarchy, the National League team owners relocated to Milwaukee to enjoy a renaissance with Warren Spahn, Hank Aaron, Eddie Mathews and Lew Burdette. The Braves remain one of the sport's most successful franchises in Atlanta.

The Triumvirate never recovered. They were offended after Frank Selee led the team to a 69–69 campaign in 1902 and fired him, thus prompting Duffy to sadly note, "Selee should long ago have left this city and taken one of several good chances instead of staying here at a very low salary." Beaneater players continued to defect to the new Huntington Avenue Grounds, the home of the new and chic Boston team. Selee took his considerable organizational abilities to Chicago, where he methodically built what became the Cub pennant winners of Tinker to Evers to Chance and Three-Finger Brown, further driving the nail into the coffin of the Boston Beaneaters.

Only James B. Billings of the Triumvirate cared about his players, and the other members of the troika, well-respected men Soden and Conant, squeezed him out in 1904. The self-immolation of the Beaneaters was complete, and even though they later changed their name to the Braves (and oddly for a brief period, the Bees), Boston had become a one-team town. By the end of the 1906 season, Soden and Conant had sold their interest in the club.

Although Duffy had not played much in 1900, he nevertheless batted over .300 for the year and in return for his efforts in setting up the new American League, he received an appointment as player-manager for the new team in Milwaukee. There, he had the opportunity to play in the field as the spirit moved him. Once he met and evaluated his new team, it took him little time to conclude that he was his best ballplayer, and he started swinging the bat again in anticipation of a new spring.

Chapter 16

McCarthy's Life
After Baseball

True to his word, Tommy McCarthy never played major league baseball again after 1896 and, uncharitably but accurately, one could say he quit playing at several points during that final season. He initially dedicated his life to his family and to his saloon, but 1897 proved far more disastrous to him as his wife Margaret died due to pneumonia on February 26 of that year, leaving him to care for three young daughters.

Unlike Duffy's wife Nora, who we know quite a bit about, Margaret McCarthy left very little trace in the historical record. Oddly, even though her husband was a major Boston celebrity, her passing attracted very little media notice, again in contrast to the sickness and passing of Duffy's first wife, Katie Gilland. Margaret McCarthy died a young woman, probably only 27 years old, and the funeral and presumably the wake were held at her home at Gates Street in South Boston. A Mass was held in St. Augustine's Church for her four days after her death, and she was buried in Boston's Old Calvary Cemetery. Her husband Tommy never remarried.

His family and friends banded around him and provided him with as much joy as possible. In October of 1897, his sister Hannah married Thomas Copell of Roxbury and McCarthy's three daughters, Sadie, Rita and Edith, served as maids of honor, all decked out in white muslin. Life went on and Tommy and his daughters banded ever more tightly together, and they endured.

With three young children looking up to him, attempting a comeback as a baseball player was out of the question.

While the saloon provided a good income to him, McCarthy could not stay out of baseball. In early 1900, Cap Anson and others publicly announced plans to form a new major league and enlisted McCarthy as their point man for a projected Boston franchise. McCarthy pounced on the prospect. It appears that he leased some land across the river at the Charles River Park in Cambridge to lay out a new ball park and otherwise invested heavily in this new enterprise. While exact figures do not exist, one newspaper estimated that the project needed the infusion of $5,000 to $10,000 in capital to make it viable.

Wealthy investors supposedly agreed to back Mac's venture, but this support proved ephemeral and Anson appeared to lose interest in the project, too. By Thanksgiving of 1900, McCarthy walked away from it all after having lost "considerable money," figuring the new league "was a dead cock in the pit." In its stead, Ban Johnson and others diligently founded their own organization, the American League, soon thereafter but Mac did not share in the economic opportunities created thereby. Even before the aborted new league drained Mac of his earnings, he had made tentative peace with baseball.

Although he never attended college and probably never even set foot in high school, Tommy McCarthy coached the Holy Cross College baseball team for five years total, serving stints from 1899–1900, 1904–1905 and 1916. Shortly after Mac's last term of service for the Crusaders, legendary Philadelphia Athletics middle infielder Jack Barry managed the school's team for almost 40 years thereafter.

While Tommy McCarthy's induction into the National Baseball Hall of Fame may have been based on his being overrated, his contributions to developing baseball at Holy Cross College in Worcester, Massachusetts, have not received their proper due. In large part, the fact that Jack Barry coached the baseball team for several decades accounts for this, yet McCarthy deserves credit in this regard and he will receive it.

Sitting atop one of Worcester's many hills, Holy Cross is a Catholic college run by the Jesuit order and founded in 1843. Known more for spawning such basketball legends as Tom Cousy and Tommy Heinsohn, it possesses a formidable baseball legacy as well.

It did not start out that way. In the late 1800s, the sport as an intercollegiate endeavor barely existed. The initial intercollegiate games for Holy Cross took place in 1876, but for many of the years that followed, including as late as 1892, no games were played at all. McCarthy succeeded Hall of Fame legend Jesse Burkett, who had led the team to a mundane 12-8 record in 1898.

McCarthy changed that of all in a hurry. Starting the season on April 15 with a 17–4 victory against Boston University, McCarthy transformed a mediocre mélange of ballplayers that first year into one of the premier programs in the United States. He also had fun defeating the Williams team, coached by his old Boston Beaneater teammate Charley Ganzell (another Beaneater, Freddy Klobedanz, sat on the bench with Mac during the game).

The penultimate game for the Holy Cross team enfolded in Worcester on May 27 when "the Cross" hosted Georgetown University, the finest team in the nation and the eventual mythical national champion. Well in advance of this contest, Tommy McCarthy personally scouted the Hoyas as they rolled over every team they faced in the Northeast.

To demonstrate the respect that Georgetown's coach and captain held for Mac's varsity, he started his ace, Doc White, a lefty who after graduation recorded 45 major league shutouts in the midst of winning 189 ballgames. Accounts vary, but perhaps as many as 4,000 fans came to the game, most of them bringing in banners draped in the school color of purple, shouting and cheering with every pitch.

Disaster struck with the first pitch from Holy Cross's Griffin to the Hoyas' leadoff batter, who crushed it out of the park. Griffin settled down and White pitched as advertised, as the Hoyas led after one inning, 1–0. After Griffin escaped from the second inning unscathed, "the Cross" erupted for seven runs in the bottom of the frame, with White serving up two home runs, two singles, a double, a walk, and to add spice to the mix, a hit batsman. White left the game in shock, as the Holy Cross squad won its biggest game ever, 11–4.

Tommy McCarthy put Holy Cross on the map of contemporary intercollegiate sports. His turn-of-the-century teams went 19-5-0 and 19-6-1, while his 1904 and 1905 clubs went 14-7-1 and 15-10-0, respectively. If Yankee Stadium is "the House that Ruth Built," Holy Cross' Fitton Field, dedicated in 1905, can truly be called "the House that Mac Built."

Not only did he build a park, Mac constructed a formidable team around some talent on that 1905 Holy Cross squad. Bill Carrigan played catcher for the Red Sox for many years and managed the team during some of their most glorious campaigns, from 1913–1916. Carrigan was succeeded in 1917 as Sox manager by another former Holy Cross player, 1905 teammate Jack Barry, who played shortstop for the Philadelphia Athletics on their famous "$100,000 Infield." Joining Stuffy McInnis at first, Eddie Collins at second and Home Run Baker at third base, Barry rounded out what perhaps remains the greatest infield in baseball history. Both Carrigan and Barry long remembered Tommy McCarthy as a key to their success as he correctly positioned these two ballplayers on the field, permitting them to flourish and attract the notice of professional teams.

And then there was team captain and star pitcher James Spring. While Carrigan and Barry always fondly recalled their association with Mac, Spring rebelled against the coach's authority. Matters came to a head in a late-season game against Yale when Mac decided that Spring needed to be relieved as a pitcher and Spring refused to get off the mound. Instead, Spring jeered at the relief pitcher to get back to where he came from, in direct contravention of McCarthy's orders. After the game, Mac tendered his resignation.

The newspapers did not say much about the incident, and what little did get mentioned tended to make Captain Spring look bad for daring to think he knew more about baseball than Tommy McCarthy. Had the issue been a simple matter of insubordination, it is highly unlikely that "the Cross" would have let Mac go. As a Catholic teaching institution in an age when no one dared to challenge church authority and remain a Catholic, it seems curious that the manager was permitted to walk while a young whippersnapper undergrad stayed on the team.

History has long neglected what occurred on the 1905 Holy Cross team, but in examining the life of Tommy McCarthy, it would be an injustice to simply write off his departure from the team as the act of a know-it-all young captain who did not listen to him. The true reason may have been covered up at the time, and in light of Mac's future experiences as a college coach, the possibility that Spring was not an insubordinate or an ingrate should not be discounted. What is true is that after Mac departed, the interim manager, Dr. George Linnehan (who played under McCarthy at the turn of the century), led the team without further controversy, causing the *Purple Patcher* yearbook writer to observe that "there was undeniably noticed a new energy in the men and they finished the season with five straight victories." What is also true is that under McCarthy, earlier in the season, Holy Cross had beaten each of those five teams.

Perhaps to set the record straight or to rehabilitate Mac's image, the *Boston*

Tommy McCarthy resigned as Holy Cross's manager before the end of the 1905 season, largely because of the actions of team captain James Spring, who is seated in the second row in the middle. Spring's career went nowhere, but two other players, Jack Barry and Bill Carrigan, loved McCarthy, and when they had the opportunity later in their own baseball careers to help Mac, they did. Jack Barry is in the second row, second from the left, while Carrigan and McCarthy are in the third row, second and third from the left, respectively. College of the Holy Cross Archives.

Globe (probably through Murnane) opined that Mac "did splendid work at Holy Cross ... McCarthy is a fine judge of a player. He knows the game, from top to bottom, and what is better still, he can impart his knowledge to others."

In addition to his service at Holy Cross, Mac also managed the Dartmouth College team in New Hampshire in the years 1906 and 1907. His teams' records were 13-8-1 and 17-9, respectively. As if to somehow make up for the treatment he received from James Spring, the Dartmouth team captain, Mike O'Brien, came down from campus to meet McCarthy in Boston and to facilitate the move, one which the *Globe* heralded as "the most important move Dartmouth has yet made in baseball, and one that is certain to boom the game at that college."

While California colleges and universities had just begun to produce such future notables as the enormously talented and dishonest Hal Chase, eastern baseball still held national primacy despite inclement springs. Dartmouth baseball boosters wanted their program to advance, and the lure of a former major league star, one who had connections in organized baseball, proved too alluring to ignore.

The 1906 season did prove eminently satisfactory to the school's fans. While the program still had its rough edges, with home plate by the campus chapel and home run balls rolling "to the front door of the Hanover Inn," the many fans who ingested hot dogs and rooted for their college decided to treat these quirks as charming. The campus press wholeheartedly approved of McCarthy's professionalism, fairly gushing that "[t]his business-like beginning by the baseball leader is commendable, and shows that past mistakes, instead of being forgotten, are to be used towards attaining success in the baseball season of 1906."

One disturbing non-baseball development had become manifest by the spring of 1906. While Mac struggled with his weight during his career and had begun to accumulate unwanted additional "love handles" about his waist in the early years of his retirement, he still had maintained a certain robust, albeit beefy appearance. But as photographs as he ascended the skipper's position at Dartmouth, when juxtaposed with portraits taken of him even two years earlier at Holy Cross starkly demonstrate, Mac had become an enormous man.

Lee Allen from the Hall of Fame later wrote that Mac "looked something like an alderman, or a wrestling champion, a president of the Fat Man's Club, or that early movie star, John Bunny." This sounds a bit unkind but it accurately depicts the serious decline in Mac's physical appearance since his peak playing days, when he ran the base-paths with as much vim and vigor as Sliding Billy Hamilton and Arlie Latham. Mac had become a huge man, easily tipping 300 pounds on his diminutive frame.

Nevertheless, Big Mac still knew baseball and he helped form a nondescript and weak-hitting squad into winners. In changing the fortunes of the Dartmouth baseball program, he may have unwittingly become a victim of his own success. For a number of years before McCarthy had managed Dartmouth, the school had insisted that its players observe strict amateur status, both during and after each season. When it occasionally discovered that one of its players had joined a summer professional or semi-pro club, the administration had punished the player severely. No issues concerning a player's amateur status had arisen in 1906, but the problem merely awaited a further reckoning.

None of these ominous rumblings were apparent during a very successful 1907 season, when Dartmouth won four more games. During its southern swing, its nine had dominated, defeating such tough opponents as Annapolis, UVA, Washington and Lee and the always formidable Georgetown nine.

Late in the season, the University of Alabama ventured to New England and Dartmouth defeated the Crimson Tide rather soundly. The University of Alabama canceled its planned game with the University of Vermont because the latter team carried two African American players on its roster. Fortunately, Dartmouth and other schools did not invoke the Jim Crow nonsense and played their schedule against Vermont. At the conclusion of the 1907 campaign, *The Dartmouth* congratulated "Coach McCarthy ... upon the gratifying results of his very effective coaching."

Despite managing a very successful ball club in 1907, the college fired McCarthy that September, voting that "it is the sense of this Council that McCarthy never be employed to coach another Dartmouth team." In addition, ten of his players received suspensions from baseball and every other campus varsity squad.

The proximate cause for the termination and player suspensions was the presence of the majority of the 1907 stars on professional teams. Most if not all of the suspended players had openly joined the roster of a touring York, Maine, club, and since they had been previously warned, the college felt it had no choice but to take this serious action. President Tucker in a campus address went so far to say, "If this demoralization continues, I am prepared, as a lover and defender of college athletics, to advise the elimination of baseball, as an intercollegiate game, from college sports."

It is unclear what role, if any, McCarthy played in the scandal. Certainly he had been hired to improve the fortunes of the program, but in his greater stress on professionalizing the team, did he abet most of his players to literally become professional in derogation of the college's warnings to the contrary?

The campus accounts do not clarify the situation and the Boston press, perhaps in deference to old friend Mac, did not exactly pick this story apart. It is conceivable that Mac knew nothing about his players joining the York team after the Dartmouth season concluded, and that he served as a convenient scapegoat for a perceived out-of-control situation.

It is more likely that Mac could not conform his practice to the requirements of collegiate sports, even in an era that did not have strict NCAA guidelines to follow. When Mac played, players and managers quite openly bet on their own teams, and the rough and tumble of professional mores simply clashed with the avowed ideals of such prestigious collegiate programs as Holy Cross and Dartmouth. His experience in Holy Cross, when he had lost his job before season's end in 1905, should have made him more sensitive to the requirement of his employers. At best, it seems he was ignorant of widespread violations of campus policies regarding amateurism; a pretty serious oversight for a manager who knew New England baseball and knew (or should have known) that almost his whole team was up in York Beach playing for pay.

Mac followed sports and he had any number of friends like Murnane in the press or other former players or team owners who must have alerted him to the presence of his players in a pro atmosphere. He easily could have taken action of his own to get his players off that club, but there is absolutely no evidence that he either tried or disclosed the professional status of his players to anyone in the Dartmouth administration. At worst, of course, he may have actively encouraged his players to make a buck on the side. In any event, between his sour ending at Holy Cross and his scandal at Dartmouth, his employment in the college coaching ranks had apparently ceased. Sadly, this had come to pass because the man could coach, but unlike Hugh Duffy, he did not know how to avoid huge headaches.

Friends like Sir Hugh and the Silver King undoubtedly told Mac that he was a fall guy who received a bum rap from Dartmouth. They would have been able to cite the unfairness of trying to build a powerhouse national baseball program without giving these poor kids a chance to make a buck once they left campus for the summer, this all in a day without an established NCAA in place to police the sport or promulgate practices for colleges and universities. Certainly, many schools knew and implicitly condoned their student-athletes using phony names and playing for pay during vacations, and Mac should have been allowed to turn a blind eye to these facts.

Behind his back, his friends probably analyzed the situation differently. Maybe Dartmouth had made an example of Mac and his players, but the school had consistently punished players that school administrators knew played summer ball for professional teams in the recent past, facts made abundantly clear to McCarthy when he got the job. Also, on the heels of his being forced to resign at Holy Cross, Mac needed to maintain a heightened state of vigilance to ensure that his players maintained their amateur status, particularly since not everyone received a second chance as he had. Either way, his friends felt sorry for him losing yet another job at the intercollegiate level.

Financially, he still had his saloon and bowling alley to fall back on for the next five years until the Avery Hotel's birth, but in terms of his participation in baseball on any level for the year 1908, Tommy McCarthy had to content himself from watching the action from the stands as a spectator. Since he had so many contacts in organized ball and due to his reputation as a skilled "baseball man," he signed up with the Cincinnati Reds, for whom he scouted from 1909 through 1912.

When not working, McCarthy still had the company of his three daughters at home and the companionship of Hugh Duffy and their largely Irish group of former ballplayers and Royal Rooters. Not wanting the good times to end, Jack Dooley formed an organization named the Winter League around 1906, and this organization became the basis for many of the booster clubs which survive today.

Once the party really got started, the Winter League held large banquets for several years in such Boston habitués as the Hotel Lenox, the Quincy House and the Boston Tavern. Mac, Duffy and Tim Murnane attended many of the League's events over the years, but with the exception of utility player Fred Lake, the old Boston Beaneaters did not appear. Honored guests at their events ranged from Hughie Jennings to Rabbit Maranville, with many speeches by local club owners and other sports dignitaries. In a typical evening, speeches were made, jokes told, songs sung and alcohol drunk.

The Winter League even played at least one game as a team against the

Standing in the second row of this Knights of Columbus team photograph, fourth from the left, is Tommy McCarthy on August 30, 1902. McCarthy continued to play in various pick-up teams for years after retiring and even got a hit in a minor league game in 1918. Boston Public Library, Print Department.

Williams Shoe club from suburban Holliston, Massachusetts, in late October 1912. Driving out in five jalopies to a large estate, the party played the local factory team and defeated them by a score of 6–1, with Tommy McCarthy getting two hits and Hugh Duffy none. In retirement, Mac had finally found a way to out-hit Sir Hugh.

Indicative of their devotion to the game of golf, the Heavenly Twins made two trips at least in the winter of 1915 to play a round together. On January 19, they ventured out on poorly plowed roads to compete in Boston's Franklin Park, and on February 15 they again braved the elements for their passion for the sport. On the last occasion, McCarthy had the better of his Heavenly Twin until he drove the ball 250 yards into a tree, causing it to bounce back 150 yards. Duffy won the match by five strokes on that latter occasion.

In much warmer weather, Duffy and McCarthy and two friends enjoyed watching a Red Sox game against the St. Louis Browns in August in the then-brand new Fenway Park. Although they did not see the Sox's star lefty Babe Ruth pitch that day, future Hall of Fame pitcher Herb Pennock pinch-ran and the home team had its own version of the Heavenly Triplets in their outfield of Tris Speaker, Duffy Lewis and Harry Hooper. The powerful Sox defeated the hapless Browns that day, 2–0, as Duffy and McCarthy were further entertained by the Browns manager, Branch Rickey, who kept jumping out of his dugout to argue with the umpires. In a few decades, Rickey would more than redeem himself by hiring Jackie Robinson to break the color barrier created largely by Cap Anson in the late 1800s.

In 1914 and 1917, Mac scouted for the Boston Braves, the lineal descendant of the old Boston Beaneaters. Much had changed in his old team — the Triumvirate no longer operated the show — but under manager George Stallings, it accomplished the seemingly impossible feat of advancing from last place in the National League at the Fourth of July that year to first place at the end of the season. He received one last chance to manage the Holy Cross varsity in 1916, with his team compiling a 10-8 record.

In 1918, he rekindled his managing dreams by managing the minor league Newark Bears. In one game, despite his fifty-five years of age and rotund frame, he inserted himself as a pinch-hitter and singled, but was thrown out trying to stretch the hit to a double. During his time with Newark, he also helped develop a promising young right-handed pitcher named Eddie Rommel, who ultimately won more than 170 games in the major leagues, and would have won a lot more had he been able to strike out anyone.

It is unclear what if anything Mac did in 1919, but by the next year he had joined the scouting staff of the Boston Red Sox, then managed by Ed Barrow, in their first post–Babe Ruth year. Barrow, as will be seen, soon left to join Ruth in New York as a team executive, and Hugh Duffy succeeded Barrow as Sox manager for 1921. Mac scouted sporadically during this period, as he experienced poor health for much of the time.

Uncle Wilbert Robinson, Mac's old minor league teammate, also gave him a job coaching for the Brooklyn Dodgers. Mac may not have lasted the full year there, but he did coach Hall of Famer Zach Wheat and a young rookie named Casey Stengel. It did not hurt one to have his best friend Hugh Duffy as the Sox skipper, and Mac had been hired to scout for 1922, and perhaps also 1921, in the same organization as Sir Hugh.

Although Tommy McCarthy had suffered from double pneumonia during the winter and early spring of 1922, by May 31, the *Globe* reported that he "was feeling fine again and searching for a fast infielder for the Red Sox."

Chapter 17

Hugh Duffy's Long Goodbye

Milwaukee Brewers manager Hugh Duffy was sore and the more he thought about his team, the madder he became. His club had just come off losing the last three games in a series in Philadelphia in 1901, the inaugural year of the new American League.

It was not supposed to be this way. After Duffy and McCarthy assisted Connie Mack in establishing an AL franchise in Boston, Duffy became the manager of the Milwaukee entry in the new league. This managerial hiring may have been a payback for Duffy assisting Mack in the establishment of the Boston American League squad, as Mack had managed a Milwaukee minor league team in 1900. Since Duffy seemingly still had some baseball talent to exploit, hiring him as a player-manager was also a savvy move as it provided the Brewers with a legend who could still play ball.

Unlike gentlemen patrician managers like Frank Selee, Duffy, along with Connie Mack and John McGraw, were going to manage their squads with strict controls, and to the extent they had any team captains, they relegated captains to mere figureheads. Seven years before Boston Cardinal O'Connell surveyed his archdiocese and proclaimed, "The Puritan has passed, the Catholic remains," these forceful Irish-Catholic personalities had begun to change the rules for their co-religionists who aspired to become major league managers. New sheriffs were in town.

Problem was for Duffy, in his zeal to strip his old Beaneater team of its stars, he and Tommy McCarthy had helped form the core of the Boston American League dynasty in the making. Duffy must have privately fumed to see Jimmy Collins managing the emergent Red Sox to victory. Collins was a good man in Duffy's estimation — sober, Catholic and serious enough — but he had never coached a team, never mind managed one. And here he had erstwhile Beaneaters Chick Stahl and Buck Freeman (and from Cleveland, a rejuvenated Cy Young) challenging for the pennant, while Duffy made do with has-beens and never-will-bes.

Although he had helped stock the Boston American League team with quality former Beaneater players, Duffy could not alter the fact that his team possessed very little major league talent. Besides Duffy, the Brewers had Tommy McCarthy's old Brooklyn Bridegroom teammate, Honest John Anderson, still playing some outfield but mainly ensconcing himself at first base. Among the regulars, only Anderson and Duffy hit over .300 for the club that year.

Since Pink Hawley was one of the very few pitchers that held Duffy hitless in 1894, he received a last chance to redeem a largely disappointing major league career. The staff "ace," Bill Reidy, lost 20 games for the Brewers in 1901. Basically, Duffy had the talent of an expansion franchise at his disposal, but since the American League had just formed, everybody shared this issue.

Too kindly to rip his own players in print or scream at them in private, Sir Hugh generally did not take out his frustrations on them. He had a healthy enough self-image that he did not seriously blame himself for the misfortunes of his team, so he casted about for a scapegoat for the hapless predicament in

For years, it was assumed that this photograph was taken around the time Duffy began to manage the Milwaukee Brewers in 1901. It is now believed to have been shot in June 1907 at a benefit game for the family of the late Chick Stahl between the Red Sox and the Providence minor league team. In the center of this photograph is Hugh Duffy flanked on the left by Sox catcher Lou Criger and to the right by Tim Hurst. Boston Public Library, Print Department.

which he and his charges found themselves. It did not help matters that virtually all season the Brewers had to labor under persistent rumors that they were going to disband at season's end or move to St. Louis.

As Duffy had done throughout his ballplaying career, he did not venture far to find a reason for his shortcomings, since umpires had proved the bane of his existence virtually from the time that he began playing at Hartford in 1886. And Duffy, like many ballplayers and managers in turn-of-the-century baseball, disrespected an umpire named Al Manassau the most. Poor Al Manassau became the lightning rod for Duffy's anger.

If Hugh Duffy could not achieve supremacy for his team in the American League, then he and his charges wanted to make the life of Al Manassau miserable. Although Tim Murnane at the *Globe* counted Duffy as one of his best friends, even he found the constant riding of Manassau by Duff objectionable, stating as early as June 9, 1901, "The brewers [*sic*] finding the day lost, turned their attention to umpire Manassau. Capt. Duffy kept up a continual nagging of the official every time he passed him, for which he got as a rebuke, 'I want nothing to do with you.'"

On that occasion, the Brewers' Billy Gilbert, having already been tossed from the game, came back on the field and stomped on the umpire's foot, causing him to jump in the air in agony. Hugh Duffy did not seem to mind that this happened, and by his abuse of the umpire, at the least tacitly encouraged it to occur.

The Silver King scolded the team on this occasion and felt that even at that point they probably set out to get even with him for a previous offense, real or imagined. He also criticized some of Manassau's previous recent work, when he "had been altogether too arbitrary in putting people out of the game, as he did manager Manning in Chicago last week." For Murnane the matter was not complicated: Manassau had to perform his job better and the Brewers had to lay off the umpires. Neither Manassau nor the Brewers' players (or Manager Duffy) heeded these balanced observations.

In all fairness to the Brewers, Manassau had severe problems with other clubs as well. Only a week later, on July 16 in a game between Cleveland and Boston, "[b]ecause of several decisions a crowd followed Umpire Manassau after the game and pelted him with cushions and bottles, and it was only through the interference of the Cleveland players that he was not mobbed."

By the end of July, Duffy's fury grew as his team had reached a point of winning only about one out of every three games it played, and no salvation appeared on the horizon. His own players had not improved, and attempts to inject his team with youth and talent failed when he could not recruit promising youngsters from Beloit College and the University of Notre Dame, essentially because the players' parents did not want their sons joining such a hapless franchise.

Sir Hugh expressed his anger to the press by maintaining, "If this thing keeps up I will be fit for a loony farm. [To lose] the games by rank errors is enough to drive a man to drink." Inevitably, matters continued to gyrate rapidly out of control during the Brewers' 8–4 loss to Detroit in Milwaukee on August 6. On that occasion, "The spectators threw bottles at umpire Manassau and came near mobbing him. Duffy was put out of the game for disputing a decision." The proclivity of allegedly responsible people like Duff to escalate tensions with Manassau, together with league inactivity to address tensions, foreshadowed a cruel conclusion to this situation.

On August 8, the Brewers traveled to Cleveland and seemed poised to redeem themselves after their pummeling in Detroit. Leading 4–3 with two outs and two men on base in the ninth, the Brewers best pitcher, Bill Reidy, needed only to retire Detroit's good-hit/no-pitch pitcher, Jack Bracken, to seal the win. Bracken had different thoughts as he hit a pitch deep to left field along the foul line that Al Manassau called fair, which led to both men on base scoring and sealing Milwaukee's defeat.

The Brewers players came after Manassau, loudly protesting the call. Rather than moderating the conflict, Duffy went haywire, frantically scampering from his post in center field to Manassau "and after arguing a moment with [him] landed a right swing to the umpire's jaw." An estimated three hundred fans poured onto the field and a donnybrook erupted, involving at least these spectators and Brewers third baseman Bill Friel and shortstop Wid Conroy. Only the concerted efforts of the "Cleveland ballplayers, [Brewers] first baseman Anderson and the police prevented further trouble." Fortunately for Duffy, the local constabularies did not arrest him for his clear assault and battery on the poor umpire.

When Duffy met the press that evening, he lied about the incident, choosing to adopt a posture made famous by O.J. Simpson 105 years later by weakly maintaining that he did not assault and batter the umpire, but if he had, he would have "done it a different way." Absurdly, he claimed, "I did not hit Manassau, as I was trying to protect him, unless I did so by accident. It will go hard with me if Manassau reports that I struck him. We have lost 25 games by his worse than incompetent work. If such a man forces me to get out of the game I will quit it altogether."

Duff mistakenly threw a punch at an umpire and magnified his error by speaking to the press when silence should have dictated his actions. A large and hostile gathering of people had witnessed him battering Manassau, so it made little sense to maintain his innocence. Furthermore, he revealed his deep feelings of hostility to his victim by blaming him for 25 Brewers losses. By that point, most people in baseball had long evaluated Manassau's shortcomings, but had concluded that his decisions hurt all teams equally. The 25 losses? The buck stopped with Sir Hugh.

As the manager, Duffy ultimately bore the responsibility for his team's inability to win. While watching someone he detested make calls against his team frustrated him to no end, he did not assign blame to the right person, but rather goaded Manassau and set an example for his players and fans to similarly disrespect and abuse the ump. In the end, of course, Duffy ended up tucking it to himself.

Punishment came swiftly as Ban Johnson immediately banned the Brewers' manager. Upon further reflection, Johnson fined Duffy $50 and suspended him for ten days, stating, "It is the most serious offense I have had to deal with in my experience and I cannot understand how Duffy could so far forget himself. It is partly my own fault because I have not jacked him up short before when he had transgressed to a lesser extent."

Duffy's outburst did not even have the effect of firing up his team as they dropped ten out of its next twelve games. The Brewers were a poor team before Duffy lost his composure and they did not prosper without their manager and best player. Sadly, the punishment did not deter the other clubs' ballplayers such as Iron Man McGinnity or Frank Shugart from pummeling umpires they did not agree with.

The incident stands today as one of the worst blemishes on Duffy's reputation. He lost his head and committed a crime for which the justice system never punished him. Also, he revealed himself as a hothead while serving in a position where he needed to protect his players and maintain the dignity of his office. He lied about his involvement in the fiasco and did it in a fashion that particularly insulted the intelligence of his organization and the public. Finally, by blaming Manassau for his club's poor record, he merely highlighted his own worse than incompetent work.

After serving his suspension, he returned to managing three games at Boston to see his team swept, losing to old teammate Ted Lewis, the immortal George Winter and Cy Young, who shut the Brewers out. He could not hit a thing in this series, probably due to his lingering upset with the situation and his own lack of timing caused by his recent idleness.

One fun footnote emerged at the end of this season, in which Duffy eked out a .302 average for the year. He is the only player ever to retire with at least a .300 average in four separate major leagues: the National, American, American Association and Players' League.

Unfortunately for Duffy, his American League average constituted about the only fun thing that happened to him in 1901, as the Milwaukee Brewers lasted only one season, moving to St. Louis as the newest incarnation of the Browns. The old American Association "Browns" that Tommy McCarthy starred with had undergone a metamorphosis into the National League's future Cardinals. Either way, Brewers/Browns ownership had settled on Jimmy McAleer (later, one of Duffy's good friends) as the new manager, meaning a change had come. For his part, Duffy stayed in Wisconsin the next two years with another Milwaukee club, this one an entrant in the minor leagues. In that endeavor Duffy and his team met with success.

Although Duffy did not follow the team to St. Louis, he had fallen in love with Milwaukee and its fans, a not unrequited love as events transpired. In 1901, as an Irish-Catholic managing in what was then a heavily German-American town, he utilized his considerable personal charm and diplomacy to win over the local cranks. The fans fell for it, dubbing him "the Duffmeier."

In 1902 and 1903, the Duffmeier managed the Milwaukee minor league entry in the Western League to third- and first-place finishes, proving that a good manager becomes a great one if he has the personnel. More importantly, he gained experience as a manager and improved his marketability with his increased experience. It also displayed his business acumen, as he acquired a part ownership in the club and a long-term contract to manage it. One more note: Duffy always performed much better as a minor league manager or a major league coach/instructor than he did as a major league manager, a trend that began during this period.

Duffy's long-term contract to manage the Milwaukee minor league team prove short-lived, after the Philadelphia Phillies tabbed him as their new manager for 1904, replacing Chief Zimmer, who had left the cupboard relatively bare. As his first act as the new manager, Duffy subjected his team to a steamboat ride from Philly to Savannah, Georgia, during the gale season. No one enjoyed these excursions. On the way home, the entire team, save for six players with cast-iron stomachs, spent most of the time on the railings of the boat throwing up. Duffy felt so seasick that he did not even attempt eating on one of the days.

The papers commended Duffy for working the players harder than Chief Zimmer did, and he spent hours having the team practice their hitting, with an emphasis on bunting. The players lost several pounds of excess weight, but unfortunately the team had not improved itself much with any considerable infusion of talent, and thus struggled throughout the year. Although Duffy had endured a tempestuous year when he first managed in the majors with the Brewers, a gentler skipper emerged with the Phillies. Duffy paid careful note to publicly and privately praise his young players, and got the most that he could out of the meager talent pool at hand.

He had some pretty good young outfielders to mold, including the largely and unfairly forgotten Sherry Magee, but his pitching staff scared no one. In 1904, Duffy's first year at the helm, the team staggered to a last-place 52-100 record, but in 1905, with the addition of Kid Nichols (10 wins) and Togie Pittinger (23 victories, second in the league to Christy Mathewson) as pitchers, they came in fourth with an 83-69 mark.

It looked bright for the Phillies as the 1906 season commenced but the promise of the year before did not hold as the team failed to advance beyond fourth place, and they actually backtracked to 71-82. At the end of the campaign, Duffy found himself fired again.

Duffy shifted from managing the Phillies to co-owning the Providence minor league club from 1907–1909. The other owner was Fred Doe, chiefly credited today with being one of the prime movers behind the institution of Sunday baseball games. The two clashed over ownership philosophies, and Duffy ended up effectively muscling Doe out.

While Duffy ended his business relationship with Tommy McCarthy initially on bad terms prior to ultimately patching up hurt feelings, there is little to indicate that Duffy and Doe ever spoke to each other again. If they did, the friendship between them had certainly ended.

As Duffy's relationship with Doe waned, another opportunity to manage arose in 1910, this time extended by Duffy's old friend Charlie Comiskey, now the owner of the Chicago American baseball club. As so often occurred in Duffy's managerial career, he jumped on the chance to manage again either just after the team's fortunes shifted for the worse or long before they eventually improved.

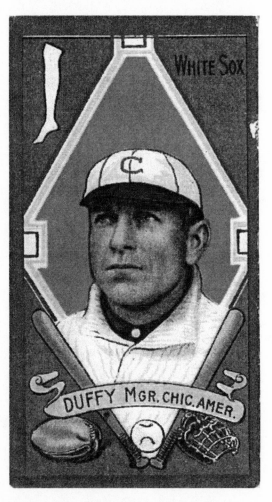

Duffy had some very good pitchers to work with in Ed Walsh, Frank Smith and Doc White (the latter from Georgetown University fame), but he also had a roster containing one of the weakest hitting set of regulars in baseball history. Chick Gandil of *Eight Men Out* infamy played on that team and either would not or did not choose to hit, leading Duffy to dump him. Only infielder Hal Lord batted over .248.

In retrospect, the crucible upon which Duffy chose to make or break his fortunes with the White Sox was an old Providence player he once controlled,

Hugh Duffy as manager of the Chicago White Sox. Although he worked for his old friend Charlie Comiskey, Duffy found that Commy's wish to win one more championship superseded any loyalty for old friends. Collection of Donald Hubbard.

shortstop Lena Blackburne. Everyone wanted Blackburne but Comiskey parted with either ten thousand dollars or lesser money and one or two players to obtain his services from Duffy's old Providence franchise. Commy did not like to part with money, but bidding wars had erupted in the major leagues, with Pittsburgh Pirates owner Barney Dreyfuss throwing a then-incredible $22,500 at pitcher Martin O'Toole around this time.

Commy liked spending money even less when Duffy's protégé proved to be a complete bust. Lena never hit the ball, and for a couple of years it appears that the White Sox suspended him. Had Blackburne played in the 1950s or 1960s, he would be the type of guy whose baseball card one kept getting instead of the coveted Willie Mays, Sandy Koufax or Mickey Mantle card. Blackburne's one minor claim to fame is that he developed a "rubbing mud" used to take the shine off of baseballs without otherwise affecting them.

No one liked shiny new baseballs out of the box, particularly the pitchers and fielders who had to grip them. Blackburne apparently found the perfect Delaware mud to rub over the balls and make them fit for professional use. Blackburne's ingenuity did nothing for his manager and mentor in 1910, though, because Duffy had sold Comiskey on two things: One, the team needed to be rebuilt on youth and, two, money had to be spent on good players. Comiskey wanted a pennant without laying out much dough, and Blackburne's bust flied in the face of those aims.

While Blackburne's career stalled in Mudville, pitcher Doc White co-wrote a song with Ring Lardner called, "Little Puff of Smoke, Good Night," which a Miss Mayhew sung at the American Music Hall, an event many of the Sox witnessed. White then hatched plans to go on a vaudeville tour in the off-season as part of a quartet with other big leaguers, namely Addie Joss, Artie Hofman and Jimmie Sheckerd. Ed Walsh caught the bug as well and investigated whether interest existed for his own theatre aspirations.

Duffy, for his part, only sang the blues as he commenced the 1911 campaign on life support. In March, Comiskey delivered the kiss of death by trumpeting, "Why, Duffy is going to win the pennant this year and you haven't heard of me letting a winner go.... Now I have been satisfied with Duffy. I know what he was up against last year." Maybe so, but Chicago obtained ambitious outfielder Jimmy Callahan (a former manager who had not played ball for years), and the rumors circulated that unless the White Sox dramatically improved, Callahan had a right of refusal on the manager's job.

After a very frustrating 1910 season, Duffy resuscitated the team in 1911 to a better than .500 record, moving his team from sixth to fourth in the standings and winning nine more games. Late in the season, Comiskey waxed about how he wanted to win one more pennant before he died and again denied rumors of Duffy's demise, but after the 1911 campaign ended, Comiskey had seen enough and fired his old Chicago Players' League teammate. Duffy never forgave Comiskey for this slight, but in all fairness to "Commy," Duffy's bottom line as a team skipper never approximated the stature he achieved as an active player.

As often happened after a negative experience, Duffy returned to Milwaukee, where he managed the minor league team for one year. Although Duffy often recharged his batteries in that great midwestern city, he and his wife were first and foremost New Englanders, and since they lived most of their married life with his in-laws, he ultimately had to chart a way to return there.

What Duffy lacked as a manager, he made up for as a businessman, and from 1913–1916 he gained an ownership interest in the Portland, Maine, minor league team. More than a quarter of a century had elapsed since Duffy led his Lowell team past the Portlands in their league championship. That was Sir Hugh's last stop before joining the Chicago Colts, and now he led a Portland squad on his own.

The Portland team that Duffy managed and at least co-owned constituted part of the New England League with its commissioner none other than the Silver King, Tim Murnane. Nicknamed the Portland Duffs after its leader, the club finished second in the league race to the Lowell entry, a reversal in the standings in the penultimate 1887 race.

Duffy led his team to a third-place finish in 1914 and then the next year the Duffs took the pennant outright. However, after that year the New England League ceased to exist, so Murnane organized a new Eastern League, whose owners and representatives met in April 1916 to formulate the rules and other matters pertaining to the new entity. Hugh Duffy represented his Portland club and met up with Sliding Billy Hamilton, who appeared on behalf of the Worcester squad. Duff's team led in the league race for most of the season before giving up the top slot in the final weeks.

By the end of the 1916 season, Duffy had decided to take his team out of Portland and requested and received unanimous league approval to relocate outside of his old Maine location. But rather than pack up his balls and bats and seek a new venue for his minor league team, Duffy learned that Fred Mitchell had decided to leave his coaching post at Harvard. At the very last second, Duffy submitted his application to coach there. He got the job and Mel Webb, a protégé of Tim Murnane's at the *Boston Globe*, wrote a very long column lionizing Sir Hugh and his many accomplishments both on the field and as a very successful manager of the Portland teams. Upon his appointment as the Harvard skipper, Duffy sold out his interests in the Portland club.

Around this time, he also received an offer to scout for the Boston Red Sox, a natural position to have since presumably Duffy had the opportunity to observe the best collegiate ballplayers on the East Coast. He signed on with the Sox for three years, from 1917 through 1919. The Sox continued their dominant play through their famous 1918 pennant, but had begun the irreversible decline in fortunes under notorious team owner Harry Frazee by the next campaign.

Through little fault of Duffy's, the Harvard nine did not thrive during his tenure there. As America had just entered World War I, many Harvardians, ballplayers included, signed up to fight in the war. Duffy's men preferred the aviation corps, as his team basically wasted away on him. He had no team to coach other than on a very informal level in 1917, with only a slight rebound in personnel in 1918.

With the war's end in the fall of 1918, Duffy fielded a team for the spring of 1919, but they met with very little success on the diamond, despite the fact that he coached seven of his hitters to .300 or better averages. After that season, it became confusing. Supposedly, Harvard offered Duffy a new contract for 1920, but then it appears as if the university actively recruited a new manager, with Jack Slattery hired as the next Harvard skipper. By all appearances, Duffy had been fired. Luckily, he did not stay inactive for long, because in December 1919, the Toronto minor league club named him as its manager for the next season.

Chapter 18

Final Days

Tim Murnane spent much of the day on February 7, 1917, in fairly typical fashion, working until 7:00 P.M. at the *Globe*, bolting down a quick dinner and then striding hurriedly to the Shubert Theater to meet his wife to cap the day off with a show. Once inside, he stood by the coat-checking window as his wife went to powder her nose for a few minutes. When she returned, a crowd had gathered around the motionless prostrate figure of her husband sprawled on the floor. A priest was summonsed from a church nearby, but he arrived too late to administer the last rites of the Catholic Church to Murnane. The Silver King had died.

Hugh Duffy had just seen him a few nights earlier when he had accompanied Murnane, Fred Tenney and Red Sox owner Harry Frazee to a Knights of Columbus smoker in Brockton during a blizzard. It was a typical hot stove gathering of the war years. Murnane loved to speak at such events, and relished the company of his friends in the sports world and fans alike. Eulogizing him in the press, Duffy stated, "Tim Murnane was the best friend I ever had.... In the many years we had been associated, I had learned what an entirely lovable character he possessed."

Hugh Duffy's real best friend, Tommy McCarthy, echoed these sentiments, harking back to his first memories of Murnane chasing down Ross Barnes and organizing the Boston Unions, reminiscing that "we have always been close friends.... No player ever did so much for the National game."

The Silver King's funeral Mass was the social event of the year in Boston. Cardinal O'Connell made an appearance along with a platoon of priests, including a relative of Murnane. Honey Fitz and Mayor Curley showed up and pretended not to hate each other for a day. All types of newspapermen logged in to pay their final respects to a writer whose achievements surpassed all of them, but who always had the class not to say so. Of course, Duffy and McCarthy came into church and each dipped his right hand into the holy water font and made the sign of the cross before walking down the aisle, genuflecting, and taking a seat at the pew, kneeling to say a prayer for their old friend. In the Catholic Church there is a cherished doctrine that the living pray for the dead, and the saved form a communion of saints, who pray for the living. Mac and Duffy prayed for old Tim Murnane, and they believed that Tim in turn tried to intercede on their behalf with God. Some things never change.

But some things do. Duffy and McCarthy were no longer the most prominent sports in attendance. Looming over both of them, as he took his seat in the church, knelt George Herman Ruth, commonly nicknamed "the Babe." Murnane's last column did not mention the Heavenly Twins, but it did pay homage to the Red Sox's star left-handed pitcher, a resident of nearby Sudbury.

Obviously the passing of Murnane hurt Duffy and McCarthy on a personal level, but it seemed to affect Mac more. Sir Hugh had figured out how to make money and position himself in such a way to ingratiate himself with an employer or a powerful person, but Mac never cultivated this talent. He relied upon the Silver King to periodically tout him in his columns to try to get his old Union Association outfielder some work.

Tim Murnane died shortly after this photograph of him was taken, but in his long life he played ball, wrote millions of words of peerless newspaper copy and acted as the conscience of baseball. He also claimed to have discovered Hugh Duffy and Tommy McCarthy and no one argued with him on those points. National Baseball Hall of Fame Library, Cooperstown, N.Y.

Fortuitously for Mac, after the Red Sox let Barrow go, they cast about for a new manager, and in November of 1920, they announced the hiring of the other Heavenly Twin, Hugh Duffy, as their new skipper. Duffy's latest foray into managing constituted his fourth attempt at leading a team decidedly down on its luck. Everyone knows the story of how Red Sox owner Harry Frazee sold Babe Ruth to the New York Yankees supposedly to ensure financing for his Broadway show, *No, No, Nanette*. What is less covered but also important is the dumping of talented Red Sox players other than Ruth to the Yankees. By the time Duffy took the helm of the team in 1921, the Red Sox were, like the Kansas City Athletics of the 1950s, essentially a minor league feeder team for the Bronx Bombers.

For instance, after Duffy's hire and before the 1921 season even began, the Sox had traded away talented right-handed pitcher and future Hall of Famer Waite Hoyt to the Yankees along with star outfielder Wally Schang and a couple of other players for Muddy Ruel, Del Pratt, Sammy Vick and Hank Thormahlen. Ruel turned into a pretty good catcher, albeit after the Sox got rid of him two years later, and Pratt was a decent infielder and hitter, but the trade still stunk.

The keys to the trade were Waite Hoyt and Hank Thormahlen. Hoyt's career path was on a strictly upward trajectory while Thormahlen's once-promising career had begun to fizzle the year before. Boston management touted Thormahlen as a sleeper who might surprise people, but he never again surprised hitters with his repertoire as he went 1–7 while he pitched for Boston. Hugh Duffy started his tenure with his new team at a competitive disadvantage with the Yankees, a team that kept gypping Frazee on his deals for players.

In retrospect, Duffy undertook a huge fool's errand, but he may have rightfully analyzed the situation quite differently. The Sox had been baseball's dominant club since the turn of the century and had won the World Series as recently as 1918. Losing Ruth was massive, but the Red Sox had replaced aging stars like Cy Young or lost superstars like Tris Speaker in the past and always rebounded. And Duffy may not have been fully aware of just how bad an owner Frazee was, or at least not have appreciated the depths of his financial plight.

Still, warning signs abounded along the road. Duffy had to shuttle back and forth to New York to meet Frazee at his offices there, a peculiar place to meet the owner of a Boston franchise. Also, the Sox hired Jimmy Burke, the Brown's ex-manager, and it appeared as if Duffy had a co-manager helping him run the team.

Even if Duffy wanted to be the manager of the Red Sox in the worst way, he could not have missed the import of these decisions by Frazee. Decades before the Chicago Cubs and their owner Phil Wrigley instituted a brief and disastrous college of coaches experiment, where managers rotated throughout the season, Frazee teetered on the cutting edge of a truly horrendous idea.

Nevertheless, hope sprang eternal as the Red Sox fans and assorted celebrities saw Hugh Duffy's train off from Boston in early March 1922 for the team's spring training site in Hot Springs, Arkansas. Among the dignitaries was Tommy McCarthy, who reportedly "fairly hugged Hughey as the Sox manager passed through the gate to the train."

As stated earlier, in May, Tommy McCarthy apparently had recovered from pneumonia and intended to search for quick infielders, a fact that did not augur well for Joe Dugan's future with the Red Sox. Dugan had been picked up in the off-season in a deal with Philadelphia, and Duffy had tried to convert this promising ballplayer into a shortstop, contrary to his natural inclination to play third base. Dugan hit well for the Sox, but apparently vocally expressed a desire to play in New York.

In mid–July, Dugan got his wish, as Frazee made another one of his idiot deals with the Yankees, swapping Dugan for $50,000 and a gaggle of worthless ballplayers. Maybe Dugan was unhappy playing shortstop for a poor team, but the Sox should have traded him to a team that was not on the verge of domi-nating the American League and could potentially ensure a return of one or more players of equal value. Instead, Frazee further dismantled his club and handed the Yankees another young phenom.

Tommy McCarthy never did sign a superstar infielder for the Sox because soon after the *Globe* ran its hopeful update on his condition, his physician diag-nosed him with cancer. On August 5, 1922, surrounded by his three adoring daughters in their home on Columbia Road in St. Peter's Parish in Dorchester, Tommy McCarthy died. The official cause of death was carcinoma of the intes-tine, with a secondary cause of death of abscess of the lung, post-pneumonic. Carcinoma of the intestine is often associated with chronic alcoholism, and while we do not know for certain that Tommy McCarthy died due to sustained alcohol abuse, it is the author's opinion that he did.

Hugh Duffy raced back to honor his best friend, who had his funeral Mass celebrated at St. Peter's Parish, after which he was buried next to his wife in the family plot at Old Cavalry Cemetery in Roslindale, Massachusetts. A sad Duffy served with Jack Dooley as one of Mac's pallbearers as hundreds of Mac's friends came out to his funeral. Duffy had lost the best friend he ever had.

Shortly thereafter, the Sox staged a benefit game for McCarthy's estate at Fenway Park between the Sox and a collection of major league "all-stars" assem-bled for the event. Originally it had been planned to help Mac during his sick-ness, but now it turned into his valediction. Babe Ruth failed to show but the all-star team fielded a woman baseball player, Lizzie Murphy, and Jack Kennedy's grandfather, Honey Fitz Fitzgerald, sang "Sweet Adeline," his sig-nature song for the crowd. Old ballplayers such as Wilbert Robinson and Ty Cobb wrote checks and Mac's three daughters received the proceeds.

The McCarthy benefit was one of the few worthwhile events that occurred at Fenway Park that summer, as the Red Sox wheezed to a 75-79, fifth-place finish. In December of 1922, Harry Frazee gave Hugh Duffy an early Christ-mas present by firing him as the manager of the Red Sox, installing Frank Chance of Tinkers to Evers to Chance fame. As the estimable Fred Lieb noted, "[t]he 1922 season finished Hughie Duffy as manager: his 'crime' was that he tumbled into the cellar with the humpty dumpties Frazee turned over to him."

After suffering through two campaigns with a badly depleted roster, Frazee deemed Duffy expendable, although ironically Duffy had one more year to run on his contract. Frazee kept him on the team payroll for the next year as scout and general girl Friday.

In the midst of his housecleaning, Frazee sent another future Hall of Famer pitcher, Herb Pennock, to the Yankees in another bonehead trade that further decimated the Red Sox. Although Duffy's managerial stint did not pan, he not only continued to work for the Red Sox in 1923, but kept working for them for more than thirty years thereafter. Having lost his two favorite companions in Tim Murnane and Tommy McCarthy, Duffy made a new best friend that would remain with him forever: the Boston Red Sox.

And his new best friend often tried Sir Hugh's patience the most. Hugh Duffy lived long enough to witness the collapse of Jim Crow in major league baseball's ban of African-Americans, with the advent of Jackie Robinson starting at second base with the Brooklyn Dodgers.

By way of a historical footnote, before Jackie Robinson met Branch Rickey and began to plan for his debut with the Dodgers, he actually participated with two other African American players in a tryout with the Boston Red Sox in 1945, and none other than Hugh Duffy ran the audition. Reality is not so glorious, as the Red Sox front office only begrudgingly granted the audition in the midst of political pressure from city councilor Isidor Muchnick and famed Boston sportswriter Colonel Dave Egan.

A common misconception is that the city of Boston at the end of World War II had no tolerance for the presence of anything but lily-white players on its two major league teams' rosters; this is simply untrue. Thirty years later, when court-ordered busing came to the city schools, rioting did break out, principally in the Caucasian neighborhoods. But this sense of racial hostility did not exist anything to this level as the Second World War concluded.

It should be noted that the Boston Braves, the lineal heirs of the old Beaneaters, desegregated early, and Sam Jethroe earned Rookie of the Year honors in 1950.

It was the front office of the Boston Red Sox that did its level best to keep African American players out of Fenway Park, a feat that succeeded until 1959, when the team finally desegregated with the arrival of Pumpsie Green. It started from the top with owner Tom Yawkey, but there were many other executives of the team, principally Joe Cronin and Eddie Collins, who supported this unctuous policy. Richard A. Johnson has termed the relationship between and amongst the purported Boston Red Sox brain trust of this period as "Croney Island," a group cattled into a groupthink mentality that could not conceive of African American ballplayers playing for the team.

When the Red Sox's hands were forced in 1945, the tryout was a farce. Duffy ran it and a few people watched. There is varying accounts of what happened but the most probable scenario is that a very standard tryout of Negro League stars Robinson, Sam Jethroe and Marvin Williams occurred and that they were told at the end to fill out forms.

The charade ended there. Jackie Robinson harbored resentment against Yawkey and Cronin for as long as he lived, although he did not seem to have any strong feelings one way or the other about Duffy, who probably seemed to him to be a genial figurehead.

There are also conflicting accounts of what Duffy said and did thereafter. One has him urging the Sox to sign this unbelievable talent, Jackie Robinson. Boston's African American paper, the *Guardian*, felt that Duffy sincerely wished to see the odious racial barrier broken. He spoke to the paper and expressed that he was "highly impressed with the trio of colored ball players...." Gushed Duffy, they were "[g]ood boys ... hustlers. We were glad to give them a tryout. They're the same as anybody else.... Got a soul same as I have. Deserve the same chance as anybody."

While team general manager Eddie Collins veiled himself in silence, the *Guardian* felt that Duffy and [coach] Larry Woodall "more or less put their okay on colored players this week." While the *Guardian's* sports editor felt that Duffy was sincere, he did express skepticism concerning the devotion of other Sox officials for desegregation, a well-conceived feeling as events transpired.

Boston Braves president Bob Quinn had predicted years before this tryout that Jim Crow's days were numbered. The Braves jumped on the bandwagon once the Dodgers and Jackie Robinson smashed desegregation forever, but the Red Sox remained opposed to the whole concept of equality. It was ironic, of course, because in their pursuit of racial inequality, their team slid into a separate and unequal existence of their own. As the other franchises desegregated, the Sox continued their bigotry and wooden-headedness to place themselves at a competitive disadvantage by refusing to fill their rosters with African-American stars. Richard A. Johnson has convincingly maintained that it was "the Curse of Jackie Robinson," and not the mythological "Curse of the Bambino," that kept the Red Sox away from winning a World Series between 1918 and 2004.

At that time in Boston the "Big Four" stars were Ted Williams, Johnny Pesky, Dom DiMaggio and Bobby Doerr, and a better group of players to assist Robinson or another African-American in desegregating baseball did not exist. At his induction into the Baseball Hall of Fame, Ted Williams famously called for the admission of African-American stars into the hall, and he would have ensured that his teammates felt likewise. Dom DiMaggio and Bobby Doerr, as thoroughly honorable men, would have followed suit and Johnny Pesky would have led the crusade. Sixty years after the fact, Pesky still talked passionately of his deep respect for Robinson as a ballplayer and an educated and classy man. He would have very verbally checked any of his teammates who thought otherwise, if only the team brain trust had given him the chance.

Likewise, it is doubtful that Duffy harbored any bias toward others, as he was a gentle soul unless provoked by umpires. It is also true that after Jackie Robinson tried out, Duffy did not go on a public crusade in the press demanding that his team break the Jim Crow restrictions. In an age when even one of Jackie Robinson's own managers with the Dodgers initially questioned Branch Rickey as to whether African-Americans were even human beings, Duffy saw all God's children as endowed with a soul, all equal in the eyes of God. He may have broken the racist barrier and brought Jackie Robinson and World Series' victories if he served as the Sox general manager in 1945, but he did not and a sad legacy crippled the Sox for decades to come.

Remember, too, that Duffy suffered to a much lesser extent than any African-American, but still suffered from the prejudice of Cap Anson, one of the men most responsible for segregation in baseball. For this reason alone, Duffy had reason to distance himself from the legacy of Cap Anson. If Anson advocated strongly for something, it had to be wrong, in the mind of Hugh Duffy.

While the Red Sox did not embrace Jackie Robinson, they did continue to employ Sir Hugh as a scout and instructor for the team. In 1943, a rookie named Sam Mele came up to the team with the daunting task of patrolling the

Hugh Duffy could charm the snakes out of the ground. Although Red Sox pitching star Lefty Grove had a reputation as being sullen, in this picture taken circa 1940, he beams in the presence of the much-older Duffy. National Baseball Hall of Fame Library, Cooperstown, N.Y.

outfield with entrenched legends Ted Williams and Dom DiMaggio. Sixty-four years after meeting Duffy, Mele remembered with striking clarity the instruction he received both in batting and hitting.

Approaching his 80th birthday in 1943, Duffy taught Mele and other Sox youngsters the fine art of batting, stressing "contact, contact, contact!" This philosophy probably accounted for Duffy's relatively low amount of walks, when juxtaposed to someone in his own time period and his height, Billy Hamilton, who walked much of the time. He also inculcated in them the proper mechanics in tracking down a ball in the outfield to the right, left and, most dangerously, behind them. Always patient and encouraging, Duffy conveyed both his love of the game and his life-long pursuit of getting the edge over the other players. Mele felt that Duffy was the Johnny Pesky of the mid-twentieth century Sox, a beloved figure who continued to inspire Sox players and fans to love the game and improve one's level of play.

Johnny Pesky recalled that just before he shipped off with the navy in World War II, he saw Duffy walking around Fenway Park with his little bat, convinced that this older man had to have been at least 100 years old. He further remembers how Duffy and Williams used to talk at length with each other and what a humorous pair they made walking around together, with Williams at about 6' 3" in height and Duffy about nine inches shorter. Williams would ask him about the pitchers of his era and Duffy would regale him with tales of Kid Nichols and Cy Young.

Duffy also wore his heart on his sleeve regarding his view of the world and it was well known that he was a daily communicant in church. When told about Duffy's earlier exploits and temper, Pesky remarked that by the time he met him, Duffy "must have done a 180" because there was no more decent and fine person by that time then Hugh Duffy, a man who was unfailingly polite to everyone and never drank, swore or smoked. When informed that Sam Mele had equated Pesky with Duffy, Johnny Pesky was deeply touched and honored.

Not only did Duff continue to instruct young ballplayers, he also served as a scout and signed many East Coast ballplayers for the team. For years, he ran a school for local players in which he coached them in baseballology while simultaneously winnowing down the list of potential Sox signees.

Above all else, Hugh Duffy was a gifted teacher. With the Red Sox and with Boston College and Harvard, he taught in a kind and patient manner, teaching young men to improve their skills on the ball field while leading by his own peerless example in how to act like a gentleman. Because he had to work in mills at a young age, like most youngsters in America in the nineteenth century, he never acquired a diploma or a degree that licensed him to teach school to people in their late teens or early twenties, so he taught baseball.

One of his most attentive students, Ted Williams, loved Hugh Duffy. While Williams scientifically broke down pitchers, pitches, strike zones and all types of mechanical minutiae, Duffy also favored keeping it simple. However, baseball's greatest hitter, Williams, inevitably gravitated to Duffy, the player with the highest single-season baseball average. Duffy kept Williams' temperament in check with constant encouragement and talked with him extensively, once quipping that Teddy Ballgame always talked hitting with him, adding "that was all he ever wanted to talk about." The keep-it-simple philosophy of Duffy in many ways was an act. Duffy disguised his true nature that kept him talking in the off-season with Tommy McCarthy in taking advantage of a rule to implement a new tactic and which also impelled him to listen to Williams in his pursuit of batting excellence.

In point of fact, Duffy never lost his desire to become a better batter, even as he approached his 90th birthday. For exercise, he swung a bat several times every day on his porch at his home in the Brighton section of Boston. After all, he never knew when he might be needed to pinch-hit again. He professed a desire to live to 100 years old, at which time he wanted friends to throw a "beer party" for him.

Duffy continued to work for the Red Sox until he became severely ill during the summer of 1954. Ted Williams went to Duffy's house on four separate occasions during this period to visit him, gestures that Sir Hugh must have cherished. It is difficult to believe that old friends like Jack Dooley also did not stop by as well as various nieces and nephews, as his condition worsened.

On October 19, 1954, Hugh Duffy literally became a Heavenly Twin when he met up again with Tommy McCarthy.

Chapter 19

Where There's a Will
There's a Way

Pensively, Michael Bowlby reviewed the few items of mail awaiting him when he arrived home. Waiting for him at the bottom of the stack was a catalog from Leland's, an auction house in New York that took celebrity memorabilia, primarily sports-related, on consignment for auction.

Leland's knew how to market their product. Page after page of colorful advertisements for signed baseballs, old team pennants, uniforms of old ballplayers and various other sundries unfolded for the sports memorabilia enthusiast, of which Bowlby considered himself to be.

The other mail could wait. Bowlby pretended not to be impressed, but in reality he could be a kid again, thumbing through the colorful catalog while grabbing a late supper. Earnestly he scanned the merchandise and the historical comments accompanying each item. Most of the commentary contained information and trivia that he already knew, but he voraciously digested its contents as if he had never read them.

Bowlby had just ended a rather typical day at work. As a title examiner in some of the local Registries of Deeds, he pored through hundreds of old papers every day in detail in order to prepare a title report for the attorneys who hired him. In order to make a living, Bowlby not only had to thoroughly review each title, but also had to prepare several title reports each day. He read with extremely poor eyesight, corrected by powerful contact lenses. He could be excused if his head spun at the end of the day, although generally it did not.

One of the perks of the job, besides being able to dress as he wished, was to indulge his passion for sports by occasionally going down to the Registry of Probate in each county and pulling old legal documents prepared for ancient ballplayers, usually their last will and testament, and gazing upon their signatures. For a brief moment the players came alive for him, an added dimension to reading about them or looking up their statistics in an encyclopedia. He had seen and held a number of documents signed by famous ballplayers, including the immortal Babe Ruth.

Whenever he finished finding his treasure and inspecting it, he carefully returned it to its file and returned the file to the clerk who had retrieved it for him. Like a fine museum piece, Bowlby greatly respected artifacts of the past. However, he never purchased an item in a Leland's auction, and since he had shifted his memorabilia collecting interests largely to Civil War items, he briefly wondered how he got on their mailing list.

Laconically, he thumbed through the Leland's catalog until he locked onto an advertisement, on page 22, for a probate document of the Suffolk County, Massachusetts, Court. It featured an item purporting to be the return of service in the estate of Abbie Wright, which contained the signature of her husband, the legendary George Wright.

As an avid baseball fan and historian, George Wright proved no stranger to Bowlby. Indeed, during one of his free moments at the Suffolk Registry of Deeds, Bowlby had requested some of the probate documents that contained the signatures. Periodically he checked on them, like a particularly appealing museum exhibit, and then returned to the more mundane tasks that awaited him. Years ago he had even seen George Wright's autograph on one of the probate documents. It was the best museum in the world; it was free and, best of all, no one told Bowlby when it was time to go.

During one visit, Bowlby had again requested some of the ballplayers' documents, and noticed that the wills he had once seen there had disappeared without a trace. As disgusted as he felt at the time, he did not report the absence of the wills. He simply felt that someone had stolen them, but that he could do nothing about it. How could they ever find the thief?

Abruptly, he changed his tune when he saw the Wright document in the Leland's catalog. A surge of white-hot anger telegraphed its way through Bowlby's body. "This is stolen!" he exclaimed to himself. He instantaneously knew what had happened to at least one of the papers he had sought.

He pointed out the display ad of the Wright document to his wife and related his theory about it to her. When his wife asked why he thought so, he pointed out that this document had been filed with the Suffolk Registry of Probate.

Bowlby pulled out his blue felt marker and started putting his considerable alarm about this matter on a yellow sheet of foolscap. One of the lawyers he knew called this the Bowlby Blue. In meticulously neat handwriting, which actually resembled printing, Bowlby composed a letter in one draft the next day to the Register of Deeds of Suffolk County, Rich Iannella, whom he had never met. Dated October 21, 1998, Bowlby wrote:

> I have been a title examiner for many years in Suffolk and Middlesex Counties. I received this auction catalog [which he mailed with the letter] this week and noticed one of the lots appears to be a probate citation that was stolen from

Suffolk Probate. I am assuming it was from Suffolk as George Wright died in Boston in 1937 (He is a baseball Hall of Famer). I know you have the authority to pursue the recovery of this document and hopefully find out who consigned it so you can instigate legal action. I personally had discovered that several wills and other documents were missing from other probates of baseball hall of famers, including Mr. Wright, documents I had viewed years ago. If I can be of assistance, please contact me.

Bowlby wanted Rich Iannella to see his letter immediately. He carefully placed the letter and Leland's catalog in a package, and requested that someone in his title company assigned to work in Suffolk County deliver it to Iannella that day.

He had never done anything like this, but then again, who had? It was whistle blowing, but the subject matter of his report, the theft of wills, seemed so creepy. Bowlby hoped that someone would pay the proper attention to this matter to ensure that this missing document, presumed stolen, might someday return to its rightful place in the public archives. He hoped that this matter would not fall between the cracks. He had a feeling that it would not.

Technically speaking, every single one of the hundreds of letters and packages of mail received by the Suffolk County Registry of Probate in Boston theoretically was delivered to and seen by its register, Rich Iannella. Indeed, many old-timers still addressed every piece of their correspondence directly to him, knowing full well that a subordinate would open it and attend to it without it going further. At some quaint time in Massachusetts history, perhaps the register did review every piece of correspondence, although those days were long since past.

Like all of his immediate predecessors, Iannella had already devised a system so that assistants opened the mail and directed it to the appropriate department. Fittingly, only letters from key members of the executive and legislative branches of the Massachusetts government, or personal letters, generally came directly to his attention.

Early on the morning of Monday, October 26, 1998, Iannella received a letter attached to a rather large and colorful catalog. It contained Michael Bowlby's correspondence, hand-delivered by someone from his office so that only Iannella could review its contents. Bowlby felt that it demanded Iannella's immediate attention and also believed the issues raised were just too unusual and serious for anyone else in the office to address.

Incredulously, Iannella followed the path of Bowlby's writing. In one short page, Iannella knew that the concerns raised did not emanate from a crackpot. He jumped his way through Leland's catalog to the twenty-second page to the Wright papers, and nearly flipped out. No way the probate department would ever let a document like that outside of its vault. Within minutes of starting the letter, Iannella knew that something seriously wrong had occurred.

Iannella went right to work on the case. He ran down the hall to the office of his director of community outreach, Bob Kavin, an authority on the authenticity of documents that he had developed during his work for years in the city council offices at city hall. Kavin had even worked for Iannella's father for twenty-two years, and Rich trusted him and valued his judgment.

Iannella shoved the Leland's catalog, open to page 22, at Kavin and said, "Come take a look at this thing! Is it real?" Kavin grabbed the catalog, looked at the purported Wright document and without hesitation exclaimed, "That's one of ours!" Iannella asked, "How can you be sure?"

Like Sherlock Holmes to Iannella's Watson, Kavin patiently provided him with the solution, which once explained, seemed so painfully obvious. He marched down the hall of the probate court offices and took out an old probate index and found the Abbie Wright estate information. He then took a magnifying glass and carefully scanned the picture of the Abbie Wright return of service in the Leland's catalog. They matched. Kavin explained that just by looking at the exhibit, he noticed a return with clerk's handwriting in the upper left area of the document. He also pointed out tiny red notations on its face, something typically placed inadvertently on a will by a clerk reviewing it line by line before filing it away.

Kavin also hypothesized that either a lawyer or court officer swiped the document. Kavin countered the skepticism that he met in Iannella's eyes with solid logic. While anyone from the general public might take a will that a celebrity had signed, only a person sophisticated in probate law and procedure would know that probate documents of a relative might also be signed by that celebrity in his or her capacity as executor or heir. Iannella nodded, secure that he had come to the right person about this matter.

Iannella knew what to do next. He placed a telephone call to the chief justice of the Massachusetts Probate Court, the Honorable Sean Dunphy, and detailed the matters that had just reached his attention. Iannella had already decided he needed to take a trip down to New York to the Leland's Auction House at East 22nd Street to view the purported Wright document, and if it proved authentic, to take appropriate steps to return it to Boston.

Iannella felt so strongly about this matter that while he requested authorization from Judge Dunphy for the payment of his expenses for the trip, he made it clear that he would pay the whole freight for the investigation if he had to. Dunphy appreciated Iannella's dedication to the matter, but assured him that his expenses would be reimbursed in full and wished him luck. Iannella spent most of the rest of the day arranging an investigation that no one knew how to conduct, since nothing like this had ever happened to anyone's knowledge. Still, he solicited advice from all quarters.

He placed a call to District Attorney Ralph Martin. Convoluted conspiracies and malicious murders were one thing, but Martin had heard of nothing like what Rich Iannella described. This was just plain weird. He too wished Iannella well and asked him to contact him upon his return. While he sympathized with Iannella, this matter had to be handled exclusively by the Register of Probate's office. At least for now.

Iannella called Kavin, a veteran of Boston political wars and the internal and internecine battles within city hall, and asked him to accompany him to New York in an effort to retrieve the Wright document. Iannella felt that he needed Kavin to take an actual peek at the original document in order to authenticate it before he demanded its return to Boston. Plus, he felt that he might need a corroborating witness to the events about to transpire.

Nervously, Iannella then placed a call to Leland's. He held himself out as a sports enthusiast, and requested an appointment for a private viewing of the Wright document. Iannella picked up what he thought was a typical New York attitude when the Leland's representative said, "Can't you just read what's in the book?"

Deflecting this comment, Iannella pressed for the appointment for the private viewing. Perhaps by now the Leland's representative felt that Iannella was displaying a typical Bostonian attitude. Nonetheless, they set the appointment up at the Leland's Auction House.

His adrenaline really pumping now, Iannella sketched out the trip in his mind. He did not see the trip as a glorified junket because he did not want to see the Big Apple all that much. As a life-long resident of Boston, he felt that his city contained most of what he needed in a major city, and if he was to take a vacation, he much preferred to retreat to somewhere sunny like Florida or Cape Cod.

Nonetheless, he packed that evening for his flight to New York the next day. He packed lightly, but remembered to bring a letter that Kavin had drafted for him to Michael Heffner, the managing director of Leland's, in which he would reveal the true nature of his trip and demand the return of the Wright document, should it prove authentic. He also packed an affidavit, which in part demanded the return of the Wright document.

Iannella booked a flight late that afternoon for he and Kavin on Delta Air Lines from Logan to JFK. Like good civil servants, they flew coach. To top it off, Kavin even negotiated a reduced fare for himself. They did everything to save a buck except handle the other passengers' luggage and assist in serving drinks on the flight.

Upon arrival, they grabbed a cab into town. Iannella had reserved a room for himself at the Hilton, but Kavin opted for a sentimental favorite, the Pennsylvania Hotel outside of Penn Station. Big bands had once played there, and Kavin could hum the bars of an old Guy Lombardo hit about the place, "Pennsylvania 65000."

Once in town, Kavin went to McSorley's in the Bowery, New York's oldest bar, for a drink. Long celebrated as a venue for people "slumming it," the bar had more realistically resembled a yuppie meeting hall for several years. Kavin did not stay there for long.

He then strolled over to Wallenbys' to meet up with an old school friend, a patent-trademark lawyer who practiced in the city. Over drinks and dinner, Kavin explained what he and Iannella had discovered that day and what they planned to do the next morning.

The patent lawyer listened with rapt interest to the yarn told to him by Kavin, an accomplished storyteller. Kavin's twinkling blue eyes had never lost their youthfulness, and they had a way of augmenting a good tale as they danced to the flow of the story. At the end of Kavin's recount, the patent lawyer felt that whoever stole the Wright document probably made the same mistake people who appropriate trademarks and patents make all the time. Oftentimes they feel that they are taking something without intrinsic value, and by doing so, this makes it somewhat better than an outright theft of a tangible object with a price tag affixed to it. But the lawyer pointed out that the will belonged to the public in one sense, but also on a private level, it contained a family's history and genealogy, and thus possessed a value far beyond the mere paper that held its sentiments.

Ultimately, it was not a thief's prerogative to decide whether something should be taken or not, or rationalize the act of theft itself. What has no value to one person might be priceless to another person. So it seemed to Kavin.

Much had changed in New York from the first time that Kavin visited there until he found himself in town on a bit of detective work, although one could still carve out a slice of the past if one knew where to go. New York was always a fun place to visit, to reminisce about past trips there, and to recall the way the old town used to be, the way people once seemed to be. He spent a wonderful evening with his friend, but before business started for him and Iannella the next morning, Kavin had an appointment for a sound sleep in the old Pennsylvania Hotel. He paid his check and bid his friend a good evening, and stepped onto the pavement of old New York again.

On the next morning, Iannella had not had the opportunity to absorb anything other than the rudimentary biographical facts concerning George Wright. Instead, Iannella bolted down a quick breakfast at the Hilton, and elsewhere Kavin grabbed a bagel, coffee and a paper. They barely needed the coffee to stay awake as they finally had time to contemplate the imminent nature of their mission since the 10:00 A.M. meeting gave them ample time to regroup. Iannella instinctively knew when he first saw the evidence of the advertisement in the Leland's catalog what he had to do, but now he had to execute his plan, and that presented challenges of their own.

He felt glad that he had someone from his office with him that morning. He knew that the theft of the papers, which by all appearances had occurred, was absolutely wrong, and he did not doubt that his plan constituted the proper course to follow. Clearly, the theft of the person's will did not materially differ, to his way of thinking, from robbing the graves of the dead. Ironically, the act of originally taking the wills paled in comparison to the efforts associated with attempting to restore it to Iannella's court.

Thus, he felt slightly uneasy about his first foray into the world of cloak and dagger. In an ironic twist, in order to unwind the effects of what his gut indicated to him was a deceptive act, Iannella needed to engage in a deception of his own with Leland's in order to review the Wright document. Unfortunately, by his very nature, Iannella did not engage in deceptions, and as he ventured inexorably to the Leland's Auction House, he wondered if he could be good at it.

Soon, however, he could tip his hand. He grabbed a cab and met Kavin about a block down from the Leland's Auction House, located at 36 East 22nd Street in Manhattan. Initially they walked past the building before they backtracked and located it. Entering the building, they had to buzz the Leland's office before going any further. They jumped in the elevator together, a tight fit in a tiny little compartment, until they ascended to the seventh floor offices.

Once they got to the Leland's reception area, they exchanged pleasantries before asking to see the prize that barely forty-eight hours earlier neither one of them knew existed. To Kavin, the Leland's office looked like a college dorm room, and not in a bad way, in that it was plastered with memorabilia, mainly sports-related with a tip of the hat to the entertainment world. Even though Kavin did not count himself as much of a sports fan, he came away impressed by the quality and quantity of valuables hanging on the walls.

Rich Iannella, the Suffolk County register of probate after the time that George Wright's will was restored. He played a critical role in retrieving other ballplayers' wills that had vanished and assisted law enforcement in apprehending the individual who was ultimately punished for this crime. Collection of Donald Hubbard.

A Leland's employee ushered Iannella and Kavin into a room filled with files and one glass table, upon which he laid the purported return of service of Abbie Wright, signed by her surviving husband, George Wright. Iannella removed the document from its plastic cover and asked Kavin,

"What do you think?" Having seen hundreds of old documents in his career, Kavin immediately knew that he held the genuine article. "This is ours!" he exclaimed.

The Leland's employee had not left the room, but had attended to other matters, seemingly oblivious to his guests from Boston. Iannella asked for permission to open up the document, which had been folded up. After receiving the go-ahead, and upon inspecting all of its pages, Kavin detailed how he had concluded that the return of service belonged to their court.

Authoritatively, Kavin gave Iannella a primer in the authentication of old official documents. In the left-hand corner of the return, the court had affixed the legal notice that had run in the local paper, announcing the probating of the will. This was a standard probate practice of the time, not a lawyers or layman's custom. Back then, when a probate clerk reviewed the document before allowing it to be filed, he (and back then it almost always was a he) held a red pen and read along with the document, inadvertently placing red dots along the page as he reviewed it.

That was not all. The document contained the Massachusetts Court's notes, something never seen in a copy. The penmanship that had been added since the lawyer had drafted the will also provided a tell-tale sign that it was not a copy. Back then, Kavin explained, the court clerks had to constantly take penmanship classes so that no matter which court official had written on the document, the handwriting from one clerk matched perfectly with the handwriting of all of the other clerks.

Finally, the document contained the Massachusetts standard ink, which Kavin explained until the mid–1970s legally had to consist of a certain blend and only a few firms in the Commonwealth even manufactured it. Again, no lawyer or layman could have done this because they did not have access to the mandated brand of ink.

At that point, Iannella formally tipped his hand. He turned to the Leland's staffer and bluntly stated, "We've got a problem." When asked what the problem was, Iannella proclaimed, "This document belongs to the Commonwealth of Massachusetts and we've got to take it back."

And that is what happened. Leland's cooperated fully in returning the Wright document to Iannella, and he and Kavin had every reason to believe that they had accomplished a valuable public service. While Iannella remembered what Bowlby had written about the other missing wills and knew that some loose ends remained to be investigated, to his mind, no other wills had been stolen and not much more needed to be done in this matter.

In this, Iannella's instincts uncharacteristically deserted him on one of the few occasions in the matter. For at the very moment of the same day that he and Kavin had lifted off on their flight back to Boston from their foray to Leland's, a very worried woman named Sandra Parker had just concluded the first day of a frantically fruitless search in the probate records of Bloomington,

Illinois, for a missing will. It had been signed by one Charles "Old Hoss" Radbourn, the legendary Providence and Boston Hall of Fame pitcher.

Around this time, too, a rumor began to circulate that a signature of Old Hoss Radbourn was being shopped around, a truly significant development in the memorabilia collecting community since very few autographs of his were thought to exist. In Bloomington, R. C. Raycraft, the son of the estimable memorabilia and Americana expert Donald Raycraft, decided to track down the matter for personal reasons since his brother had written an article about the will in the past.

His curiosity sufficiently ripened, he called a journalist friend named Steve Arney to accompany him on his mission. Like Iannella taking Kavin to New York, R. C. Raycraft felt it prudent to have a witness with him in the event that the will had vanished. Finally, on October 28, 1998, late in the afternoon, they went to the same location where his brother had uncovered the will almost ten years earlier and requested to see a copy of the document. It was gone.

The clerk directed the two friends to the circuit court clerk, Sandra Parker, a pert redhead whose job in Illinois roughly paralleled Iannella's in Boston. The circuit court clerk since 1989, she had worked at the courthouse an additional ten years before she ascended to her current position. While she did not know Raycraft, she got along famously with Arney, as he covered many of the stories that emanated out of her court. The two friends related the nature of their search and offered their conclusion that someone had stolen Old Hoss' last will and testament.

Parker had never heard of Old Hoss, and she did not know the history of the inquiries made to Raycraft's father, so she cautioned them not to jump to any conclusions. "Before you say that it is stolen," she told them, "it might simply be misfiled."

With that hope in mind, she went to work with one of her assistants to find Old Hoss' will. Since genealogists frequently ordered numerous files under the family name that they were searching, she hoped that a researcher had ordered up every Radbourn probate file, and in the process of being disorganized, placed the will in someone else's file.

The search of each Radbourn probate file did not yield the will, nor did a search of the entire box that housed what remained of Old Hoss' probate file. In one particularly dark corner of the record room, she had to use a flashlight to see. Late that night, she concluded that indeed someone had taken the will. Like Iannella and Kavin's experience earlier that afternoon in New York, it had been a very bad day. The next morning she reported the theft of the will to the police and spent the balance of that day continuing her search for the will and answering questions about it in front of television cameras.

Their suspicions that a theft had occurred confirmed, Arney and Raycraft commenced writing a series of articles under the same by-line in the *Pantagraph*, a local Bloomington newspaper, concerning the disappearance of the

Radbourn will. In their articles, the two friends not only traced the progress of the investigation of the will's disappearance, but also wrote perceptively, sometimes movingly, about their subject, Old Hoss Radbourn.

Bowlby's warning had proven correct; wills had disappeared all over the place, many in Massachusetts but some in Illinois, New York, Connecticut and throughout the Mid-Atlantic. In addition to Rich Iannella's office, the Boston FBI, Steve Blair from the Boston Police Department and Detective Howard Springer of the McLean County Sheriff's Department (Bloomington, Illinois) coordinated their investigative efforts.

Eventually, Iannella ascertained that at a minimum, numerous losses had occurred. In addition to the George Wright signed documents, wills executed by Hall of Famers Tom Connolly, Hugh Duffy, Thomas McCarthy, Joe McCarthy, Johnny Evers, Jackie Robinson, James O'Rourke, Ned Hanlon, Connie Mack, Harry Wright and Hoss Radbourn had disappeared. In addition, wills signed by such lesser luminaries as John Kelleher, George Fair, Sam Wright, George Haddock, Sam Curran, Jack Slattery, Miah Murray, Buck O'Brien, Tom Smith, Denny Sullivan and Jack Manning had vanished. Ultimately, suspicion arose that the will of Jack Chesbro had been stolen, along with famous

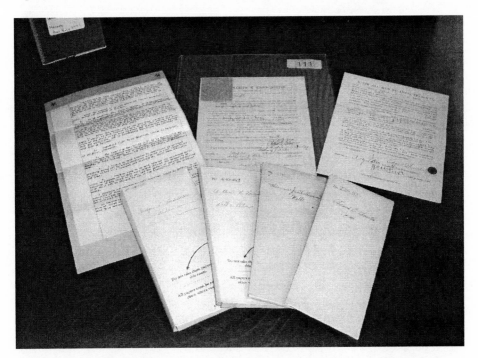

These documents are some of the probate records signed by baseball legends that were recovered through the diligence of Rich Iannella and law enforcement officers. Collection of Donald Hubbard.

America artist Fredric Remington. At least one document signed by Babe Ruth likewise had been lost.

Some wills, such as those of Hugh Duffy and Hoss Radbourn, were returned. Others, such as the wills of Tommy McCarthy and Jackie Robinson, are still missing. The author of this book once saw Ned Hanlon's lost will advertised in a publication and reported this to Iannella and the FBI; it has been returned to its rightful place.

Ultimately, Boston Police Detective Steve Blair arrested a Suffolk County (MA) probation officer for the theft of the Wright documents. The probation officer had access to old archival files in the basement of the old court house and had stolen wills and the supporting documents that contained the authenticated signatures of baseball stars. The probation officer lost his job and was placed, ironically enough, on probation. He had to pay back some of the victims who had spent money on his stolen documents.

The thief had justified his actions to the FBI agent who investigated him on the basis that, in his opinion, what he committed was in essence a victimless crime. The documents were old and largely forgotten and their disappearance hurt no one. That is nonsense, of course, because before the thief had resorted to crime, he had shown at least one friend how to order a mortgage with Babe Ruth's signature on it, thinking it a neat thing to show a friend. Other people knew the autographed documents were at the registry as well, and without doubt many of those folks enjoyed touching an item of memorabilia once touched by the Babe. The thief had even shown Bowlby at least one of the signed documents years earlier.

More tangibly, in researching old baseball players, one has only a limited amount of resources to check in order to try to learn about these men, never mind to attempt to construct a biography of their lives. Since the Hugh Duffy will (and perhaps supporting inventories and accounts) had been restored to the Suffolk Probate Court, they served as useful instruments to gain information about Sir Hugh.

Valuable leads concerning the identities of his heirs and the name of his attorney came from gleaning these public records. An exact inventory of the assets that he owned at the time of his death assisted in ascertaining the types of investments he dabbled in and the certainty that even at the age of 87, Duffy had shrewdly accumulated a considerable nest egg for himself, despite never having the wealth of an Al Spalding. And it is a very neat experience to hold a document that this wonderfully gifted man once read and signed.

Since Tommy McCarthy's will has never returned to its archives and remains lost, one can only surmise the financial condition he found himself in at the close of his life. Not only had his will been stolen, but his inventory and final account had likewise disappeared, perhaps because his executor may have been Hugh Duffy, who as a fiduciary would have signed many of the probate forms.

But since the documents have vanished, we do not know who Tommy McCarthy's executor was and what assets he owned at the time of his death. He may have been nearly destitute toward the end of his life, or he may have accumulated a substantial portfolio of his own. Unless those documents, or at least a copy of them, come to light, we shall never know.

Stealing a person's last will and testament is a disrespectful and disgraceful act to commit. Ironically, the theft did lead to a renewed interest in many of these mostly forgotten ballplayers, and directly culminated in the creation of the biographies of Hugh Duffy and Tommy McCarthy. That task was made considerably more difficult by the disappearance of Tommy McCarthy's entire estate file.

Chapter 20

Heavenly Twins Yes,
but Hall of Famers?

Unlike Tommy McCarthy, Hugh Duffy lived to appreciate his induction into the Baseball Hall of Fame in 1945. But did either man deserve the honor bestowed upon him?

Let us start with the easier of the two, Hugh Duffy, whose Hall of Fame plaque reads:

> Brilliant as a defensive outfielder for the Boston Nationals, he compiled a batting average in 1894 which was not to be challenged in his lifetime — .438.

That is pretty good for a lead-in, to which we quickly add that he arguably was the first ballplayer to hit for the triple crown (recent data suggests that he just missed out on the RBI jewel in the crown), finished with a final average of over .300 in four separate major leagues and retired with a .326 batting average. Of course, not all of this data fits into a Hall of Fame plaque, but this sounds like a person deserving of his induction into the Cooperstown shrine.

Now when you read Tommy McCarthy's Hall of Fame plaque, it shockingly inspires scant awe: One of Boston's "Heavenly Twins" under Manager Frank Selee.

> Outstanding baserunner who stole 109 bases for the Browns in 1888. Pioneer in trapping fly balls in the outfield. Holds N.L. record for assists in outfield — 53 with Boston in 1893. Played 1268 games in major league.

Hardly a ringing endorsement for a baseball Hall of Famer. Starting with the first sentence, it seems as if he is in the hall because of his relationship with Duffy (the other Heavenly Twin) and Frank Selee, his brilliant manager. It tells us little about him other than with whom he associated. Between the lines, though, it does inform the modern reader how important it was in the middle of the twentieth century to form a constituent part of a famous aggregation of players, such as the "Heavenly Twins" or "Tinkers to Evers to Chance."

The second line of the spiel cites a pretty impressive total of stolen bases for one year of his career (it actually overstates the total, for in 1888 Mac stole 93 bases, not 108), but does not speak to his career-long abilities to grab a base. As we know, the older Mac got, the larger he became, and by the 1890s quite often he figuratively carted a piano across the field with him. The third line, concerning his pioneering role in trapping balls, is unimportant because while this skill thrilled crowds in the nineteenth century, it never served much use on a regular basis. With the advent of larger ballparks and outfields in the twentieth century, trapping disappeared (quite literally in the infield with the infield fly rule) even if one tried to master this art.

His plaque ends with a couple more factoids: that he made a boatload of assists in 1893 and played more than 1,200 games. The assist record sounds nice, but outfielders do not make the Hall of Fame based on their fielding ability, and relatively few infielders or catchers do, either. An outfielder ideally should run like a deer and make catches like Willie Mays, but even if one does not, the player still may gain induction into the hall by leading the league in hitting or bashing a ton of home runs.

The fact that Mac played 1,246 games is an indictment of the brevity of his career, not a testament to him mythically scaling Olympus. Cal Ripken, Jr., holds the all-time consecutive games played record and all told starred in slightly over 3,000 games. Granted, comparing many Hall of Famers to Ripken for endurance and longevity is absurd, but Mac's career at best lasted thirteen years. Even if we accept the Union Association as a major league, the low number of games played by McCarthy testifies more to the lack of his devotion to the game and the maintenance of proper physical conditioning. All in all, an odd resume for enshrinement in the hall.

In *The Politics of Glory*, Bill James sets forth 15 factors in what he termed the Keltner Test to assist judging a player's relative worthiness for the Hall of Fame. Some of the factors do not strictly apply to Duffy and McCarthy because, for instance, one measure of greatness is the number of All-Star Games he participated in, and these exhibitions did not exist in the nineteenth century.

Still, some of the criteria are very helpful in analyzing the Heavenly Twins. For example, "Was he ever regarded as the best player in baseball? Did anybody ever suggest that he was the best player in baseball?"

In 1894, the year Hugh Duffy hit for what remains the highest average in baseball, no one exceeded his performance on the ball field. Duffy seemed to believe that in 1887, with Lowell, he had reached a pinnacle, but while he was probably the finest minor league player, his next two years with Anson in Chicago proved that he still needed to improve as a hitter.

Tommy McCarthy never came close to consideration as the finest baseball player in any year that he played. Routinely overrated as an outfielder and as a batter, McCarthy was never praised by anyone to such a degree that they designated him the finest in the land.

Another factor in the Keltner Test is, "Was he the best player on the team?" With Duffy, by logical extension, he was the best player on his team in 1894, but with the Boston Beaneaters, he was probably the best player on the team for the many of the years he played there with the exception of pitcher Kid Nichols. In 1901, when he served as the player-manager of the Milwaukee Brewers, he distinguished himself even at that late stage in his career as the best player on his team.

McCarthy was the best player on the St. Louis Browns in 1890, but most of his former teammates had jumped to the Players' League that year. He also had a very good year in 1889, and had a couple of notable seasons with the Beaneaters, but he did not dominate any of those teams.

Another factor to consider: "[W]as he the best player in baseball at his position? Was he the best player in the league at his position?" Pundits often spoke of Duffy and McCarthy as the best players at their positions in the outfield, particularly during their time with Boston. In retrospect, McCarthy did not deserve these plaudits, and as time passed, few heaped this type of praise upon him. For instance, John McGraw placed Hugh Duffy on his all-time team, as did Cap Anson. Try locating McCarthy on anyone's dream team, with the exception of Hugh Duffy's mythical squad, which consisted only of Boston Beaneater ballplayers. McCarthy may have achieved primacy at his position in his second and third years with St. Louis and second and third years with Boston.

Factor four of the Keltner Test is, "Did he have an impact on a number of pennant races?" Duffy had an impact on every pennant race he participated in. In his two best years with St. Louis and Boston, McCarthy had an impact on the race. In his first year with Boston, even though the Beaneaters won the championship, Mac did not do that much for the team.

"Was he a good enough player that he could continue to play regularly after passing his prime?" With Duffy the answer is a resounding yes. Even after he had aged and slowed down, he still played very good ball for Boston. Although he did not play as regularly with Milwaukee in 1901, he still hit over .300. After he had passed his prime sometime in the 1895 season, McCarthy played rather poorly and lazed his way out of baseball by the end of the next season.

> Three Keltner factors are very similar: 1. "Is he the best player in baseball history who is not in the Hall of Fame?" 2. "Are most players who have comparable career statistics in the Hall of Fame?" 3. "Do the player's numbers meet Hall of Fame standards?"

Of course, Duffy and McCarthy both obtained induction into the hall. But had they not, neither one would be thought of by most people as the best player not admitted, although Duffy would be in contention. Mac would miss by a mile. If he had retired in modern times, it is extremely doubtful that Mac would garner enough votes to make the ballot year after year because so few voters would vote for him.

Using Baseball-Reference.com as a guide for hitting only, seven of the ten players deemed comparable to Duffy have plaques hanging in the Hall of Fame: one active player, Kenny Lofton, is not there and another, George Van Haltren, probably deserves the honor, but he antagonized too many people. In that site's Black Ink and Gray Ink Tests, Duffy grades out as somewhat above an average Hall of Famer.

By contrast, only Frank Chance amongst the ten players dubbed comparable to Tommy McCarthy is in the hall, and Chance probably does not merit his selection there. Mac's Black Ink and Gray Ink scores fall considerably below that of an "average Hall of Famer."

If you wish to argue against Hugh Duffy's right to induction into the Hall of Fame, you have an uphill climb. To advocate Mac's selection, one must throw out any analysis of Black Ink and Gray Ink or Keltner tests because your hero cannot even approach the minimum required standard.

One strong non-statistical argument in Mac's favor is his contributions to the inside aspects of the game. John McGraw appropriated the conception of the hit-and-run play for himself, but most historians will give Tommy McCarthy credit for this innovation, in whole or in part with Frank Selee. McCarthy also mastered the art of trapping the ball and was one of the earliest and most successful practitioners of stealing another team's signs. He also effectively injected himself into assisting infielders of his team with assists and even participation in double plays.

Hugh Duffy and Tim Murnane did not stand alone in proclaiming McCarthy's greatness. The *Sporting Life* in his era trumpeted him as one of the finest players in the firmament, as did many of the Boston and St. Louis dailies. Rhetorically speaking, if McCarthy was so mediocre, why did his name crop up in rumors in the mid-nineties for an even-up trade between Boston and Philadelphia for Billy Hamilton? He did contribute to the success of some fine teams of that era, including repeat pennant winners in St. Louis and Boston.

He did steal an awful lot of bases, and created a surfeit of opportunities for his team to score runs as a result of his speed. To this day, Mac stands 42nd all-time in stolen bases, an impressive feat since during the first four years of his career he rarely played, and the last two years his feet no longer propelled his large body with any speed. Still, in the career rankings, one finds him wedged between Mike Griffin and Jimmy Sheckard, neither of whom is an immortal.

Incidentally, Billy Hamilton is still ranked third all-time for stolen bases, exceeded only by Rickey Henderson and Lou Brock; therefore, to suggest that Philadelphia almost traded him straight up for Mac is meaningful, strains credulity. The point is that Philadelphia did not consummate the proposed McCarthy-Hamilton trade, and when they did deal with Boston, they received washed-up Billy Nash for Hamilton, a swap that long-time Hall of Fame historian Lee Allen called "one of the dumbest trades in history." Had Philly traded Hamilton for McCarthy, given Mac's figurative and literal baggage in the mid–1890s, it too would have constituted one of the ghastliest robberies ever.

Similarly, although Mac did contribute to the Browns' success in 1888, they had won three championships before he joined the team. With Boston, Mac signed with a team that had won the National League flag the year before he came as well as following his departure. In fact, due in part to his departure, the Beaneaters continued to win after he left.

Perhaps the more interesting question is not whether McCarthy should be in the Hall of Fame, but rather what propelled him there, given his lack of credentials?

It certainly did not hurt that the state of the art in baseball research in 1946 did not approximate what we have today, never mind what developed by 1969 when the first comprehensive edition of a baseball encyclopedia reached publication. The information existed and anybody had the opportunity to compile it and run it through an analysis, but clearly this did not occur in the way that we understand it today.

Old *Reach Guides* and newspapers did give a competent year-by-year analysis of batting and fielding statistics, and ideally, these statistics lent themselves to some sort of a spread sheet analysis, but no evidence exists that this occurred.

Until he died, Hugh Duffy charitably deflected praise for his past accomplishments by frequently maintaining that Tommy McCarthy was the best outfielder that he ever saw, high praise indeed. Sir Hugh did not lavish praise on Billy Hamilton because Sliding Billy did not have the same friends, hang around the golf courses in Boston or go to the same church as he and Tommy McCarthy did. He probably bore no ill will toward Hamilton because of his nature, but Duffy regarded McCarthy like family and felt obligated to brag about his old buddy to whomever listened to him.

Hamilton stole many bases like Mac did, but when Mac left the ballpark, he did not retreat to riding horses and skating in the country. He hung out in his bar or other bars and befriended sportswriters, other ballplayers, politicians and influential fans. In the outfield, Mac trapped balls, made a ton of assists, involved himself in double plays, and routinely threw punches at opposing players and teammates alike.

Hamilton and Mac both played for Harry Wright, a very mild-mannered and dignified man. But Wright scuttled Mac, and Mac ended up with a lunatic like St. Louis Browns owner Chris Von der Ahe. While Hamilton may have bragged too much about his base-stealing prowess, Mac had his money taken from him by Von der Ahe's goons in St. Louis; Mac then waited a bit and had Von der Ahe arrested in Boston. Hamilton did not punch teammates and opponents alike, and when he had a problem with an umpire, generally did nothing more than glare at the ump like he had just used Hamilton's toothbrush. You could picture McCarthy with a dirty uniform by the end of the third inning, while strangely enough, one had difficulty conjuring this image up for Sliding Billy Hamilton even after he slid into base.

You could have a beer with Mac; you could not with Hamilton.

It is worth wondering if some sudden surge or some backroom bartering brought Tommy McCarthy into the Hall of Fame, and it seems that none of this occurred. At the time of his election, a handful of people elected veterans into the Hall of Fame, namely Connie Mack, Ed Barrow, Sid Mercer, Harry Cross, Grantland Rice, Bob Quinn, Mel Webb and Stephen Clark. Here is where it gets interesting.

We know Connie Mack today as the manager of two dynasties for the old Philadelphia Athletics, whom he managed from 1901–1950. He also played for a number of years in the major leagues, coming to Washington as the catcher in 1886, thus necessitating his Hartford club to hire a young Hugh Duffy as his replacement. During his career as a catcher, he had the best view in the park to see Tommy McCarthy, Hugh Duffy and Billy Hamilton hit and steal bases.

And yet, Tommy McCarthy received enough votes for election into the hall in 1946 and Billy Hamilton had to wait another 15 years for his posthumous recognition. Instead, Mack saw what he wanted to see, and Mack helped give Mac the nod at the expense of Sliding Billy Hamilton and any number of more qualified nineteenth century candidates.

One possible link between Mack and Mac was uncovered fairly recently by *Boston Globe* reporter Bob Duffy, who maintained that Mack, McCarthy and Hugh Duffy played instrumental roles in bringing American League baseball to Boston circa 1901. They worked together to accomplish a goal and succeeded. While McCarthy and Duffy did not become franchise magnates, and they may not have even profited financially by doing so, they certainly financially damaged their old National League Beaneaters' team by helping create the future Red Sox. Their efforts in establishing the American League also financially benefited Connie Mack.

So Mack and Mac were friends, and in a looser sense, business associates. But other folks sat on the committee also. What about them? Mel Webb achieved fame as a Boston sportswriter, mainly remembered today as the man who did not include Ted Williams in the MVP voting in the year that Teddy Ballgame hit .406, thus supposedly costing him that recognition.

Webb certainly knew McCarthy, so well in fact that Mac contributed some very thoughtful comments to a column Webb penned about proposed changes in baseball published in the *Globe* in 1917. At that time Webb referred to McCarthy as "one of the game's leading scouts."

More importantly, Webb socialized with Hugh Duffy repeatedly over several decades in covering the Red Sox, and Duffy told anyone who asked him that Tommy McCarthy, not he, was the finest outfielder he ever knew. Of course, this clashed with the truth and Duffy knew it, but it helped deflect attention away from himself to his long-deceased best friend. Had he not known Tommy

McCarthy well or had not played on the same team with him, Duffy would never have placed Mac in the pantheon of great outfielders. But he did like him and honored his memory by wildly exaggerating his long-gone buddy's qualifications.

Since he covered the Red Sox in the 1940s, Webb either heard Duffy laud McCarthy, or at least had read a contemporary interview or account of such, and he believed it or at least knew that electing McCarthy to the Hall of Fame would warm Duffy's heart. As a protégé of Tim Murnane, Webb by extension heard all about Tommy McCarthy and his greatness in the same spirit that Duffy spoke of Mac. When McCarthy and Duffy entered the church for the Silver King's funeral Mass, one of the ushers who guided them to their seat was Mel Webb.

Ed Barrow certainly knew Tommy McCarthy as a Boston sports personality before Barrow left Boston and became an executive with the Yankees. Mac also served as a Red Sox scout in 1920, Barrow's last year with the team. Barrow managed the Red Sox from 1918–1920, with Hugh Duffy succeeding him at that post. To the extent Barrow knew McCarthy, he probably harbored positive perceptions of Mac, and if he called Duffy on the phone, he would have had his impressions reinforced by Sir Hugh.

The friendships Tommy McCarthy made in life assisted in his being elected posthumously to the Hall of Fame. This Winter League photograph taken in October 1912 may be the only one still in existence showing the Heavenly Twins together, with Duffy and McCarthy shown respectively in the front row first and second from the left. Jimmy McAleer is standing third from the left and Nuf Ced McGreevey is standing sixth from the right, while Jack Dooley is seated at the extreme right. Collection of Peter Nash/Baseball Fan Hall of Fame.

Sid Mercer and Harry Cross may not have been involved much in the vote since they both died in the mid–1940s. Grantland Rice succeeded them and probably participated in the 1946 vote, but it is a bit difficult to ascertain who actually cast a ballot. It is hard to believe that Rice did not vote for McCarthy, as he tended to elevate good athletes to the pantheon of the gods. Stephen Clark was tied to the family that helped found the Hall of Fame and probably knew little or nothing about McCarthy other than what someone told him.

Bob Quinn in 1946 had just retired as a part-owner and president of the Braves and had also owned the Boston Red Sox before selling the team to Tom Yawkey in 1933. He probably saw Mac play in the 1890s, and certainly he recalled Mac fondly. More importantly, Hugh Duffy punched in on the Red Sox payroll for several of the years that Quinn ran the club, and Duffy had ample opportunity to fill him in if asked about Mac's prowess.

Circumstantial evidence might therefore help explain how Tommy McCarthy obtained election to the Hall of Fame at the expense of more qualified candidates. Since all of the voters have long since passed on and we do not have much evidence concerning how they arrived at their decision, paranoia to a marked degree and conspiracy theorems exist to fill this vacuum. Willing ignorance might explain a lot as well since a cold reading of Mac's career would not warrant even a passing consideration of his candidacy to the hall, not to mention his election. But is it paranoia if Mac only got into the hall on a friends and family plan?

The crucial link that cannot be totally discounted is Connie Mack's participation in the process. Even if he sincerely recalled Tommy McCarthy as a superstar a half-century after his last game as a Beaneater, that explains in part this poor selection but does not excuse the omission of boring Billy Hamilton, a player far better qualified than McCarthy. Simply put, McCarthy's election was no more or less a popularity contest than any junior high school class president's election. Gregarious Tommy McCarthy trumped a cold fish like Billy Hamilton.

By way of a continuing comparison, Billy Hamilton, who had a much more distinguished career than Tommy McCarthy, did not make the Baseball Hall of Fame until 1961. None of his former teammates pushed his election, and indeed, most of them were as dead as he was by that time. While Hamilton stayed involved in baseball most of his adult life, when he died only his family attended his funeral and asked that flowers not be given to them. In other words, as a private man in life, his family chose to grieve him quietly and without fanfare.

And they got their wish because baseball fans and former teammates essentially forgot about him. His family got what they professed to desire. Unlike McCarthy, Hamilton did not own a bar, was not close friends with Hugh Duffy and Tim Murnane, and did not have a particularly electrifying career. He hit the ball more often and ran faster and played longer than McCarthy, but none of this seemed to matter. He did not stick out in a crowd.

While he and his family craved privacy, his surviving daughters did not cotton to the idea that his accomplishments had passed into oblivion and that less-deserving folks kept gaining admission into the hall. In 1959, one of Hamilton's daughters, who lived in California, sent Paul Kerr of the Hall of Fame a letter that he termed "rather caustic." However, it piqued his interest, and he wrote a letter to Lee Allen, the Hall of Fame's historian, and asked him about this Hamilton fellow.

Allen wrote back a very short but comprehensive letter to Kerr and at one

point called his trade to Boston for Billy Nash one of the "most stupid" trades in baseball history. More correspondence from Hamilton's daughter in California followed, and this time it did not offend or otherwise spring from a poison pen, but rather she related charming and affectionate vignettes about her dad.

Something clicked at the hall because Hamilton went from an overlooked ballplayer to an immortal very rapidly thereafter. It was not due to his extremely strong credentials (all-time stolen base leader in 1961, still third today; sixth all-time

Billy Hamilton's somewhat retiring nature helped bury his considerable achievements, feats that only came fully to light when one of his daughters began to trumpet his cause long after his death. To this day, his 914 stolen bases are third all-time behind Rickey Henderson and Lou Brock. Collection of Richard A. Johnson.

with a .344 lifetime batting average, fourth all-time with a .455 on-base percentage), but because one of his daughters touched a chord with some of the influential people at the hall. In essence, he made the hall, like McCarthy, for all the wrong sentimental reasons. And yet, incomplete personality aside, Billy Hamilton belongs in the Baseball Hall of Fame.

Most people would conclude that Tommy McCarthy does not belong in the Hall of Fame (for those of you keeping score, his career batting average was .292 with an OBP of .364), but the argument ends there. After all, assuming all of this is true, what is there to do about it? Does the hall kick him out or, at best, place a black shroud around his plaque? And if you remove Tommy McCarthy's plaque, then the hall has its work cut out for it in determining who else to throw out.

Let us start with the players in his era who were inducted in the 1945–1946 period, and a number of them must go due to lack of qualifications.

Cap Anson was a bigot who helped institutionalize Jim Crow in the major leagues, and Boston Red Sox owner Tom Yawkey did not integrate his team until 1959; you must toss them out. What's more, even though Yawkey owned the Red Sox for decades, the team never won a World Series title during his reign. Tris Speaker and Ty Cobb did not exhibit sensitivity to minorities, so they go next.

Since Pete Rose cannot come into the Baseball Hall of Fame because he bet on his own team, we need to prune like-minded and like-acting ballplayers and managers such as Ned Hanlon, who did not even try to hide the fact that he bet on baseball.

Babe Ruth was a drunken slob who cavorted with whores, so off with his head. How about players like Orlando Cepeda, who used drugs?

Before too long, we have a Hall of Fame consisting of Branch Rickey, Jackie Robinson, Willie Mays, Hank Aaron, Tony Gwynn, Cal Ripken, Jr., Stan Musial and Christy Mathewson. Not a bad group of fellows, but it leaves out a lot of very qualified players. Fact is, baseball is such a great sport despite its quirks. It has ballparks with different dimensions and it lets in ballplayers into the Hall of Fame who do not belong and keeps others out. Tommy McCarthy could not hold a candle to Pete Rose in terms of baseball ability, and they both bet on their own teams, but McCarthy cannot leave Cooperstown and Pete Rose cannot come in. It is these endless incongruities that make baseball so fascinating.

Baseball is fascinating, as a ballplayer can be a drunk or a bigot or a wife-beater and that probably is not enough to keep that person out of the Hall of Fame, but a gambler is dead meat. Similarly, a number of nineteenth-century ballplayers clearly are not qualified to be honored by admission into the Hall of Fame, while far superior players like Ron Santo, Jim Rice and Bert Blyleven can only get in by buying a visitor ticket. Virtually no one talks about whether a football, basketball or hockey player should be in their Hall of Fame, but in baseball, the subject never gets old.

The question that has confounded folks who have pondered this matter is whether Tommy McCarthy is a Hall of Famer. It is an odd question because the analysis truly is whether he belongs in the Hall of Fame. Miscarriages of justice occur every day. If your old man is on the local youth hockey board, you have a much better chance of making the elite team than if your father is not on the board, regardless of whether you belong on the team or not. Mac made a lot of friends in life and they remembered and recognized him after his death with an honor that he did not earn by his achievements in life on the baseball field.

If he does not belong in the Hall of Fame, one fact is clear: he is a member of the Baseball Hall of Fame. If you want to know whether Tommy McCarthy is a Hall of Famer, travel to Cooperstown and go no further than the hall that houses the plaques. Tommy McCarthy's plaque is there, not far from that of Hugh Duffy. He is, in fact, a Hall of Famer.

At least one voice of the past best encapsulates why this may be. Just before Christmas in 1895, the Cleveland note writer for the *Sporting Life* positively beamed when asked about the effect he felt Tommy McCarthy would have on his new team, the Brooklyn Bridegrooms. "Out this way McCarthy is regarded as a marvel. Tom may not be the greatest batter or the greatest fielder on earth, but show me a better ball player, a better run getter and the cigars will be on me." Even in 1895, folks knew that McCarthy did not measure up statistically against his loftier peers, but enough fans and influential people felt that he possessed baseball greatness. Mac rode those sentiments all the way to Cooperstown.

Epilogue

At the beginning of Thomas Melville's great American novel, *Moby Dick*, the young Nantucket whaler, Ishmael, sits down in a makeshift chapel and listens to the preacher preach about Jonah. Not a bad sermon for a whaler to hear, particularly one about to embark on a voyage with an obsessed captain who will figuratively cause this obsession to doom himself and almost his entire crew.

Similarly, in a Boston church the week after Easter, the priest gave a sermon that dealt mostly with the Boston Red Sox. Again, not a bad sermon since most of the parishioners had embraced the hometown team with a devotion bordering on the metaphysical. St. Patrick legendarily explained the concept of the Holy Trinity to his Irish listeners by pulling a three-leafed clover out of the ground and analogizing the three leafs in one clover to the Trinity. To teach a Boston congregation, it is useful to throw a Red Sox player or two into the mix to clarify the often thorny theological points a minister, rabbi or imam wants to convey.

The priest began by asking the parishioners about Carl Yastrzemski and everyone, even the little kids, had something nice to say about Yaz. Then the priest asked about Bill Buckner and the first response was, "He was the guy who let the ball roll through his legs and cost the Sox the World Series."

The priest then related to the congregation that before this famous event occurred, the Mets had tied the game. Indeed, Sox reliever Calvin Schiraldi had not sealed the deal and pitcher Bob Stanley and battery mate Rich Gedman had participated in a passed ball (or was it a wild pitch?), which let in another costly run. Buckner's error let in the winning run to Game Six, but the Red Sox still played a seventh game afterwards, at which time the Mets won the World Series.

Being the week after Easter, the Gospel concerned the apostle Thomas, known as Doubting Thomas for expressing incredulity that Jesus had risen from the dead. The priest made the point that Thomas had received a bad rap

213

because not even Jesus' mother Mary had initially believed this. The point that the priest struggled to make (and it is debatable whether he did or not) was that like Bill Buckner, the apostle Thomas had been unfairly singled out throughout history for something that he did not exclusively feel or cause to occur. Unlike Buckner, Thomas had never let the ball roll through his legs, but that is a story for another time.

The strained analogy between Doubting Thomas and the goat horned Buckner did not persuade, but then the priest mentioned that the name Thomas is derived from the Aramaic word for "twin." Indeed, in the Gnostic Gospels, Thomas is called the twin brother of Jesus.

And that part of the sermon hit home, for a biographer who had devoted much of his waking time to a modern-day Thomas, namely Thomas McCarthy, the Heavenly Twin of Hugh Duffy. When one writes about an historical figure, it is easy to permit that person to engulf your thoughts, to appear in your dreams, and ultimately to become almost a friend. So when it became clear that Thomas meant twin, the sermon became less a Catholic one and more of an ancient Puritan one about predestination. The Catholic had passed, the Puritan remained.

Hugh Duffy (front right) and friends say goodbye for now. Collection of Katherine Dooley.

Thomas McCarthy was destined to have a twin and they were meant to charm and beguile Boston's loyal rooters, whether they be Irish Catholics weighted down by the concept of original sin or the ancestors of the stern Puritans, so fearful of the sky falling and somehow offending God to such an extent that the sky would indeed fall. The triumph of the 2004 Red Sox in the World Series not only blotted out an 86-year-old "curse," but also permitted people to believe that somehow we did not deserve futility, but could hope and expect the sun to shine.

Duffy and McCarthy came from poor families but both seized baseball as a means out of a life of drudgery and a way to make themselves and others happy. The Red Sox rooters before the 2004 season had forgotten the joy that Babe Ruth and Chick Stahl and Cy Young had brought to New Englanders when the Red Sox ruled the baseball world. With Duffy and McCarthy, most Bostonians had not forgotten those wonderful world-beater Beaneaters because they had never heard of them to begin with.

But they did win championships together. They loved baseball and they loved their families and friends. They loved being Irish, and they loved being Catholic. They loved being around ball fields and they loved Tim Murnane. They loved each other like brothers, and how they loved Boston.

The Heavenly Twins were not heavenly because they resembled nineteenth-century versions of Mother Theresa, but because when they won ballgames and world championships, their fans felt like they had temporarily entered heaven, that they had "slipped the surly bonds of earth and had touched the face of God." In Boston, baseball and God are never too far away from each other; it's just that too often we fail to make the connections. We are doubting Thomases when we should be Heavenly Twins.

Chapter Notes

Introduction

1. Nancy Lusignan Schultz, *Fire & Roses* (New York: Free Press, 2000), p. 147–190.

2. J. Anthony Lukas, *Common Ground: A Turbulent Decade in the Lives of Three American Families* (New York: Vintage Books, 1986), p. 91.

Chapter 1

1. National Baseball Hall of Fame Hugh Duffy file, reviewed 3-29-07.

2. National Baseball Hall of Fame Tommy McCarthy file, reviewed 3-29-07.

3. National Baseball Hall of Fame Tim Murnane file, reviewed 3-29-07.

4. *Boston Globe*, 1892: October 16; 1917: February 7–8, 9, 11, 18; 1922: August 6.

5. Bill James, *The New Bill James Historical Baseball Abstract* (New York: Free Press, 2001), p. 21–34.

6. 1870 and 1880 Federal Censuses.

7. *Boston Post*, August 6, 1922.

8. Suffolk County (MA) Probate and Family Court Records, Hugh Duffy Estate.

9. Lee Allen and Tom Meany, *Kings of the Diamond* (New York: Putnam's, 1965), p. 173.

10. *Sporting Life*, September 29, 1886.

11. Boston City public records.

12. Harold Kaese, *The Boston Braves 1871–1953* (New York: Putnam's, 1948 and 1954), p. 70.

13. Francis Russell, *The Knave of Boston* (Boston: Quinlan Press, 1987), p. 39.

Chapter 2

1. *Boston Globe*, 1884: June 25, July 15, July 20, July 23–24, July 27, July 30, August 2, August 6, August 8–10, August 12, August 15–17, August 19, August 21–24, August 26, August 28, August 31, September 2, September 3, September 5, September 9, September 11, September 14, September 19, September 21, September 30, October 5, October 18, October 20; 1889: January 19, February 11; 1890: September 21 and 23; 1896: September 21, 23; 1904: February 7, October 18; 1910: December 3; 1917: February 9, 18 (the poem is by W.L. Dougherty); 1920: October 3.

2. David Q. Voigt, *From Gentleman's Sport to the Commissioner's System*, Volume 2 of American Baseball (Norman: University of Oklahoma Press, 1966), p. 130, 132–133.

3. James, *The New Bill James Historical Baseball Abstract*, p. 121–134.

4. *Philadelphia Inquirer*, August 22, 1897.

5. *Boston Morning Journal*, July 11, 1884.

6. *Sporting Life*, 1884: September 24.

7. *Boston Post*, August 6, 1922.

Chapter 3

1. *Sporting Life*, 1885: April 15; 1887: March 30, July 13, July 27, August 10; 1892: April 16.

2. *Boston Globe*, 1885: April 18–19, September 3, 1887: June 21.

3. *Oshkosh in Baseball*, (Oshkosh, WI: Oshkosh Base Ball Club, 1913), p. 13.

4. *Daily Northwestern*, 1887: June 29, July 1, 2, 30, August 9, 11, October 10, 12–13.

5. Lee Allen, *The National League Story* (New York: Hill & Wang, 1963), p. 66.

6. National Baseball Hall of Fame Frank Selee file, reviewed 3-29-07.

7. Lawrence S. Ritter, *The Glory of Their Times* (New York: Macmillan, 1966), p. 53–54.

8. Richard A. Johnson, *Boston Braves* (Charleston, SC: Arcadia, 2001), p. 16.

Chapter 4

1. *Springfield Daily Republican*, 1887: May 3, 6, 14, 17 and 25.

2. National Baseball Hall of Fame Hugh Duffy file, reviewed 3-29-07.

3. *Salem Gazette*, 1887.

4. *Lowell Weekly Sun*, 1887: July 7, 9, 30, August 6, 13, 27, September 3, 10,17, 30, October 8 and 29.

5. *Boston Globe*, 1887: July 14, August 6, August 21, September 30, October 1 and 22.

6. National Baseball Hall of Fame Hugh Duffy file, reviewed 3-29-07.

Chapter 5

1. *Philadelphia Inquirer*, August 31, 1888, September 28, 1890.

2. *Boston Globe*, January 30, 1888.

3. *Sporting Life:* 1888: August 22, September 12; 1889: May 1, May 8, May 15, August 28; 1890: April 26, May 24; 1892: April 16.

4. *St. Louis Times Dispatch*, 1888: March 20, March 25, April 1, May 25, June 28, July 6, July 10, July 18, September 3; 1889: May 3–8, May 28; 1890: April 7.

5. J. Thomas Hetrick, *Chris Von der Ahe and the St. Louis Browns* (Lanham, MD: Scarecrow Press, 1999), p. 127, 131.

6. *Chicago Tribune*, 1890: August 19, September 7.

7. *Sporting News*, 1888: September 15; 1889: September 21; 1890: May 31, September 13.

Chapter 6

1. Allen, *Kings of the Diamond*, p. 174.

2. Carl Yastrzemski and Gerard Eskenazi, *Yaz: Baseball, the Wall, and Me* (New York: Doubleday, 1990), p. 39.

3. *Sporting Life*, 1888: June 13, July 4; 1889: May 29, June 5, September 11; 1890: July 5, September 13, October 11.

4. *Chicago Tribune*, 1888: July 5, 23, 27, September 5, October 9; 1889: May 10, 21, June 8, 14, 19; 1890: June 7, July 27, August 6, August 24, August 31, September 3.

5. *Boston Globe*, 1889: March 18, 1890: January 3; 1916: October 13.

6. David L. Fleitz, *Cap Anson: The Grand Old Man of Baseball* (Jefferson, NC: McFarland, 2005), p. 192–193.

7. *Sporting News*, June 30, 1888; 1890: June 21, September 6, September 13.

Chapter 7

1. *Boston Globe*, 1891: February 12, 21, 22, 24, March 7, 21, 29, May 7–8, 21–24, 26, June 7–10, 26, July 28, August 18, 26–27; 1892: March 12.

2. *St. Louis Post Dispatch*, 1891: April 7, 21–22, May 20, June 7–10, July 6, 10, 28, August 2, 19, September 13, 22, 23.

3. *Sporting Life*, May 2, 1891.

Chapter 8

1. Robert Smith, *Baseball* (New York: Simon and Schuster, 1947), p. 384–385.

2. *Sporting Life*, 1892: April 2, April 9, May 7, May 21, May 28, June 4, June 11, June 25, July 9, July 23, August 6, September 3, October 1–22.

3. *Boston Globe*, 1891: October 22; 1892: January 3, February 7, March 23, April 2, May 5 7, 23–25, May 27, June 2, July 21, August 7, October 16–25; 1929: November 19.

4. George V. Tuohey, *A History of the Boston Baseball Club* (Boston: M.F. Quinn, 1897), p. 143.

5. *Boston Post,* May 3, 1892.

6. Kaese, *The Boston Braves*, pp. 49, 61.

Chapter 9

1. *Sporting Life*, 1893: May 13, May 27, August 19, September 30.

2. *Boston Globe,* 1893: April 2, June 4, 21, August 9, September 1, 14, 22, 27–28, October 3, 22.

3. Kaese, *The Boston Braves,* p. 73.

4. Tuohey, *A History of the Boston Baseball Club,* p. 111.

Chapter 10

1. Burt Solomon, *Where They Ain't: The Fabled Life, and Untimely Death of the Original Baltimore Orioles, the Team That Gave Birth to Modern Baseball* (New York: Free Press, 1999), p 77.

2. Kaese, *The Boston Braves,* p. 76.

3. Tuohey, *A History of the Boston Baseball Club,* p. 112.

4. *Sporting Life,* 1894: April 21, May 12, May 19, May 26, July 7, July 14, July 21, August 18.

5. *Boston Globe,* 1894: May 11–12, May 18–19, May 31, July 18, 21–22, 28, September 1, 29, November 11–12.

6. *Boston Post,* 1894: May 11, August 16, October 19.

7. *Philadelphia Inquirer,* July 18, 1894.

Chapter 11

1. *Boston Globe:* 1885: June 11; 1894: December 9; 1895: November 10; 1905: August 5; 1907: April 26; 1915: September 26.

2. Kaese, *The Boston Braves,* p. 78.

3. Tuohey, *A History of the Boston Baseball Club,* Advertisement Section.

4. *City of Boston Directory:* 1900, 1913 and 1914.

5. Harold Seymour, *Baseball, The Early Years* (New York: Oxford University Press, 1960), p. 336.

Chapter 12

1. Bill Stern: *Bill Stern's Favorite Baseball Stories* (Garden City, NY: Blue Ribbon Books, 1949), p. 34–35.

2. *Boston Globe,* 1895: February 10, March 3, March 14–15, April 29, May 4, 17–19, 21 (the May 21 edition also contains the allega-

tions of religious difference on the team made by the *Cincinnati Enquirer*), July 11–12, 25, September 2, 5, 18–19, 25, October 13, November 19.

3. Kaese, *The Boston Braves,* p. 78.

4. *Sporting Life,* 1895: May 25, August 24, September 14, September 21, September 28, October 5.

5. Tuohey, *A History of the Boston Baseball Club,* p. 119.

Chapter 13

1. *Brooklyn Eagle, 1895:* January 19; 1896: March 26, May 7, June 16, 24, July 11, September 20; 1897: March 6, 8–10.

2. *Boston Globe,* 1895: October 13, November 19; 1896: February 25, March 26–27, August 11, 16, September 3, 18–19, November 18.

3. *Sporting News,* 1896: January 25, August 15.

4. *Sporting Life,* 1896: April 11, May 11, October 31.

5. *The 1897 Reach Guide.*

6. Kaese, *The Boston Braves,* p. 79.

7. National Baseball Hall of Fame Billy Hamilton file, reviewed 3-29-07.

9. *Sporting News,* 1896: January 25 and August 15.

Chapter 14

1. *Boston Globe,* 1897; April 26, May 3, 8, June 22–23–25, September 24–30, October 1.

2. *Baltimore Sun,* 1897: May 19, June 22, 25, July 25, September 25, 27, 30 October 7.

3. Tuohey, *A History of the Boston Baseball Club,* p. 129–131.

4. Solomon, *Where They Ain't,* p. 119–120.

5. Kaese, *The Boston Braves,* p. 81–82.

6. *Sporting Life,* 1897: March 27 and May 22.

Chapter 15

1. *Boston Globe,* 1899: July 26; 1900: January 20; 2006: June 9.

2. National Baseball Hall of Fame Frank Selee file, reviewed 3-29-07.

3. Kaese, *The Boston Braves*, p. 85, 99–100, 105, 110.

4. Frederick G. Lieb, *The Boston Red Sox* (New York: Putnam's, 1947: reprint, Carbondale and Edwardsville, IL.: Southern Illinois University Press, 2003), p. 11, 14.

Chapter 16

1. *Boston Globe,* 1897: October 20; 1900: January 3, November 25; 1905: May 25; 1906: January 3; 1909: April 4, October 17; 1912: October 27; 1914: December 11 and 13, 1915: January 20, February 16, August 15; 1916: February 22; 1921: May 11; 1922: May 31.

2. Archives of Holy Cross College reviewed on June 14, 2007.

3. Archives of Dartmouth College reviewed on June 19, 2007.

4. Allen, *Kings of the Diamond,* p. 193.

5. City of Boston Public Records, Births, Marriages and Deaths Division.

6. Background information regarding the Winter League was also obtained by the author's correspondence with Peter Nash.

Chapter 17

1. Allen, *Kings of the Diamond,* p. 173–174.

2. *Boston Globe,* 1901: June 9, July 16, August 2, August 6, August 8, August 14 (quoting the *Chicago Tribune*); 1916: April 25, September 23; 1917: January 18; January 20, April 1, April 17; 1919: January 24, May 15, May 21, June 8, June 12, July 21, September 30, October 21, December 8; 1920: October 3, 2001: June 9.

3. James, *The New Bill James Historical Baseball Abstract,* p. 737.

4. *Philadelphia Inquirer:* 1901: July 17, August 7–8; 1904: March 30, April 3.

5. *The New York Times,* August 8, 1901.

6. Charles Bevis, *Fred Doe,* SABR Biography Project.

7. *Sporting Life:* 1901: August 3, August 17, August 24; 1910: August 27, October 1; 1911: March 25, August 26, September 2.

8. National Baseball Hall of Fame Hugh Duffy file, reviewed 3-29-07.

9. Kaese, *The Boston Braves,* p. 99–100.

10. www.baseball-reference.com/bullpen/ New England League.

11. minorleaguebaseball.com/milb/history/top100.

12. www.baseball-fever.com, quoting in part an AP article.

13. http://baseballrubbingmud.com.

Chapter 18

1. National Baseball Hall of Fame Tim Murnane file, reviewed 3-29-07.

2. *Boston Globe,* 1917: February 7–8, 11, 18; 1920: November 6; 1921: March 6, 26; 1922: May 13, August 6, August 8–10 and 14.

3. City of Boston, Death, Marriages and Birth Records Division.

4. Howard Bryant, *Shut Out: A Story of Race and Baseball in Boston* (New York: Routledge, 2002), p. 48–49, 66.

5. *Boston Guardian,* 1945: April 14, 21.

6. *Boston Record,* April 16, 1945.

7. Interview with Teddy Lepcio, January 24, 1997.

8. Interview with Sam Mele, April 11, 2007.

9. Interview with Johnny Pesky, May 15, 2007.

10. Archives of Holy Cross College reviewed on June 14, 2007.

11. Glenn Stout and Richard A. Johnson, *Red Sox Century* (Boston/New York: Houghton Mifflin, 2000, 2004 paperback edition), p. 242, 244.

12. National Baseball Hall of Fame Hugh Duffy file, reviewed 3-29-07.

13. Lieb, *The Boston Red Sox,* p. 187.

Chapter 19

1. Interview with Michael Bowlby, October 28, 1999.

2. Interview with Bob Kavin, September 27, 1999.

3. Interview with Rich Iannella, September 27, 1999.

Chapter 20

1. Bill James, *The Politics of Glory: How Baseball's Hall of Fame Really Works* (New York: Macmillan, 1994), p. 41–49, 274–275.

2. Kaese, *The Boston Braves*, p. 72.
3. *Brooklyn Eagle,* December 17, 1896.
4. *Boston Globe,* February 4, 1917.

Epilogue

1. John Gillespie Magee, Jr., *High Flight* (Faith and Freedom, 1942).

Bibliography

Books

Allen, Lee. *The National League Story* (New York: Hill & Wang, 1963).
_____, and Tom Meany. *Kings of the Diamond* (New York: Putnam's, 1965).
Bryant, Howard. *Shut Out: A Story of Race and Baseball in Boston* (New York: Routledge, 2002).
Fleitz, David L. *Cap Anson: The Grand Old Man of Baseball* (Jefferson, NC: McFarland, 2005).
Hetrick, J. Thomas. *Chris Von der Ahe and the St. Louis Browns* (Lanham, MD: Scarecrow Press, 1999).
James, Bill. *The New Bill James Historical Baseball Abstract* (New York: Free Press, 2001).
_____. *The Politics of Glory: How Baseball's Hall of Fame Really Works* (New York: Macmillan, 1994).
Johnson, Richard A. *Boston Braves* (Charleston, SC: Arcadia, 2001).
Kaese, Harold. *The Boston Braves 1871–1953* (New York: Putnam's, 1948 and 1954; reprint, Boston: Northeastern University Press, 2004).
Lieb, Frederick G. *The Boston Red Sox* (New York: Putnam's, 1947: reprint, Carbondale and Edwardsville: Southern Illinois University Press, 2003).
Lukas, J. Anthony. *Common Ground: A Turbulent Decade in the Lives of Three American Families* (New York: Vintage Books, 1986).
Oshkosh in Baseball (Oshkosh, WI.: Oshkosh Base Ball Club, 1913).
Ritter, Lawrence S. *The Glory of Their Times* (New York: Macmillan, 1966: reprint, New York: Random House Vintage Books, 1985).
Russell, Francis. *The Knave of Boston* (Boston: Quinlan Press, 1987).
Schultz, Nancy Lusignan. *Fire & Roses* (New York: Free Press, 2000).
Seymour, Harold. *Baseball, The Early Years* (New York: Oxford University Press, 1960).
Smith, Robert. *Baseball* (New York: Simon & Schuster, 1947).
Solomon, Burt. *Where They Ain't: The Fabled Life, and Untimely Death of the Original Baltimore Orioles, the Team That Gave Birth to Modern Baseball* (New York: Free Press, 1999).
Stern: Bill. *Bill Stern's Favorite Baseball Stories* (Garden City, NY: Blue Ribbon Books, 1949).
Stout, Glenn, and Richard A. Johnson. *Red Sox Century* (Boston/New York: Houghton Mifflin, 2000).

Tuohey, George V. *A History of the Boston Baseball Club* (Boston: M.F. Quinn, 1897).
Voigt, David Q. *From Gentleman's Sport to the Commissioner's System*, Volume 2 of American Baseball (Norman: University of Oklahoma Press, 1966).
Yastrzemski, Carl, and Gerard Eskenazi. *Yaz: Baseball, the Wall, and Me* (New York: Doubleday, 1990).

Articles

Charles Bevis, *Fred Doe*, SABR Biography Project.

Newspapers and Magazines

Baltimore Sun
Boston Globe
Boston Guardian
Boston Herald
Boston Morning Journal
Boston Post
Boston Record
Brooklyn Eagle
Chicago Tribune
Daily Northwestern
Lowell Weekly Sun
New York Times
Philadelphia Inquirer
St. Louis Post Dispatch
Salem Gazette
Sporting Life
Sporting News
Springfield Daily Republican

Internet Articles

baseball-fever.com, quoting in part an AP article
baseball-reference.com/bullpen/New England League
http://baseballrubbingmud.com
minorleaguebaseball.com/milb/history/top100

Poems

John Gillespie Magee, Jr., *High Flight* (Faith and Freedom, 1942).

Index